The Other Side of TERROR

An Anthology
of Writings
on Terrorism
in South Asia

The Other Side of TERROR

edited by **Nivedita Majumdar**

OXFORD
UNIVERSITY PRESS

OXFORD
UNIVERSITY PRESS

YMCA Library Building, Jai Singh Road, New Delhi 110001

Oxford University Press is a department of the University of Oxford. It furthers
the University's objective of excellence in research, scholarship, and education
by publishing worldwide in

Oxford   New York

Auckland   Cape Town   Dar es Salaam   Hong Kong   Karachi
Kuala Lumpur   Madrid   Melbourne   Mexico City   Nairobi
New Delhi   Shanghai   Taipei   Toronto

With offices in

Argentina   Austria   Brazil   Chile   Czech Republic   France   Greece
Guatemala   Hungary   Italy   Japan   Poland   Portugal   Singapore
South Korea   Switzerland   Thailand   Turkey   Ukraine   Vietnam
Oxford is a registered trade mark of Oxford University Press
in the UK and in certain other countries

Published in India by Oxford University Press, New Delhi

© Oxford University Press 2009
Photographs © Sheba Chhachhi

081797

The moral rights of the author have been asserted
Database right Oxford University Press (maker)

First published 2009

Every effort has been made to trace the copyright holder of some of the pieces included in this
volume. The publisher would be pleased to hear from the owner of the copyright so that
proper acknowledgement can be made in future editions.

ISBN-13: 978-0-19-569696-7
ISBN-10: 0-19-569696-4

Typeset in Lapidary 333BT 11.5/13.5
by Sai Graphic Design, New Delhi 110 055
Printed at DeUnique, New Delhi 110 018
Published by Oxford University Press
YMCA Library Building, Jai Singh Road, New Delhi 110 001

For Ma
With All My Love

CONTENTS

II.— REVOLUTION AND TERROR

INDIA

NEPAL

III. — IDENTITY AND TERROR

SRI LANKA

ACKNOWLEDGEMENTS

I would like to express my gratitude to the people and institutions that have helped generously in the realization of this project. The grants from the Professional Staff Congress of the City University of New York and the Office for Advancement of Research at John Jay College have been immensely helpful. I owe a special word of thanks to Ira Raja for her interest in the project and for taking it to Oxford University Press. I am grateful for the many conversations with friends as well as the occasional advice from strangers whom I approached and who responded kindly and generously; I would especially like to thank Amritjit Singh, Saros Cowasjee, Mini Krishnan, Urvashi Butalia, Joseph Mathai, Snehlata Gupta, Elliot Podwill, and Avis Lang. My gratitude extends to Avis also for her invaluable editorial help with the Introduction. My friends and colleagues in the English Department at John Jay College provided an exceptionally warm and supportive work environment. The usually deadening process of obtaining copyright permissions turned into a wonderful opportunity for me to get in touch with writers I admire. Samrat Upadhyay, Pankaj Mishra, Jean Arasanayagam, and A. Sivanandan were encouraging with the project and kindly extended the permission to reproduce their pieces. To A. Sivanandan I am indebted in a deeper way. His magnificent novel, *When Memory Dies*, with its profound experiential rendering of history, is the inspiration behind this book. I was fortunate to work with an editorial team at Oxford University Press that was unfailingly prompt, efficient, and helpful. As always, I am grateful to my parents for their love and support; I dedicate this book to my mother, who first instilled in me the love of literature and whose courage and grace in the face of adversity now strengthens me. Finally, I thank Vivek for his love, support, and inspiration, which give meaning to my endeavours, and my little Ananya for being there.

THE MANY SIDES OF TERROR
An Introduction

I do not regard killing or assassination or terrorism as good in any circumstances whatsoever. I do believe that ideas ripen quickly when nourished by the blood of the martyrs. But a man who dies slowly of jungle fever in service bleeds as certainly as one on the gallows. And if the one who dies on the gallows is not innocent of another's blood, he never had ideas that deserved to ripen.

—Mahatma Gandhi

At the level of individuals, violence is a cleansing force. It frees the native from his inferiority complex and from his despair and inaction; it makes him fearless and restores his self-respect ... Illuminated by violence, the consciousness of the people rebels against any pacification. The action which has thrown them into a hand-to-hand struggle confers upon the masses a voracious taste for the concrete. The attempt at mystification becomes, in the long run, practically impossible.

—Frantz Fanon

Terror, that most primitive of human emotions, as well as its relative, terrorizing, a most ancient political strategy, have undergone a strange metamorphosis within the past decade. Dressed up in modern garb, they have turned into 'terrorism', suddenly the single most prominent political phenomenon on the world stage.

Let us provisionally accept the prevailing definition of terrorism as the use of violence to achieve political ends, taking note of the fact that political ends are generally claimed and also acknowledged to be legitimate ends. As per this definition, terrorism is certainly not a strictly recent phenomenon. For millennia, terrorism has lurked within the heart of war itself, an extreme and comprehensive form of politically motivated violence enacted both on land and at sea with the aim of gaining land, slaves, food, and opportunities. But beyond the armies, navies, mercenaries, and privateers that ruthlessly carried out the commands of kings for the sake of consolidating power and territory, there were, very early on, many small, cohesive groups that acted as agents of terror—sects, pirate crews, parties to suicide pacts. Seafaring raiders from Asia Minor sacked the cities of the Levantine coast and terrorized the inhabitants of coastal Egypt late in the second millennium BC. The Zealots arose in Palestine in the first century AD; the Assassins arose in Persia and Syria in the eleventh century. As for tactics, tyrannicide was considered noble in ancient Greece. Poison, fire, the Trojan horse, and other deadly or clever instrumentalities played their parts in achieving the desired ends.

In recent history, terrorism as a systematic strategy towards revolutionary aims was most prominent, indeed notorious, under the brief rule of the Jacobins, notably Maximilien Robespierre and the Committee of Public Safety, during the so-called Reign of Terror of 1793–4. The use of terror is seen in some of the writings of the Russian populists, socialists, and revolutionaries of the mid- to late nineteenth century; the same period saw the emergence of anarchists and Irish terrorists. Terrorism, however, has a special resonance in the twentieth century with its anti-colonial movements and state offensives across the world, including in Palestine, South Africa, Ireland, and India. Even as terrorism has constituted an aspect of modern political consciousness, at times more visibly than at others, its contemporary pre-eminence is a novel phenomenon.

9/11 AND ITS AFTERMATH

It was the attack on the World Trade Center in September 2001 that served to push terrorism to the centrestage of world politics. And yet what was unique about that attack? Surely not the destruction of property or even the loss of some 3,000 lives. Ghastly and indefensible as the attacks were, our war-weary world has ultimately become immune to destruction and loss of this scale. Was it, then, the sheer spectacle of the planes, the flames, the leaping bodies, and the disintegrating buildings that attracted worldwide attention? All that was surely part of the reason for the sense, whether intuitive or manufactured, or both, that 9/11 seemed different from other attacks. But there was still more to it than that. The World Trade Center in New York symbolized the success and glory of a unipolar capitalist world, and yet it was not only attacked but swiftly destroyed by a few unarmed non-citizens. The morning of 9/11 showcased the vulnerability of power against the rage of the powerless.

Post-9/11 state politics has been a narrative of power re-asserting its legitimacy through force and ideology. Unarguably, the show of force has been spectacular. After declaring a 'war on terror', the mightiest country in the world has proceeded to destroy two of the poorest nations on the planet. Frighteningly, in this so-called war on terror, more than 16 times as many people have been killed than the 46,986 people killed in all terrorist attacks worldwide since 1968.[1] In Iraq alone, a recent study shows, more than 650,000 people have died since March 2003 as a consequence of the invasion[2]—and it must be remembered that this is a country with a population of less than 30 million, in which economic sanctions imposed in 1991 had already caused more than a million to perish from preventable diseases prior to the invasion. To the death toll in both Iraq and Afghanistan, one must also add the severe toll taken by the devastation of civilian infrastructure: sewage systems, electrical grids, roads, bridges, hospitals, schools, homes, markets, a bakery on one street, a clinic on another.

The deadly war on terror has another face—reserved for its home population, the one being protected from the terror. The people at home face an attack on their rights and liberties. While the wounded nation attacks other nations ostensibly in order to 'bring democracy' to their people, it steadily undermines democratic institutions at home. War and

---

[1] http://www.unknownnews.net/casualties.html

[2] 'Study Claims Iraq's "Excess" Death Toll Has Reached 655,000, David Brown', *Washington Post*, 11 October 2006; Page A12; 'Mortality After the 2003 Invasion of Iraq; A Cross-sectional Cluster Sample Survey', Gilbert Burnham, Riyadh Lafta, Shannon Doocy, Les Roberts, *The Lancet*, 11 October 2006.

warlike situations offer one of the most effective ways of consolidating power: squelching dissent. The past century is replete with instances of ruling classes worldwide taking advantage of such opportunities. In the month after 9/11, the US government passed the USA PATRIOT Act (the acronym stands for 'Uniting and Strengthening America by Providing Appropriate Tools Required to Intercept and Obstruct Terrorism'), providing sweeping powers to law enforcement authorities, and undermining basic principles of checks and balances. The Act threatens fundamental freedoms by, for instance, enabling government surveillance of and access to medical records, tax records, telephone bills, credit card statements, and library loans, without probable cause. It permits agents of the government to enter private homes and conduct searches without informing the residents, a manoeuvre known in legal circles as the 'sneak and peek' search warrant. Under the new regime, non-citizens have been rounded up and detained, many for months or even years, without being charged with a crime or given the opportunity to meet a lawyer. In Guantánamo Bay, prisoners suspected to be terrorists are held as 'unlawful combatants'—a term that holds no meaning in international law. In order to obtain confessions, these prisoners are subjected to what the US government, including its Department of Justice, euphemistically calls 'enhanced interrogation techniques'.

The state uses a tested strategy to legitimize its excesses: it counterposes *security* to *liberties*. The country is under attack; therefore, extraordinary measures are called for. Security and safety are primal needs, understood and valued by nearly everyone. To many people, in contrast, civil liberties are an abstraction that can be relinquished with little or no sense of loss, traded in for safety. The counterposition is, of course, deeply fallacious, for civil liberties *are* a form of security—security against the state.

The deadliest ideological ploy in this alleged war on terror is the resurgence of rhetoric derived from and consonant with Samuel P. Huntington's 'clash of civilizations' theory, which argues that the fundamental source of conflict in the contemporary world is not political or economic but, rather, civilizational or cultural. 'The fault lines of civilizations,' Huntington asserts, 'are the battle lines of the future.'[3] This

---

[3] 'The Clash of Civilizations?' Samuel P. Huntington, *Foreign Affairs*, Summer 1993.

theory has been exploited to the full for the purpose of moulding the public response to terrorism. Following Huntington's thesis, terrorism can be viewed as the new mode of battle of one kind of civilization against another. Two months after the attack on the World Trade Center, President George W. Bush remarked:

Our nation faces a threat to our freedoms, and the stakes could not be higher. We are the target of enemies who boast they want to kill—kill all Americans, kill all Jews, and kill all Christians. We've seen that type of hate before—and the only possible response is to confront it, and to defeat it. This new enemy seeks to destroy our freedom and impose its views. We value life; the terrorists ruthlessly destroy it. We value education; the terrorists do not believe women should be educated or should have healthcare, or should leave their homes. We value the right to speak our minds; for the terrorists, free expression can be grounds for execution.[4]

The terrorist here is identified by his supposed *cultural* beliefs, specific to his religion and his region—in other words, Huntington's civilizational fault lines. Akin to faith in racial categories, the theory of civilizational divide holds that cultures situated on different sides of these deeply incised boundary lines have characteristics which mark them as irrevocably different, alien, oppositional. In another twist, the entire issue is cast in a millennial light as a struggle between good and evil. Speaking in the context of the 9/11 attacks, the Israeli Prime Minister, Ariel Sharon, declared:

This is a war between good and evil—between humanity and those who thirst for blood. The way of the wicked will be defeated; the way of those who profess evil will not prosper. The way of the righteous, the humane and the free, will be victorious.[5]

The problem with the civilizational perspective is not that it posits a difference in cultures. By definition, different cultures are different. It is the nature of the difference attributed to different cultures that is thoroughly objectionable. It is assumed, for instance, by proponents of a culturalist, Huntingtonesque perspective that values such as freedom

[4] In Address to the Nation World Congress Center, Atlanta, Georgia, 11 August 2001.

[5] PM Sharon Addresses the Knesset's Special Solidarity Session, Jerusalem, 16 September 2001.

and tolerance, or ideals of liberty and equality, are intrinsic attributes of the Western civilization. The civilizational perspective rejects the notion of the universality of certain values and is incapable of acknowledging that cultures may adopt several historical trajectories in their attempts to realize certain goals and ideals.

In the discussion on terrorism, the emphasis on cultural difference performs an insidious function. At the outset, it is claimed that the terrorist embodies an irreconcilably different set of values from those held by the targets of his attacks. Civilizational rhetoric thereby denies the possibility that the terrorist could have political and economic grounds for his actions. The idea that terrorism could be the outcome of specific socio-economic and political causes is simply not taken into account. The civilizational worldview is inimical to the recognition of political and economic grievances grounded in universal principles of fairness and equality. Thus, the culturalist perspective renders hollow terrorism of all political meaning.

VIOLENCE AND DISSENT

Its engagement with the phenomena of dissent and of violence is what permits terrorism to be cast as unacceptable. The right of dissent is, of course, a cornerstone of democracy; it is widely regarded as one of the most desirable principles upon which a society may be founded. And yet even as the principle might remain unchallenged, its manifestations may come under attack. Perhaps, much like the need for security, and in some senses connected to it, the need for social order is primal. Thus when dissent is expressed through a disruption of the social order—even a non-violent disruption—it can be readily viewed as questionable. Strikes, for instance, are often regarded as a nuisance; at times, they are seen as downright objectionable. Writing a petition, on the other hand, remains more acceptable. The less a given expression of dissent threatens social order, the more acceptable it is. The terrorist's dissent, inasmuch as the dissenter, is prepared to wreak havoc on the fabric of social order, and thus becomes completely objectionable—and completely dismissable.

Far more than dissent, however, it is actual violence that makes terrorism deplorable. In fact, the component of dissent is often marginalized, if not completely unacknowledged, in accounting for terrorism. Above all, it is the violence that becomes foregrounded. The violence, we are given to understand, is of a special kind—often said to be rootless, disconnected, even purposeless. But even that is not what sets it apart or makes it special. The terrorist's violence is supposedly unique because it targets innocents, people who are not responsible for the terrorist's real or imagined grievances. Indeed, no violence could be more egregious than the kind that punishes people for crimes for which they bear no responsibility. Bombing an office building, hijacking a plane, blowing up a pizzeria, or holding schoolchildren as hostages are instances of maximally egregious violence. In such instances, the *reason* for the violence becomes immaterial. Or so we are led to believe.

Does the reason for the violence—including the kind whereby innocents are targeted—ever become immaterial? If so, how do we account for the slaughter of innocents in Hiroshima, in Siberia, in Vietnam, in Palestine?

Other deadly forms of violence have become all too well known across the globe, from the US to South Africa, from China to Israel, from India to Chile. These are the forms which target, not those who are innocent, but those who are guilty—of dissent. In this category, one must include 'advanced interrogation techniques', torture, mass disappearances, imprisonment without trial, deaths in 'encounters'—all the forms of violence that make dissent, in effect, a capital crime. In each such instance, the violence inflicted on the dissenter is made out to be 'reasonable'. It is sanctioned violence that allegedly *protects* lives.[6]

---

[6] On a website that claims to meticulously detail known casualties in twentieth century genocides, Hiroshima and Nagasaki do not make to the list. The author justifies their omission in a footnote, observing, 'I often get asked if Hiroshima/Nagasaki qualify as a genocide. I disagree ... Winston Churchill and Harry Truman did not start that war: they ended it. It is even debatable if these bombings killed or saved lives: Hiroshima probably saved a lot of Japanese lives, because a long protracted invasion like the one that took place in Germany would have killed a lot more people.' If we were to agree with the author on the use of the atomic bomb, then let us imagine another possible scenario. What if the Irish Republican Army (IRA) had bombed London in the mid-1970s? Because of the heavy casualties, what if the British government were forced to arrive at an amicable settlement with Ireland? The very arguments that the author uses to justify Hiroshima could be used here—that the IRA did not start the 'war', they ended it, that the bombing of London, in the long run, saved more lives than destroy them.

In truth, the targeting of civilians—even, one might contend, if it does save more lives than it destroys—is always morally unjustifiable, whether carried out by the state or by terrorist organizations. It is an act of murder, not sacrifice, for the simple reason that sacrifice presupposes the consent of the one who is being sacrificed. Another disturbing symmetry in the targeting of civilians by states and terrorists is evident in the arena of foreign policy, an arena in which even democratic governments rarely reflect the will of the people. Instead, as Noam Chomsky succinctly phrases it, states garner a 'manufactured consent' from the people they govern. And yet acts of 'war', as well as most terrorist acts, are intended to be attacks on a country's foreign policy. *Ultimately, both states and terrorists punish people for the acts of their governments.*

The film *The Battle of Algiers* (1965), masterfully directed by Gillo Pontecorvo, shows that the deadly symmetry between acts of states and acts of terrorists notwithstanding, it is unwise to forget that these two types of perpetrators are not on the same footing. Based on the Algerian anti-colonial struggle, the movie was made only a few years after Algeria became an independent nation. The sympathies of the film, which presents a brutal indictment of French colonial ideology and of the atrocious methods used to contain the Algerian revolution, clearly lie with the revolutionaries. Even as it positions itself on the side of the revolutionaries, however, the film attains a high level of sophistication in its philosophical engagement with the nature of violence. In its depiction, for instance, both of the use of torture by French officials and of revolutionary attacks against French settlers, it invites the viewer to engage with the moral and political texture of violence. At one point, a revolutionary is questioned about the morality of targeting French civilians, and his response captures the asymmetry embedded in the relationship between the state and the militants: he replies that if the Algerians had an army like that of the French, they could fight a war which might be palatable to the French.

The violence of states is usually more egregious and less justified than the violence of terrorists. Unlike terrorists, states have entire administrative and ideological apparatuses at their command. Whatever the 'cause,' they have more options for a response. In addition, unlike terrorist attacks, the violence unleashed by states is almost always more methodical, more deliberate, more sustained and, most important, sanctioned. While not a justification of terrorism, an examination of the nature of state violence reveals the state's claim about the *unique nature* of terrorist violence to be hollow and obfuscatory. A case in point would be a statement by Ariel Sharon about 'bloodthirsty terrorist[s]', wherein he declares: 'I oppose all those who relate to innocent civilians—women and children, babes in their mothers' arms—as legitimate targets.'[7] The painful irony of that statement makes commentary redundant.

Regardless of the cause, a certain kind of violence, whether unleashed by terrorists or by states, remains unjustifiable. I am speaking of the violence directed at ordinary people living their ordinary lives. Moments before Nagasaki was bombed, minutes before the airplane flying straight into the World Trade Center became visible, there were people in the direct line of the imminent attacks who epitomized human existence— for the most part, neither noble nor vile. Some of them must have been marked by grotesque contradictions or held indefensible views; others might have borne the marks of unreciprocated love; all of them, on occasion, surely exercised generosity and tolerance. These were people unflinchingly and unavoidably engaged with quotidian minutiae and thus interconnected in their everyday reaffirmation of life. If political goals are to derive from anything, they must derive from the embrace of ordinariness, that is, human life. The kernel of justice must be to protect this ordinariness, not to target it.

Terrorism in South Asia—A Historical Outline

The Independence Movement

Terrorism was not an integral part of India's Independence Movement, though the movement did produce several revolutionary upsurges that adopted terrorism as a strategy. The earliest of such groups emerged in Bengal during the first decade of the twentieth century: the Anushilan Samiti, for instance, was formed in Calcutta in 1902 and later set up a bomb factory. Two of its members, Khudiram Bose and Prafulla Chaki, perpetrated the Kennedy murders on 30 April 1908, missing their intended target, a magistrate named Kingsford. During the same period, in eastern Bengal, the Dacca Anushilan conducted the Barrah dacoity

[7] The Knesset's Special Solidarity.

(both 'dacoity' and 'thuggee', a much older word from which 'thug' derives, are Anglicized terms that refer to armed robbery). Extremist and revolutionary groups and actions also emerged in Benaras, Punjab, Madras, and Maharashtra. Sumit Sarkar's views on the Bengal terrorism of the period capture the tenor of the movement in general:

The 'revolutionary' movement took the form of assassinations of oppressive officials or traitors, *swadeshi* dacoities to raise funds, or at best military conspiracies with expectations of help from foreign enemies of Britain. It never, despite occasional subjective aspirations, rose to the level of urban mass uprisings or guerilla bases in the countryside. The term 'terrorism' remains hence not inappropriate. (*Modern India*, 124)

World War I proved propitious for revolutionary terrorists striving for immediate and complete independence. During this period, there was considerable cooperation between Indian revolutionaries and those from other countries, including Turkey, Germany, Ireland, and Canada. Indians succeeded in obtaining both arms and funding from abroad. The famous Ghadar movement—a well-funded, committed group working for a revolutionary uprising in India that sent its members by the thousands back to India after the outbreak of the war—arose in 1913 in British Columbia and the US West Coast. With cooperation from Ghadar members, revolutionaries in Bengal organized assassinations and political dacoities, which reached their peak between 1914 and 1916. Not surprisingly, the British perceived all these activities as a threat and undertook severely repressive measures to control the groups' activities. In the mid- to late 1920s, there was a brief upsurge of revolutionary activity, including the formation of the Hindustan Socialist Republican Army in 1928 under the leadership of Bhagat Singh. Several outbursts went beyond the confines of the movement defined by the Congress Party. The Chittagong group of revolutionaries, for instance, headed by Surya Sen, committed a spectacular act by seizing the local armoury and issuing an independence proclamation on 18 April 1930. Four days later, during a battle fought against the police in Jalalabad, they lost twelve of their members.

A host of regulations and Acts were passed to contain and repress activities that challenged the colonial state. Regulation III of 1818 enabled the detention of suspects. The Press Act of 1900 regulated the publication of newspapers and other printed materials that might encourage sedition. The 1915 Defence of India Rules gave the state wide powers of detention. Among the other legislations aimed at censorship and repression were the Indian Penal Code (Amendment) Act of 1921, the Criminal Amendment Act of 1925, and the Bengal Suppression of Terrorist Outrage Act of 1932. In each case, every piece of legislation was aimed at curtailing the fundamental rights and liberties of the subject population.

Yet it is precisely the abundance of such laws that belies the fundamental insecurity and instability at the heart of the empire. In fact, the repeated enactments and amendments expose the constant need felt by the state to contain the ever-present, and ever evolving, threat to its authority. It was as if each new piece of intelligence about the restiveness of the population once again rendered existing legal provisions inadequate. The state had embarked on a hysterical drive to treat ever-emerging symptoms while continuing to nurture the underlying disease. In thus isolating terrorism as an issue of law and order, unconnected to the legitimacy of the political regime, colonial governance provides the model approach followed by states in their encounters with terrorism. Ranabir Samaddar draws an interesting parallel between the response of the British empire and the response of regimes in our own time, noting how in each case the state approaches terrorism as an aberration that can be solved through the detailed profiling of terrorists and how the state becomes baffled when this strategy does not work:

… [E]ach year the [British] colonial administration produced history sheets of persons and organizations, detailed their caste identities or caste basis, behavioural proclivity, and the dress, the look, the handwriting style, the manner of speaking … So we have in government files the photograph of a baboo, of a coolie, of a terrorist-baboo, of a raider. And then, as if the government wanted to resolve once and for all the enigma of who could be a terrorist, we find in the files pages and pages on a terrorist's love for death. Thus, for instance, the government wanted to know why Charu Chandra Bose, who was hanged in 1909 and who had one useless hand, had joined the movement, why just a few days before he assassinated the public prosecutor in the Alipur conspiracy case had he gone to a studio to photograph himself, why had he wanted to meet his relatives before his death, why he, a meek and silent person, had done 'this,' and thus possibly solve the enigma of Charu's identity … Even today the counter-insurgency experts who are engaged, for instance, in pacifying Palestine have not solved the enigma of why a young woman, aged eighteen and a mother of two sons, photographs herself and allows herself to be photographed before she leaves on a mission? Who is a Palestinian terrorist, a Tamil terrorist, or a guerrilla of Peru?

Terror after Colonialism

Certainly the post-colonial era is an improvement on the regime of colonial constitutionalism, which not only denied rights of representation to the colonized but also categorised all challenges to the state's authority as criminal. Only after a pitched battle—at times fought directly by the subject population, at others on behalf of that population—did the post-colonial regime emerge. In essence, the new regime's constitution and laws had to incorporate the fight against colonial authoritarianism.

Nationalism is the ideology that emerged in the subcontinent as the mobilizing discourse against British rule, and while taking its place as the dominant mode of national cohesion, nationalism became the new normative force, claiming to represent the interests and aspirations of the entire nation. As a result, nationalist ideology had to perform a double manoeuvre: it had to be sufficiently porous to allow disparate social groups and their sometimes divergent interests to be incorporated into its fold and, at the same time, had to suppress aspects of these interests so as to encourage the task of *nation-building*.

In India, the class and cultural formation of the post-Independence elite determined the particular character of the nascent nation. In the intricate ideological process of nation-building, two sets of interests were both co-opted and marginalized—those of the economically oppressed and those of ethnic minorities. The co-optation was largely rhetorical, achieved through inclusive slogans that stressed the eradication of poverty and celebrated the nation's cultural diversity. In practice, however, the construction of the nation followed a path that remained indifferent, if not hostile, to the economically underprivileged and to cultural minorities. *Terrorism, as a phenomenon in post-colonial India, is intricately connected to this fundamental failure at the heart of the process of nation-building, which engendered the disenchantment of certain of the nation's core constituencies.*

It is not a coincidence that in post-colonial India, terrorist strategies have been adopted by two kinds of movements: struggles around economic issues and those around issues of identity. Among the former is the Naxalite movement, which emerged in the late 1960s and continues into the present. Among the latter are the movements in Kashmir, Punjab, and the North-East. To point to the failure of the nation-state is not to claim that movements against the state are necessarily entirely justified either in their aims or in their methods. Nevertheless, it is essential to recognize the connection between such movements and the frustrated aspirations that they represent. This connection gives the lie to the official stance that the adoption of strategies of terror automatically renders a movement unjustifiable. In the post-colonial period, in fact, the official position regarding terror and counter-terrorism operations shows a continuity with the positions held during the colonial period.

Kashmir

Arguably, the current Kashmir conflict has roots in the repressive Dogra rule in the region, dating back to the eighteenth century, as well as the more recent appearance of the British. More relevant to the present discussion, however, is the controversial 1947 accession of Kashmir to India.

In the early 1940s, Sheikh Mohammad Abdullah emerged as a popular leader, articulating local aspirations for an independent Kashmiri homeland. Such a Kashmir was envisioned to be inclusive and egalitarian, a socialist and secular state. Arrested by the then Dogra ruler, Sheikh Abdullah remained in prison while Hari Singh, the next Dogra ruler, played India and Pakistan off against each other and finally signed the Instrument of Accession by which Kashmir became part of India. Because of the special circumstances under which Kashmir was joined to India, it was agreed that a plebiscite would be held to obtain the consent of the Kashmiris. It never took place. Through Article 370 of the Indian Constitution, Kashmir was granted special status, a very controversial state of affairs. Meanwhile, Sheikh Abdullah, who was released from prison after the accession, was imprisoned once again in 1953, mainly because India's Central Government under Nehru was threatened by his massive popularity and his overtures to Pakistan. After the Sheikh's imprisonment, a puppet regime was installed in Kashmir.

Kashmir remained central to the dispute between India and Pakistan, with each country claiming its proprietorship over the region. Three full-scale wars and several smaller ones have been fought over Kashmir by the two countries. The present phase of the movement can be traced back to 1989, when Kashmiri youth took to the streets. Since then, the conflict has been shaped by diverse factors and forces, from grassroots nationalist aspirations to mercenaries and militants trained in Pakistan. The movement and its ramifications have wrought havoc in the lives of Kashmir's people. Tourism, which had been a mainstay for the economy of the region, came to a standstill for over two decades. The loss of livelihood and the breakdown of security have resulted in large-scale displacement. The inhabitants of the valley have been victimized by both the militants and security forces. It is estimated that over a million people have been displaced, an additional 70,000 have died, and around 10,000 are said to be missing in illegal detention. The number of women who have either lost their husbands or whose husbands have been missing for several years (the latter group is often called 'half-widows') stands at over 15,000.

The Indian state is gravely implicated in the Kashmir imbroglio. As mentioned earlier, the promised plebiscite regarding accession to India was never held. The marginalization of Sheikh Abdullah and the installation of puppet regimes did nothing to restore the faith of the Kashmiri people in the Indian state. To be sure, the insurgency is aided by forces from across the border. But instead of treating the involvement of Pakistan as only one significant aspect of the Kashmir issue, the Indian state has always made it the centerpiece. By first reducing a complex issue to one of illegal foreign involvement, the government paved the way for a focus on tough counter-insurgency operations as the primary solution.

Several acts aimed at countering terrorism have been applied to Kashmir, with disastrous consequences for the local population. The Armed Forces Special Powers Act (AFSPA), promulgated in 1990, provides sweeping powers to law enforcement authorities at the expense of basic civil rights. The Act, for instance, empowers members of the security forces to use lethal force 'against any person indulging in any act which may result in serious breach of public order, acting in contravention of any law or order for the time being in force, or the carrying of weapons'. AFSPA, which has its origins in nineteenth-century British colonial legislation and is based on a 1942 colonial ordinance

intended to suppress the Indian independence movement,[8] is linked
to the Disturbed Areas Act, also promulgated in 1990. Provisions in
the latter permit the armed forces to arrest, without warrant, not only
someone who may have committed an actual offence but also anyone
who may be liable to commit a cognizable offence in future. Given the
legal immunity bestowed by these Acts on agents of the state, it is not
surprising that cases of custody deaths, rapes, disappearances, murder,
and torture abound.

The North-East

The turmoil in the North-East also has its roots in the colonial period.
The British practice of indirect rule in the hill areas of the North-
East insulated the region from the spread of pan-Indian nationalism.
The colonial policy of indirect rule, allegedly aimed at promoting the
cultural survival of the hill tribes, fostered separate religious, social,
and national identity in these regions, achieved primarily through the
creation of an Inner line under the East Bengal Frontier Regulation
of 1873. The insulation of the region from its neighbours for many
decades offered Christian missionaries a magnificent opportunity for
unrestricted proselytizing and conversion. In fact, Virendra Singh Jafar,
while commenting on the policy of forced isolation of the region,
asserts it to be a method 'for carrying out political, anthropological,
and ecclesiastical experimentation on a scale thereto unknown in the
annals of colonial rule.'[9]

   Unfortunately, independence did little to mitigate the political and
social isolation of the region. The North-East never benefited from an
enlightened perspective that would both integrate it with the rest of the
nation and nurture its unique culture. Instead, the Sixth Schedule of
the Indian Constitution, though well intended, has only reinforced the
separation of the region from the mainland. Initially, the hill tribes were
retained within the state of Assam, and Assamese was imposed as the
official language of the state, thereby preparing the ground for widespread

---

   [8] Information and quotes from http://hrw.org/reports/2006/india0906/4.
htm#_Toc144362278
   [9] Virendra Singh Jafa, 'Insurgencies in North-East India,' in Responding to
Terrorism in South Asia, ed. S. D. Muni, Manohar, 2006, p. 78.

discontent. During the ensuing decades, the region has been ravaged by several insurgencies demanding statehood or secession. The geopolitical location of the region has proved to be a major factor in sustaining these movements, ensuring the inflow of arms from and the provision of sanctuaries in the neighbouring countries of China, Bangladesh, and Bhutan. The Central Government has often colluded with insurgent outfits for short-term political gains in ways which, rather than addressing local grievances, have served to exacerbate the existing situation.

Military solutions to the insurgencies have predictably yielded little success. The strategy of resettlement, for instance, was practised in a limited way in the Naga hills and—at a much larger scale, involving 90 per cent of the population—in the Mizo hills. The operation consisted of regrouping—in other words, displacing—the rural population so as to isolate the insurgents and also gain much greater freedom and flexibility to conduct military operations in the depopulated regions. Although the military declared that the gains from this strategy were immense, the local population perceived it more as a form of collective punishment. In a society where access to their land is the lifeblood of the people, displacement has caused widespread resentment and has, in fact, strengthened the insurgents' cause.

Faced with the limited success of military operations, policymakers proposed the development approach, requiring massive investment in the region. This approach has indeed been attempted, albeit in a half-hearted fashion. Corruption, inefficiency, subversion by the underground economy of the insurgent network, and a general lack of political will have, however, scuttled the possibility of sustainable economic development. As a result, a somewhat circular analysis has emerged: the lack of success of the development approach is invoked to argue that the approach itself is flawed and should be traded for a hard-line military solution, which would presumably revive the widespread resentment that was originally exacerbated by military solutions.

The fact remains, though, that development has never been promoted in the North-east with sufficient political and administrative will. Consider the Union Liberation Front of Assam (ULFA), for instance, which takes a strong anti-immigrant stance. The ULFA holds that 'illegal Indian immigration' drains or rechannels the resources of the state away from the actual Assamese, the traditional inhabitants of the region. Even though the issue thus posited is one of identity, its underlying cause is economic. This is not to argue that even a sustained programme of economic development of the North-east would necessarily quash the separatist aspirations represented by insurgent bodies. But removing the economic base on which these identity-based movements often ride would, at the very least, weaken them.

Punjab

The separatist movement which made the strongest imprint on the Indian national consciousness is the fundamentalist movement that emerged in Punjab in the early 1980s, of which the central demand was a separate homeland for adherents of the Sikh religion. The Sikhs suffered immensely during the Partition and holocaust of 1947, but because of their eastward migration during those years, they became for the first time the majority population in certain areas of eastern Punjab. Yet there arose a sense of dissension and unease among some Sikhs, who felt marginalized in the new nation. The government tried the appeasement approach, and with substantial state investment in dams and canals, as well as the onset of the 'Green Revolution', the Sikh population as a whole prospered. Feelings of marginality, if not persecution, based on their national minority status, however, remained strong among sections of the population. After prolonged agitation, the Sikhs gained a major victory in 1966 in the form of a 'Punjabi Suba': a formally constituted, Punjabi-majority state within India, named (of course) Punjab.

During the ensuing years, Sikh fundamentalism continued to grow, fuelled in strong measure by the rise of Hindu fundamentalism. The emergence of the populist leader Jarnail Singh Bhindranwale in the late 1970s, with his gospel of fundamentalism and separatism, marked a turning point for the movement. Bhindranwale, whose following was especially strong among the rural unemployed and the underprivileged, made common cause with the influential Akali Dal, a party that largely represented the interests of well-to-do farmers. Between Bhindranwale and the Akali Dal, they mounted a massive and violent agitation, based on a set of demands that could be construed as leading to a separate homeland, the proposed republic of Khalistan. Its worst fallout was the resultant suspicion and violence between Hindus and Sikhs both inside and outside Punjab. For its part, the Central Government refused to

engage seriously with the root causes of the movement and also chose
to underestimate its strength. A political solution to the crisis was
rendered impossible by an inexplicable dragging of feet and a politics
of brinkmanship between the Akalis at the local level and the Congress
at the Centre.

On 6 June 1984, the Central Government, under Prime Minister
Indira Gandhi, sanctioned Operation Bluestar—the army's storming
of the Golden Temple in Amritsar to defeat Bhindranwale and his
forces, who had armed themselves with sophisticated weapons and
fortified themselves within the temple. While Bhindranwale was killed
and his supporters defeated by the massive force deployed by the army,
Operation Bluestar turned out to be one of the worst possible courses
of action undertaken by the government to tackle terrorism. Apart
from considerable damages to a site deeply venerated by the followers
of the Sikh religion, over 500 unarmed civilians were killed during the
operation, whose timing coincided with one of the holiest days in the Sikh
calendar. The government's actions were roundly condemned by a unified
Sikh population, most of whom held no brief either for Bhindranwale or
for his fundamentalist creed. In fact, noted journalist Khushwant Singh, a
staunch critic of the Khalistan movement, compared Operation Bluestar
to the British massacre of Jallianwala Bagh in 1919.[10]

In a reprehensible terrorist retaliation, Indira Gandhi was
assassinated less than five months later, on 31 October 1984, by her
own Sikh bodyguards. The assassination was followed by some of the
worst communal riots since 1947, in which Sikhs were targeted all over
the country, though mostly in Delhi. During the three days following
the assassination, some 6,000 Sikhs lost their lives, and some 50,000
ended up in refugee camps. A massacre of such scale, as shown by
several reports and inquiries, could only have been the result of a state-
engineered pogrom.[11]

As Hindu-Sikh relations hit an all-time low, terrorist attacks
continued in the form of shoot-outs and explosions, claiming over
20,000 lives by 1993. Egregious acts by the militants included opening
fire in crowded public areas, attacking passengers on public buses and

---

[10] *My Bleeding Punjab*, UBSPD, 1992, p. 73.
[11] Ibid., pp. 96–7.

trains, murdering labourers, and assassinating public figures and security officials. The movement was brought to a finish by the mid-1990s through a ruthless campaign by the state, whose own pattern of gross violations of human rights included arbitrary arrests, torture, prolonged detention without trial, disappearances, and the summary killings of Sikh civilians and suspected militants.

The Naxalite Movement

In April 2006, at a meeting of chief ministers, Indian Prime Minister Manmohan Singh described the Naxalite movement as the 'single biggest internal security challenge' ever faced by India.[12] In December 2007, at another chief ministers' meeting, he reiterated that sentiment. 'Not a day passes without an incident of Left-wing extremism taking place somewhere or the other,' he said. 'We need to cripple Naxalite forces with all the means at our command.'[13]

The Naxalite movement, which has maintained a noticeable presence in several parts of the country for several decades, began in 1967 with a peasant uprising in Naxalbari, a village in northern Bengal near the Nepalese border. Initially led by armed members of the Communist Party of India (Marxist) (CPI-M), the movement later broke away to form the Communist Party of India (Marxist-Leninist) (CPI-ML). Its continuity derives from the same causes that facilitated its emergence: rural poverty, the social humiliation of the underprivileged, the recourse to repression to silence protests. In the late 1960s and early 1970s, the Naxalites were certainly also inspired by the international climate of radicalism.

The movement, begun in the countryside, spread to the cities during the 1970s. There, it attracted mainly educated, unemployed youth. Economic development was not keeping pace with the expansion of opportunities for higher education, and the education system itself had become archaic in its substance and corrupt in its functioning. The disillusioned and frustrated youth was strongly energized by the peasant movement for rights and recognition. Charu Mazumdar, the prominent Naxalite leader, called on the students to give up on bourgeois education

[12] http://www.rediff.com/news/2006/apr/13naxal.htm

[13] http://www.expressindia.com/latest-news/Naxal-menace-worries-PM-pledges-action/252445/

and join the workers and landless peasants. While some students did go to the villages in response to his call, those who remained in the cities turned their energies into radicalizing the student movement. As Sumanta Banerjee has pointed out, the fact that the educated Naxalites were not rooted in working-class movements proved to be disadvantageous in the long run: 'As a result of the concentration on this explosive section of the urban population, poised for action, the industrial proletariat received very little attention, to the detriment of the movement at a later stage.'[14]

The urban movement was characterized by a strong component of iconoclasm. It began with organized attacks against schools and colleges that were perceived to be relics of a colonial era, continuing the practice of producing a stratum of the oppressive elite and contributing nothing more to society. Attacks were also directed against statues of nineteenth-century social reformers and other political leaders. Soon, however, the movement turned its attention to living targets. As state repression gained momentum, especially in the countryside, targeted attacks began in the city. This 'annihilation programme' targeted people in uniform: police officers, paramilitary personnel, traffic constables. This programme was followed by another: capturing the rifles of security officials, the goal being to build an arsenal. Despite the sheer brutality of the Naxalites' attacks, the movement did enjoy considerable popular support because of the general disenchantment against the oppressive police force.

Before long, a monumental counter-offensive was mounted by the state. After local police proved ineffective in wiping out the movement on their own, the military was called in to help tackle the situation. In September 1970, the West Bengal government revived a colonial-era law, the Bengal Suppression of Terrorists Outrages Act of 1936. Later that very year, another law was passed—the West Bengal Prevention of Violent Activities Bill, which gave wide-ranging powers to the state. Thus empowered with draconian anti-terrorist laws, it launched a campaign including arrests on suspicion, torture, 'encounter' killings, and disappearances, and even took to shooting down unarmed prisoners inside jails. Other strategies included encircling localities and searching

---

[14] Sumanta Banerjee, *India's Simmering Revolution: The Naxalite Uprising*, London: Zed Books, 1980, p. 178.

each house; arresting 'suspects', which meant arresting almost every youth who could be found; and on-the-spot shooting of recognizable Naxalite cadres. The police also mobilized unemployed local hoodlums to hunt down CPI(M-L) activists. The Naxalites' lack of a principled and coherent programme, combined with these powerful anti-insurgent operations, brought this phase of the movement to an end.

At present, the Naxalite influence is spread in over thirteen states, including Maharashtra, Madhya Pradesh, Uttar Pradesh, Chhattisgarh, Jharkhand, West Bengal, and Bihar. While different outfits operate in various areas, they are loosely united as the Communist Party of India (Maoist). They are waging a violent struggle with over 10,000 armed members. The sheer breadth of their presence in the poverty-stricken regions of the country testifies to a certain level of popularity among the sections they are fighting for, that is, the lower castes, peasants, and landless labourers. There is a major state offensive to combat the movement, including the involvement of government-supported vigilante groups like the Salwa Judum in Chhattisgarh. While the official line is that Naxalism is a result of poverty and discrimination, the state remains unable to devise a solution in line with that assessment.

Nepal

Nepal recently made headlines the world over by achieving a rare feat—the successful culmination of a communist revolution. While the communist movement in Nepal goes back to 1949, the present phase of Maoist insurgency can be traced back over just one decade. On 4 February 1996, the Communist Party of Nepal (Maoist) presented 40 demands to the prime minister, warning that if these demands were not met, a 'people's war' against the government would ensue. Among the demands were the drafting of a new constitution, a declaration that Nepal would henceforth be a secular state, a whittling-down of the royal family's privileges, and the introduction of work permits for foreigners. The government paid little heed to the demands and warnings, and the insurgency began soon thereafter. Over the past decade the 'people's war' has claimed well over 10,000 lives including those of Maoist guerrillas, police, alleged police informers, and civilians. According to independent observers, more innocent civilians have been killed in 'fake' encounters promulgated by Nepal's army and police than Maoist guerillas killed in real encounters. And, as is almost routine in counter-insurgent operations, there have been extra-judicial killings in captivity as well as disappearances of persons in police custody.

The most remarkable aspect of the Nepalese insurgency, however, is its tremendous mass base among the underprivileged, who constitute the overwhelming majority of the country, and also, to a considerable extent, among the middle classes. This is not surprising, given that the movement bases itself on the deep-rooted socio-economic grievances of the peasants, the workers, and large numbers of the unemployed. Indeed, the Dhami Commission Report, the product of the government's own systematic effort to analyse the Maoist movement, ended by recommending socio-economic reforms very similar to those demanded by the Maoists. It also admitted to massive police brutalities and the targeting of innocents by security personnel. In 2006, after fighting a decade-long battle with a state aided by international players such as the US, the UK, and India, the Maoists joined the Seven Party Alliance (SPA) to form an interim government and initiated a peace process. In December 2006, the SPA and the Maoists finalized a draft interim constitution, which relegated the king to the margins, stripping him of most of his powers, including his status as supreme commander of the army. Elections for the Constituent Assembly, initially scheduled to be held in June 2007 and subsequently delayed until November 2007, were held in April 2008. The Maoists won a majority of seats in the elections and at its first session held on 28 May 2008, the Constituent Assembly voted to abolish the monarchy and declared Nepal a federal democratic republic.

Sri Lanka

This small island nation has been torn by civil war for over two decades. The underlying issues have to do with both ethnicity and economics. The Sinhalese, the main ethnic group, comprise three-quarters of Sri Lanka's inhabitants, while the remainder of the population includes Sri Lankan Tamils (about 12 per cent), concentrated in the north and east of the island; Muslims (about 8 per cent); Up-country Tamils (about 5 per cent), primarily tea-plantation workers from the hill country in the south-central part of the island; and a smattering of Christian Burghers. The conflict is between the two largest groups, the Sinhalese and the Sri Lankan Tamils, and is connected in important ways to the two class-based Marxist insurrections that took place in the country, the first in 1971 and the second in 1988–9. Both were the handiwork of the People's Liberation Front (PLF), and both involved only the Sinhalese segment of the population. Staged primarily by rural Sinhalese youth, the insurrections were grounded in a strong sense of socio-economic deprivation, manifested in extremely uneven industrial development and rural poverty. The first insurrection ended with a government operation that killed more than 15,000 citizens; in the second, more organized insurrection of 1988–9, a similar military crackdown cost over 50,000 lives. Other than its heavy-handed military response, the government did little by way of substantive reforms to address the issues raised by the insurrections, except for one course of action which ended up fuelling the inter-ethnic conflict.

Instead of creating more employment and educational opportunities for all, the government instituted programmes that would benefit the majority Sinhalese population at the expense of the Tamils. The criteria for university admissions, for instance, were changed so as to reduce the number of Tamils and increase the number of Sinhalese. The disaffection caused by the new education policy became a major cause of Tamil militancy. But the seeds of the Sinhala-Tamil conflict were sown much earlier, and by the time of independence in 1948, the separate nationalist identities of the two groups were deeply entrenched. The Sinhalese used their numerical dominance to cast aside ideas of secularism and a pluralistic polity in favour of a race-based nationalism.

Yet in spite of their numerical preponderance, the Sinhalese political elite forged an identity of being an embattled people protecting a religion (Theravada Buddhism) and language (Sinhalese) followed by a minuscule fraction of the world's population. From that perspective, the Tamils represent an intrinsic cultural threat because even though they may be a minority within Sri Lanka, their language (Tamil) and religion (Hinduism) are *regionally* far more powerful. Therein lies the logic for the flourishing of Sinhalese nationalism. As a result, in 1955, the country abandoned the two-language policy and adopted an official Sinhala-only policy of Sinhala, and in 1972, Buddhism was enshrined in the constitution as the religion that was to be fostered and protected. Such institutional marginalization of the Tamil population, combined with the shrinkage in educational and employment opportunities fostered by the post-1989 reforms, caused the emergence of militant Tamil nationalism. The present state of hostilities has been fostered by repeated and often systematic attacks on Tamils during the riots of 1958, 1977, 1981, and 1983—attacks in which the complicity of the government has been only too evident.

The central Tamil nationalist demand is for a separate homeland, Eelam, carved out of the areas where the Tamils constitute a clear majority, that is, the north and north-east. The movement began developing in the early 1980s, when several organizations claimed to represent Tamil demands. Eventually the Liberation Tigers of Tamil Eelam (LTTE) emerged as the sole voice of the population, mainly by decimating all the other organizations. The LTTE, with its leftist ideology and organized structure, is now the central player along with the government in a civil war that has claimed around 70,000 lives and caused the displacement of nearly two million people. Suicide attacks have been the main weapon used by the LTTE against political, economic, and military targets. They have had a high rate of success in their attacks: among the many people whose lives they have taken were two prominent political leaders, former Indian Prime Minister Rajiv Gandhi, in 1991, and Sri Lankan President Ranasinghe Premadasa, in 1993. There have been several rounds of negotiations and ceasefire agreements between the government and the LTTE, but the situation remains highly unstable and volatile, with no meaningful political solution in sight.

LITERATURE

While the need for 'understanding terrorism' is often articulated with urgency, the process remains mechanical and myopic, characterized by cut-and-dried discourses abounding in empirical evidence with only modest attention being paid to social and political conditions. Literature, by personalizing the political and politicizing the personal, illuminates terrorism in ways that cannot be achieved through any other vehicle, and without which our grasp of terrorism remains incomplete. In literary texts, the social element is not merely a background condition for the emergence of the terrorist. Rather, the intimate portrayals of ordinary people help to show how the conditions of everyday life can fuel the politics of terror. Movements that have been designated as terrorist may at times appear in a sympathetic light when viewed from the perspective of a loved one. At other times, the innate human capacity for empathy reorganizes the lines that separate the soldier from the civilian, the terrorist from the victim, the state from the militant. Outside literature, terrorism is often explained as a product of cultural difference or psychological aberration. In literature, however, regardless of whether terrorism is cast in a sympathetic light or unequivocally rejected, the phenomenon is invariably embedded within a context that is both historicized and humanized.

The literature relating to militant nationalism in the colonial era not only recreates a tumultuous period but is surprisingly relevant to our own period. Bankim Chandra Chattopadhyay's *Anandamath* is widely accepted as one of the most influential texts to engage with the independence movement. Published in the early 1880s, the novel is set in the Bengal of a century back, around the time of the famine of 1770 and its aftermath. Written at the formative stage of the nationalist movement, the novel encapsulates Bankim's conviction that cultural regeneration is a prerequisite for political self-expression. The particular nature of cultural regeneration favoured by the writer—specifically, its communal character—has been a subject of much discussion. A Hindu cultural re-awakening, Bankim believed, was essential for the success of the fight against British colonialism. Over the past century, the novel became a crucial source in shaping the ideology of militant Hindu nationalism. Indeed, the text has, for the most part, come to be identified with a Hindu sectarian ideology, to the exclusion of its other motivating force: anti-imperialism.

The fact that *Anandamath*—informed by the twin energies of the cultural and the political, specifically identity formation and nationalism—turned out to be significant for its vision of a Hindu identity, rather than its anti-colonialism is, I believe, instructive for contemporary global politics. Terrorism, most commonly associated with an Islamist perspective, is generally construed as a product only of religious fundamentalism and nothing more. But just as in Bankim's novel, religion is often only an integument for deeper economic and political issues. This point is best illustrated by the Palestinian case, wherein it is the political, economic, and social grievances that drive the movement, albeit outwardly cloaked in religious garb.

The history of *Anandamath*, and its role in the shaping of the sub-continent's history, offers yet another lesson. The celebration of sectarian identity, *regardless of its initial motivating energy*, takes on an insidious life of its own. This can be seen in the continuing life of the novel's famous song, *Vande Mataram*. Often interpreted as signifying national pride, it has also been sung by Hindu rioters while targeting Muslims. Thus, even when the forging of religious identity may be only incidental to a militant political movement, it unleashes its own inescapable dynamics.

The works of two of South Asia's literary giants, Rabindranath Tagore and Sarat Chandra Chattopadhyay, offer a fascinating glimpse into the debates around militant politics. Sarat Chandra's *Pather Dabi* (1926; translated as *The Right of Way*), with its charismatic revolutionary protagonist, Savyasachi, made an indelible imprint on the times, despite the book having been banned by the British Indian government very soon after its publication. In Savyasachi, Sarat Chandra created the ideal anti-colonial hero, the scholar-warrior par excellence, whose dazzling physical powers are matched only by his amazing scholarship. Continually on the run from the British authorities, he ably justifies his doctrine of revolutionary terrorism. For him, the 'unscrupulous, naked, selfish, and brute' colonial power can be resisted only through the use of force. Any other form of intervention becomes a politics of reform, not revolution: 'You mustn't waste your time trying to improve the lot of factory workers. Nothing worthwhile can be achieved that way. Their true emancipation can come only through revolution ... revolution can't be achieved through peaceful means. Violence is essential for its success ... No government has given in peacefully to the right of the people for self-determination.'

After the book was banned, Sarat Chandra requested that Tagore join the extensive protest against the ban. Not surprisingly, the request was denied. By the time *Pather Dabi* was published, Tagore had constructed a well-developed critique of militant activism, and was making the case in his essays and fiction that the task for India lay in recognizing and reforming the social and spiritual life of its people rather than in the pursuit of the political. Sarat Chandra's novel directly challenged the core of the poet's political philosophy. A few years later, Tagore published *Char Adhyay* (1934; translated as *Four Chapters*), in which he fictionalizes his critique of collective action, in general, and of patriotism, in particular. It is a novel that can readily be read as a reply to *Pather Dabi*. In *Char Adhyay*, an underground terrorist movement is led by Indranath, who, while comparable with Savyasachi in his intellectual and physical powers, does not elicit the reader's admiration or sympathy. Unlike Savyasachi, Indranath does not have his creator's endorsement: he has been constructed as the anti-hero. His perspective on violence, which he views to be an essential means for his political goal, is clinical and instrumentalist. The instrumental approach pervades other aspects of his character, notably his relationship with the members of his group. He destroys their individuality and their selfhood, treating them as puppets advancing a great cause. Indranath's unwitting destruction of all that is worthwhile is consistent with Tagore's belief that 'the life of a country cannot be saved by killing its soul'.

If *Char Adhyay* is meant to be a literary critique of *Pather Dabi*, it does not, in my opinion, quite succeed in its objective. Tagore's novel argues that preserving the distinction between means and ends, between political action and its goals, is crucial; to its author, the danger is that the use of force becomes more than a mere means in the hands of patriots 'who have no faith in that which is above patriotism.' But Savyasachi is not one of those patriots. He clearly envisions political independence itself as only a means of realizing the full potential of the individual: 'My sole aim in life is to achieve the independence of India, but I've never made the mistake of thinking that there can be nothing greater in life. Independence is not an end in itself. Religion, peace, literature, happiness are all greater than that. It's for their fullest development that freedom is essential; else of what use is it?' Sarat Chandra, it may be argued, shared Tagore's cultural and individual ideals. But unlike Tagore, he also believed that political freedom was a necessary precondition for realizing those ideals. And if, therefore, the attainment of that freedom necessitated a certain kind of violence, then it had to be accepted.

The pre-Independence literature on terrorism anticipates some of the concerns that would, decades later, animate the literature on terrorism in the post-colonial era. The enmeshing of the personal and the political, and of the tortured connections between methods and goals, remains central to the literature of the contemporary era. K.S. Duggal's short story, 'Her Due of a Daughter', set in Punjab, exemplifies the literary probing of a political phenomenon. The story begins with a dreaded terrorist, Malikat, firing into a crowded marketplace; it ends with the capture of the terrorist by the authorities. But in the course of six pages, the terrorist becomes an increasingly sympathetic figure, ruffling the reader's received notions. After the shooting, Malikat is unable to join members of his group who are on a mission to rob a bank in a particular town. The reason he backs off is that a girl from his own village is married to a man from that town; to Malikat, a young girl from his village is like his own daughter, and to loot a bank in the town where she lives would be like committing a crime against his child. And so, instead of joining his fellow militants in their adventure, Malikat decides to visit the girl with a gift that would be the proper due of a daughter. While thus coming out of hiding to perform the role of a 'father', the terrorist is captured.

The story raises several questions. Do the writer's sympathies lie with the militants? Why does he portray a dreaded terrorist in a sympathetic light? However, if the writer had wished to generate a favourable impression of the movement, it is doubtful that he would have begun his story with a trigger-happy terrorist shooting into a market. It seems to me that the subject of engagement here is the terrorist, the person, rather than terrorism, the phenomenon. The story rescues the terrorist from the blanket condemnation of terrorism by reinserting him where, in a fundamental sense, he has always belonged: amongst his community. One might say that Duggal recognizes that the dominant language on terrorism eschews complexity in the make-up of a terrorist—perhaps out of fear that recognizing a terrorist's communitarian sensibilities would somehow undermine the stance against terrorism—and has sought to remedy the omission. Ashis Nandy, in an insightful essay on the nature of Indian terrorism, adopts a similar stance, distinguishing between the simplifying rhetoric of the 'modern nation-state, which shapes so much of the available theories of terrorism', and an assessment that while questioning terrorism also allows for a recognition of the 'multi-layered nature of human personality and social relationships.' Nandy, like the writer of the story, makes an argument for a more nuanced appreciation of terrorism—the kind that is fast receding from the dominant discourses on it.

In Mahashweta Devi's justly famous *The Mother of 1084*, we have a searing re-assessment of both the 'terrorist' and 'terrorism'. Narrated from the perspective of a bereaved mother, the novel offers an intensely intimate portrayal of both a militant and a movement. For its protagonist, Sujata, the only way of reconnecting with her murdered son, Brati, is by educating herself about the movement for which he sacrificed himself.

The reader accompanies Sujata in a voyage that is both political and personal as the shallowness and criminality of the bourgeois order is exposed. Sujata realizes that while she herself had always been repulsed by the values and lifestyle of her upper-middle-class family, for her son and his comrades, the issue was more than merely personal. Their rebellion against middle-class ideals and mores was part of a larger struggle against capitalist exploitation. Even as the locus of the actual movement was the countryside, this novel, set in Calcutta, focuses on the way the movement played out in urban centres. It rehearses well-known aspects of the movement, such as the committed involvement of bright young students cutting across socio-economic barriers. But the poignancy of the novel lies in its exposure of the brutal repression unleashed by the state in countering the insurgency. The complicity of the intelligentsia, with the state in its silent response to the draconian counter-insurgency, is repeatedly foregrounded. Sujata wonders at the reputation of Calcutta as a politically conscious and progressive city. She knows that intellectuals of the city protested against the oppression in Vietnam and Bangladesh, yet notices that they managed to remain quiet on analogous happenings in their own city. By thus comparing the repression in Calcutta with that of Vietnam and Bangladesh, Mahashweta Devi highlights the colonial aspects of a post-colonial state.

The novel remains remarkable for its empathy with a young, idealistic generation who embraced the ideal of a violent and radical restructuring of society. For Sujata, however, the ideal cannot be abstract; she is able to reach out to her lost son only by gaining a concrete sense of the ideals that moved him, and so she searches out answers and clues to various aspects of her son's life and beliefs which had remained hidden to her while he was still alive. In this quest, she meets her son's lover and comrade, Nandini, who was imprisoned and tortured for a year and is now under house arrest. Nandini has contempt for Sujata's generation, which has neither the language nor the sensibility to appreciate the struggle waged by their children. In contrast, Nandini cherishes the feelings that motivated their struggle in the first place. Far from being loyal to an abstract set of ideals, they had pledged allegiance to all that is joyous in everyday life:

Brati and I would walk all the way from Shyambazar to Bhowanipur, just talking all the way. Whatever we saw on the way—the people, the houses, the neon signs, red roses in a wayside florist's stall, festoons on the streets, newspapers pasted on boards near the bus stops, smiling faces, a beautiful image in a poem in a little magazine picked up at one of the stalls on the way, crowds clapping like mad at a political rally on the maidan, snatches of lilting tunes from Hindi films, everything spelt ecstasy, we couldn't hold the joy, we felt explosive.

Sujata connects the dots between this raw love for life and a movement aimed at demolishing exploitation and untruth. And, like the reader, she is left to wonder how the likes of Brati and Nandini could have been condemned as terrorists unmoored from civilized values and deserving of the full wrath of the state.

But where does idealism end and terror begin? Are the strategies of terror justifiable if informed by politically desirable goals? How do the methods of terror and ideologies of fanaticism become merged? These questions have haunted writers from disparate movements in South Asia. The Punjabi poet Pash, for instance, who was murdered by terrorists at a young age, documents the sinister consequences of the marriage of religious fanaticism with terror. His poems, such as 'Begging for Alms of Faith', remain remarkable for their empathy for ordinary people victimized by such forces. In literary tracts from other settings, such as Mitra Phukan's 'Hope', we have a similar engagement with the costs borne by common people, in whose alleged interest the movements are fought. Set in a battle-weary Assam, 'Hope' poignantly portrays the havoc wrought on families who lose their loved ones to a cause that is not their own. In the story, a man has simply disappeared, and there are no clues regarding his whereabouts. But the narrative is not about him. It is about the real and imaginative life journeys of his mother and his wife, who will forever be haunted by his absence.

Other costs are incurred by the vulnerable sections of society, especially as a consequence of identity-based movements. As feminist theorists have shown, women are typically made to bear the burden of communitarian identity in ways that deprive them of their interests and aspirations. Neerja Mattoo illustrates the issue in her discussion of the devastation visited on women's lives in Kashmir since 1990. She writes of the transformation of the Government College for Women in Srinagar from a liberal, multi-cultural haven for inquiring, independent minds to a constricted mono-culture occupied by subjugated and disciplined subjects. Mattoo, who was a student of the college in the 1950s and later became a teacher there, describes the period of the 1950s to the 1970s as 'heady', when 'everything seemed within reach, anything possible'. In the country as a whole, belief in progressive social transformation still held sway; within Kashmir, women's achievements were significant enough to have changed the gender landscape of education, business, and government. It was especially significant, as Mattoo notes, because all this was made possible even without the presence of an organized women's movement in the state. But the gains turned out to be temporary: with the onslaught of an identity-based separatist movement, women were once again relegated to the backwaters. An illustrious principal of the college had exhorted the women to always hold their heads high; but in a transformed landscape, 'safety lay in abject submission, whether to the orders of the militants or the state'.

A. Sivanandan's *When Memory Dies*, a novel of epic proportions, traces the history of Sri Lanka for close to a century. Indeed, it is this novel—in particular, its depiction of the militant Tamil movement with profound humanism and a meticulous historical vision—that inspired the present anthology. In a sharp departure from the prevalent discourses that take ethnic conflicts or terrorism in the country as a given, this novel provides a deeply contextualized reading of militancy. It documents how the communalism of the majority Sinhalese population, aided by state repression, gave birth to Tamil resistance. The resort to terrorism is shown as the last desperate means adopted by the Tamil youth to redress the steady disenfranchisement of their community. Para, a prominent character, insightfully sums up the motivation and nature of the movement: '[T]he British took away their past, the Sinhalese took away their future. All they have is the present. And that makes them dangerous.'

A striking achievement of Sivanandan's novel is that while it remains completely empathetic with the cause of the militants, it also unequivocally rejects their methods. *When Memory Dies* shows the deterioration of an idealistic movement motivated by social justice into a top-down organization governed by dogma. Vijay, another of the novel's prominent characters, tries to explain to a young friend the contradictions in the methods adopted by the LTTE: 'That way liberation never comes, and you know it. Socialism is the path to liberation, not just its end.' He offers a telling commentary on the 'suicide pill'—something that has come to symbolize Tamil terrorism in general:

It was such a symbol of waste, of no-hope, of death as a way of life. It had such a finality about it. Maybe it was alright at the beginning when it symbolized a heroic refusal to inform, at least it implied choice; but now that it had been raised to dogma, belief, ideology, it symbolized the end of choice. And the end of choice was the beginning of terror.

The writings anthologized herein illuminate those aspects of terrorism that often remain buried in the dominant discourses. For their authors, terrorism is not automatically to be taken as a grotesque, irremediable cancer arising incomprehensibly within a society, but is rather an inevitable outgrowth of our social and political order. At times, terrorism can be understood only by reaching out to the terrorist, as in Mahashweta Devi's work. In stories such as Chandani Lokugé's 'A Pair of Birds' and Mohan Bhandari's 'Comb Your Hair, My Dear', the focus is on the inextricable connections between the domestic and the political, between personal relationships and social commitment. Other texts, such as Agha Shahid Ali's 'The Floating Post Office', Samrat Upadhyay's 'A Refugee', or Bitopan Barua's 'The Hunt', explore the dark contours of terror from the perspective of its victims. Strategies of counter-insurgency are interrogated, sometimes through a sheer exposure of its brutal methods, as in Anita Agnihotri's 'Encirclement'. Confidence in easy distinctions is sometimes exposed, as in the haunting Sri Lankan story 'In the Garden' by Jean Arasanayagam. There we have a soldier on a mission to liberate civilians from Tamil militants. But as he walks through the deserted room of an abandoned house, the distinctions between soldier and civilian, between liberator and aggrandizer, get blurred: 'War has its own distinctive language. A "terrorist" is killed. A "soldier" sacrifices his life ... Who's to decide who's what ... We're all groping blindly in the jungle, while day by day the war is carried deeper and deeper within, into our innermost beings.'

August 2008   Nivedita Majumdar

I

FREEDOM AND TERROR

ANANDAMATH

Bankim Chandra Chattopadhyay

Bhabananda was sitting in the monastery singing Hari's praises when an extremely spirited *santan* called Jnanananda came up to him, looking crestfallen.

'Why so serious, Gosai?' asked Bhabananda.

'There seems to be a problem', said Jnanananda. 'Because of yesterday's fuss, the baldies only have to see someone in saffron to seize him![1] All the *santans* have stopped wearing saffron robes, with the exception of our leader Satyananda, who set off alone towards the city. What will happen if he's captured by the Muslims?'

'There isn't a Muslim in Bengal who can hold him against his will', replied Bhabananda. 'I know Dhirananda's gone after him. Still, I'll go to the city myself and see what's happening. You guard the monastery'.

Bhabananda then went into a private room and removed some clothes from a large chest. Suddenly his appearance changed: instead of the saffron robes he was now decked out in pleated trousers and a long, loose shirt, with a waistcoat and turbanlike headdress, and pointed shoes. The trident shape and other marks of sandalpaste from his face had gone, and his handsome features with their jet-black beard and moustache assumed a wonderful glow. Anyone seeing him now would

[1] 'Baldies': an uncomplimentary reference to Muslim men as 'shaven' or 'lopped'.

take him for a young man of Moghul descent. Thus attired but armed, Bhabananda left the monastery.

About two miles away stood a couple of small hillocks covered in jungle. Between the hillocks lay a secret place in which a large number of horses were kept. This was the stable of the monastery's inhabitants. Bhabananda untethered one of the horses, mounted it and galloped towards the city.

As he sped on he was suddenly brought to a halt, for there on the side of the road by the gurgling stream's bank—like a star fallen from heaven or a dart of lightning that had dropped from the clouds—lay the radiant form of a woman. Bhabananda saw no signs of life; an empty poison box lay by her side. Bhabananda was shocked, upset, afraid. Like Jibananda, he had never seen Mahendra's wife and child before, but whereas Jibananda had had the means to guess at their identity, Bhabananda had none. He had not seen the monk and Mahendra being led away as captives—nor was the child still there. From the empty box he could see that some woman had taken poison and died.

Bhabananda sat by the body and spent a long time in thought with his cheek resting in his hand. He touched the woman's head, armpits, hands and feet, and examined her in a number of mysterious ways. At last he concluded that there was still time, but even if he saved her, what then? This thought preoccupied him for a long while. Finally, he went into the forest and returned with the leaves of a certain tree. Crushing the leaves in his hands, he squeezed out some juice, and parting the woman's lips and teeth allowed the juice to trickle down his fingers into her mouth. Then he put a few drops in her nostrils and began to rub her body with the liquid. He repeated the process a number of times, now and then placing his hand near her nose to see if she breathed.

At first it seemed as if his efforts were in vain. But after persevering thus for a long time, Bhabananda's face brightened—he felt a faint breath of air on his fingers! He squeezed out some more of the juice, and gradually the woman's breath grew stronger. Feeling an artery, he saw that her pulse was beating. Finally, little by little, like the first flush of dawn from the east, like the first opening of the morning lotus, or like love's first awakening, Kalyani began to open her eyes. When he saw this, Bhabananda lifted her still half-recovered body onto his horse, and galloped into the city.

Before evening had fallen, the whole Order of Children had been informed that the monk Satyananda and Mahendra had been confined as prisoners in the city jail. Then, arriving in ones and twos, and in their tens and hundreds, the Order of *santans* began to surge into the forest that surrounded the temple. Everyone was armed, with the fire of anger in their eyes, pride in their faces, and a pledge on their lips. First a hundred came, then a thousand, then two thousand—thus did the number of men begin to grow.

Then, standing at the entrance of the monastery with sword in hand, Jnanananda cried out in a loud voice, 'For a long time we've been wanting to smash the nest of these weaver-birds, to raze the city of these Muslim foreigners, and throw it into the river—to burn the enclosure of these swine and purify Mother Earth again! Brothers, that day has come! The teacher of our teachers, our supreme preceptor—who's full of boundless wisdom, whose ways are always pure, the well-wisher of all, the benefactor of our land, who has pledged to give his life to proclaim the Eternal Code anew, whom we regard as the very essence of Vishnu's earthly form, who is our way to salvation—today lies captive in a Muslim jail! Is there no edge to our swords?' He thrust out his hand and cried, 'Is there no strength in this arm?' Striking his chest he roared, 'Is there no courage in this heart? Brothers, cry out 'O Hari, enemy of Mura, of Madhu and Kaitabha!' We worship Vishnu—who destroyed Madhu and Kaitabha, who wreaked the downfall of such powerful demons as Hiranyakashipu, Kamsa, Dantavakra, and Shishupala, by the loud whirling of whose discus even the immortal Shambhu became afraid, who's invincible, the giver of victory in battle. It is by his power that we have infinite might of arm! He is all-powerful. Let him but wish it and we will conquer in battle. Come, let's raze that city of the foreigners to the dust! Let's purify that pigsty by fire and throw it into the river! Let's smash that nest of tailor-birds to bits and fling it to the winds! Cry 'O Hari, enemy of Mura, of Madhu and Kaitabha!'

Then from thousands of throats in that forest all at once rose a most fearful cry, 'O Hari, enemy of Mura, of Madhu and Kaitabha!' Thousands of swords clashed as one, thousands of spears and shields were raised aloft, the slapping of thousands of arms began to sound like thunder, and thousands of bucklers began to grate on the rough backs of the massed warriors! Terrified by that great din the animals fled from the forest.

Screeching with fear, the birds rose into the sky and covered it. Just then hundreds of wardrums resounded all at once!

Crying 'O Hari, enemy of Mura, of Madhu and Kaitabha!' the massed ranks of *santans* began to emerge from the forest. In the dark of the night, with firm and steady tread and calling loudly on Hari, they headed in the direction of the city, their armour rustling, their weapons clattering, with a clamour from their voices, and occasional shouts to Hari in the din! Steadily, solemnly, wrathfully, mightily, that *santan* army reached the city and threw it into terror. Suddenly seeing this thunderbolt, the inhabitants fled in all directions, and the sentinels of the city became confused and unable to act.

The Children went straight to the royal jail, smashed it open and slew all the guards. Then they freed Satyananda and Mahendra, and lifting them above their heads, began to dance in triumph. There was a great hubbub of chanting to Hari, and once Satyananda and Mahendra had been freed, the *santans* set fire to as many Muslim homes as they could find.

'Go back!' cried Satyananda, when he saw this. 'There's no need for such a pointless and evil course of action!'

When they heard about these depredations of the Children, the region's authorities despatched a group of the district's sepoys to quell them. Not only were these armed with guns, but they also brought a cannon with them. When the Children heard that they had arrived, they came out of the Forest of the Monks to join battle. But what chance do staves and spears and a few guns have against a cannon? The Children were defeated, and they began to run away.

...

After the victory, the conquering band of heroes surrounded Satyananda on the banks of the Ajay River and began to celebrate in various ways. Only Satyananda grieved—for Bhabananda.

Thus far the Vaishnavas had not indulged much in the musical sounds of battle, but now, out of nowhere, thousands upon thousands of different kinds of drums, gongs, pipes and horns sounded together. The whole area, forest, river and open ground, was bursting with the sounds and echoes of the victory din. After the Children had celebrated in this way for a long time, Satyananda said, 'Today the Lord of the world has been merciful to us, and the *santan* code has triumphed! But one task remains. We cannot forget those who have been unable to celebrate with us and who have sacrificed their lives so that we could rejoice. Let us perform the rites for those who have been slain on the battlefield, and especially for that Great Soul who achieved this victory for us by sacrificing his life. Come, let us perform Bhabananda's rites with great ceremony'.

Then, repeating *Bande Mataram,* the company of *santans* proceeded to perform the rites for the dead. A great many gathered together, and with chants to Hari and many loads of sandalwood, prepared a pyre for Bhabananda. They laid him on it and lit the flame; then, walking round the pyre they began to chant *Hare Murare.* These were devotees of Vishnu, not members of some Vaishnava sect, so they cremated their dead.

When this was over, only five—Satyananda, Jibananda, Mahendra, Nabinananda and Dhirananda—remained in the forest to confer in secret.

Satyananda said, 'The vow for which we gave up every other code of life and all our joys is now fulfilled. No longer is there a foreign army in this region, and those who remain will be unable to withstand us even for a short time. What should we do next?'

Jibananda said, 'Why don't we capture the capital now?'

'My view precisely', said Satyananda.

'Well, where's our army?' said Dhirananda.

'Why, here it is', answered Jibananda.

'Where?' said Dhirananda. 'Do you see anyone about?'

'They're resting in various places', said Jibananda. 'As soon as you sound the call, they'll be here'.

Dhirananda said, 'Not a single one will turn up'.

'Why not?'

'Because everyone is out looting. The villages are now unprotected. They'll plunder the Muslim villages and the silk factories and go home. You won't find a single one about. I've gone and looked for them'.

Disheartened, Satyananda said, 'At any rate we are now in command of this whole region. No one is left to oppose us. So proclaim *santan* rule in Barendrabhumi, collect taxes from our subjects and assemble an army to conquer the city. When people hear that Hindus are ruling, many soldiers will gather under the *santans'* banner'.

Then Jibananda and the others paid obeisance to Satyananda and said, 'We bow down to you, highest Maharaj! At your command we'll set up a throne for you right here in this forest'.

For the first time in his life Satyananda showed anger. 'Shame!' he exclaimed. 'Do you think I'm an empty vessel? None of us are kings. We are renouncers! Now the Lord of heaven himself is the king of this land. When you conquer the city you can crown anyone you wish king, but know for sure that I'll not change my celibate state for any other. Now each of you go to his own work'. The four prostrated to the monk and rose up.

Without letting the others know, Satyananda motioned to Mahendra to wait. The others left and Mahendra remained. Satyananda said to him, 'All of you took a vow in Vishnu's shrine to follow the *santan* code. Both Bhabananda and Jibananda broke their vow, and Bhabananda today decided to pay the penalty. I'm always worried about when Jibananda too will surrender his life to make amends. Yet I live in the hope that for a secret reason unknown to you he won't be able to die just yet. You alone, however, kept your promise. The Children's task is now completed, and you had promised that until that was done you would not set eyes on your wife and daughter. But now that our task is accomplished, you can go back to living as a householder'.

Eyes streaming with tears, Mahendra said, 'Master, with whom can I live as a householder? My wife has taken her own life, and I've no idea where my daughter is or how to find her. You've told me that she's alive, and that's all I know'.

Then Satyananda called Nabinananda and said to Mahendra, 'This is Nabinananda Goswami, most pure of mind, and a dear disciple. Nabinananda will tell you how to find your daughter'. He made a sign to Shanti, who understood. She paid her respects to Satyananda and was about to leave when Mahendra said, 'Where will I meet you?'

'Come with me to my hermitage', said Shanti, and walked on ahead.

Respectfully touching the monk's feet, Mahendra took his leave and accompanied Shanti to her hermitage. It was now late at night. Even then, without resting, Shanti headed for the city.

When everyone had left, Satyananda lay prostrate by himself on the earth, and placing his head on the ground, began to meditate on the Lord of the world. The night had turned to dawn when someone came up, touched his head and said, 'I have come'.

Roused and startled, the monk said in great agitation, 'You have come? But why?'

'Because it is the appointed time', said the other.

'My Lord', said the monk, 'excuse me today. On Magh's approaching full-moon day, I will carry out your command'.

KARMAYOGIN
Early Political Writings

Aurobindo Ghose

The final indiscretion of Sir Edward Baker was also the worst. We do not think we have ever heard before of an official in Sir Edward's responsible position uttering such a menace as issued from the head of this province on an occasion and in a place where his responsibility should have been specially remembered. We have heard of autocrats threatening contumacious opponents with condign punishment, but even an autocrat of the fiercest and most absolute kind does not threaten the people with the punishment of the innocent. The thing is done habitually—in Russia; it has been done recently in Bengal; but it is always on the supposition that the man punished is guilty. Even in the deportations the Government has been eager to impress the world with the idea that although it is unable to face a court of justice with the 'information, not evidence' which is its excuse, it had ample grounds for its belief in the guilt of the deportees. Sir Edward Baker is the first ruler to declare with cynical openness that if he is not gratified in his demands, he will not care whether he strikes the innocent or the guilty. By doing so he has dealt an almost fatal blow at the prestige of the Government. If this novel principle of administration is applied, in what will the Government that terrorises from above be superior to the dynamiter who terrorises from below? Will not this be the negation of all law, justice and government? Does it not mean the reign of lawless force and that worst consummation of all, Anarchy from above struggling with Anarchy from below? The Government which denies the first principle of settled society, not only sanctions but introduces anarchy. It is thus that established authority creates violent revolutions. They abolish by persecution all the forces, leaders, advocates of peaceful and rapid progress and by their own will set themselves face to face with an enemy who cannot so be abolished. Terrorism thrives on administrative violence and injustice; that is the only atmosphere in which it can thrive and grow. It sometimes follows the example of indiscriminate violence from above; it sometimes, though very rarely, sets it from below. But the power above which follows the example from below is on the way to committing suicide. It has consented to the abrogation of the one principle which is the life-breath of settled governments.

THE PERSONAL RESULT

Sir Edward Baker came into office with the reputation of a liberal ruler anxious to appease unrest. Till now he has maintained it in spite of the ominous pronouncement he made, when introducing measures of repression, about the insufficiency of the weapons with which the Government was arming itself. But by his latest pronouncement, contradicting as it does the first principles not only of Liberalism but of all wise Conservatism all over the world, he has gone far to justify those who were doubtful of his genuine sympathy with the people. Probably he did not himself realise what a wound he was giving to his own reputation and with it to his chances of carrying any portion of the people with him.

A ONE-SIDED PROPOSAL

A writer in the *Indian World* has been holding out the olive branch to the advanced Nationalist party and inviting them into the fold of the body which now calls itself the Congress. The terms of this desirable conciliation seem to us a little peculiar. The Nationalists are to give up all their contentions and in return the Bombay coterie may graciously give up their personal justified afterwards in quarrelling with the good faith of the Moderates merely because they themselves had chosen to enter the Convention on conditions which would have meant hopeless ineffectiveness in that body and political suicide outside? If infants in diplomacy choose to cherish an obstinate admiration for their own Machiavellian cleverness or mere bookmen who do not understand the A.B.C. of practical politics, elect to play the game with past masters of political statecraft, the result is a foregone conclusion. We have exposed over and over again the hollowness of the pretensions of this measure to figure as a great step forward in Indian administration or the beginning of a new progressive era in Indian politics, but we did not need the publication of the Regulations to open our eyes to this hollowness. Lord Morley's own statements, the nature of things and of humanity and the clauses of the Reform Bill itself were a sufficient guide to anyone with even an elementary knowledge of politics.

The Nasik Murder

The tale of assassinations is evidently not at an end; and it is difficult to believe that they will be until a more normal condition of things has been restored. The sporadic and occasional character of these regrettable incidents is sufficient to prove that they are not the work of a widespread Terrorist organisation, but of individuals or small groups raw in organisation and irresolute in action. The Anglo-Indian superstition of a great Revolutionary organisation like the Russian Revolutionary Committee is a romantic delusion. The facts are entirely inconsistent with it. What we see is that, where there is sporadic repression of a severe kind on the part of the authorities, there is sporadic retaliation on the part of a few youthful conspirators, perfectly random in its aim and objective. The Nasik murder is an act of terrorist reprisal for the dangerously severe sentence passed on the revolutionary versifier Savarkar. It is natural that there should have been many meetings in Maharashtra to denounce the assassination, but such denunciations do not carry us very far. They have no effect whatever on the minds of the men who are convinced that to slay and be slain is their duty to their country. The disease is one that can only be dealt with by removing its roots, not by denouncing its symptoms. The Anglo-Indian papers find the root in our criticism of Government action and policy and suggest the silencing of the Press as the best means of removing the root. If the Government believe in this antiquated diagnosis, they may certainly try the expedient suggested. Our idea is that it will only drive the roots deeper. We have ourselves, while strongly opposing and criticising the actions and policy of the bureaucracy, abstained from commenting on specific acts of repression, as we had no wish to inflame public feeling; but to silence Nationalism means to help Terrorism. Our view is that the only way to get rid of the disease is to disprove Mr. Gokhale's baneful teaching that violence is the only means of securing independence, to give the people hope in a peaceful and effective means of progress towards that ideal, which is now the openly or secretly cherished ideal of every Indian, and to that end to organise peaceful opposition and progress within the law. If the Government can retrace their steps and remove the ban from lawful passive resistance and self-help and the Nationalist Party, while holding its ultimate political aim, will define its immediate objective within limits which a Radical Government can hereafter consider, we believe politics in India will assume a normal course under normal conditions. We propose to do our part; we will see whether the Government thinks it worth their while to respond. They ought to be able to understand by this time that Nationalism and not Moderatism is the effective political force in India.

THE HIGH COURT ASSASSINATION

The startling assassination of Deputy Superintendent Shams-ul-Alam on Monday in the precincts of the High Court, publicly, in daylight, under the eyes of many and in a crowded building, breaks the silence which had settled on the country, in a fashion which all will deplore. The deceased officer was perhaps the ablest, most energetic and most zealous member of the Bengal detective force. It was his misfortune that he took the leading part not only in the Alipur Bomb Case in which he zealously and untiringly assisted the Crown solicitors, but in the investigation of the Haludbari and Netra dacoities. The nature of his duties exposed him to the resentment of the small Terrorist bodies whose continued existence in Bengal is proved by this last daring and reckless crime. Under such circumstances a man carries his life in his hand and it seems only a matter of time when it will be struck from him. We have no doubt that the Government will suitably recognise his services by a handsome provision for his family. As for the crime itself, it is one of the boldest of the many bold acts of violence for which the Terrorists have been responsible. We wish we could agree with some of our contemporaries that the perpetrators of these deplorable outrages are dastards and cowards; for, if it were so, Terrorism would be a thing to be abhorred, but not feared. On the contrary, the Indian Terrorist seems to be usually a man fanatical in his determination and daring, to prefer public places and crowded buildings for his field and to scorn secrecy and a fair chance of escape. It is this remarkable feature which has distinguished alike the crimes at Nasik, London, Calcutta, to say nothing of the assassination of Gossain in jail. With such men it is difficult to deal. Neither fear nor reasoning, disapprobation nor isolation can have any effect on them. Nor will the Government of this country allow us to use what we believe to be the only effective means of combating the spread of the virus among the people. All we can do is to sit with folded hands and listen to the senseless objurgations of the Anglo-Indian Press, waiting for a time when the peaceful expression and organisation of our national aspirations will no longer be penalised. It is then that Terrorism will vanish from the country and the nightmare be as if it never had been.

ANGLO-INDIAN PRESCRIPTIONS

The Anglo-Indian papers publish their usual senseless prescriptions for the cure of the evil. The *Englishman* informs us that it is at last tired of these outrages and asks in a tone full of genuine weariness when the Government will take the steps which Hare Street has always been advising. It seems to us that the Government have gone fairly far in that direction. The only remaining steps are to silence the Press entirely, abolish the necessity of investigation and trial and deport every public man in India. And when by removing everything and everyone that still encourages the people to persevere in peaceful political agitation, Russia has been reproduced in India and all is hushed except the noise of the endless duel between the omnipotent policeman and the secret assassin, the *Englishman* will be satisfied,—but the country will not be at peace. The *Indian Daily News* more sensibly suggests police activity in detecting secret organisations,—although its remarks would have sounded better without an implied prejudgment of the Nasik case. If the police were to employ the sound detective methods employed in England and France, it would take them a little longer to effect a coup, but there would be some chance of real success. It is not by indiscriminate arrests, harassing house-searches undertaken on the word of informers paid so much for each piece of information true or false, and interminable detention of undertrial prisoners in jail that these formidable secret societies will be uprooted. Such processes are more likely to swell their numbers and add to their strength. The *Statesman* is particularly wroth with the people of this country for their objection to police methods and goes so far as to lay the blame for the murder of Shams-ul-Alam on these objections. If we had only submitted cheerfully to police harassment, all this would not have happened! The bitter ineptitude of our contemporary grows daily more pronounced and takes more and more refuge in ridiculously inconsequent arguments. Is it the objectionable methods or our objections to them that are to blame? We may safely say that, whatever influences may have been at work in the mind of the assassin, the occasional criticisms of vexatious house-search in the Bengali journals had nothing to do with his action. The *Statesman* does not scruple, like other Anglo-Indian papers, to question the sincerity of the condemnations of Terrorist outrage which are nowadays universal throughout the country, and to support its insinuations it has to go as far back as the Gossain murder and the demonstrations that followed it. These demonstrations were not an approval of Terrorism as a policy, but an outburst of gratitude to the man who removed a dangerous and reckless perjurer whose evil breath was scattering ruin and peril over innocent homes and noble and blameless heads throughout Bengal. We do not praise or justify that outburst,—for murder is murder, whatever its motives,—but it is not fair to give it a complexion other than the one it really wore. If it had really been true that a whole nation approved of Terrorism and supported the assassin by secret or open sympathy, it would be a more damning indictment of British statesmanship in India than any seditious pen could have framed. The Chowringhee paper's libellous insinuation that the secret societies are not secret and their members are known to the public, has only to be mentioned in order to show the spirit of this gratuitous adviser of the Indian people. Nor can one peruse without a smile the suggestion that the Hindu community should use the weapon of social ostracism against the Terrorists. Whom are we to outcaste, the hanged or transported assassin, or his innocent relatives?

THE PARTY OF REVOLUTION

Be the fault whose you will, ours or the Government's, the existence of an organised party of armed Revolution in Indian politics is now a recognised factor of the situation. The enormous strides with which events have advanced and a sky full of trouble but also of hope been overcast and grown full of gloom and menace, can be measured by the rapidity with which this party has developed. It is only five years since the national movement sprang into being. The cry was then for self-help and passive resistance. Boycott, Swadeshi, Arbitration, National Education, were the hope of the future, the means of self-regeneration. In five years everything has been struck to the earth. Boycott has almost disappeared, Swadeshi languishes under sentence of arrest, Arbitration died still-born, National Education is committing suicide. A tremendous disintegration has taken place and we look amazed on the ruins of the work our labour and our sacrifice erected. It is a huge defeat, an astonishing catastrophe. And on those ruins grim, wild-eyed, pitiless to itself and to others, mocking at death and defeat with its raucous and careless laughter Revolution rises repeating the language of the old-world insurgents, cherishing a desperate hope which modern conditions deny, grasping at the weapons which the Slav and the Celt have brought into political warfare. The seeds which the *Yugantar* sowed in its brief, violent and meteoric career have borne fruit in unexpected quarters and new-born journals repeat in foreign lands and in the English tongue the incitations to revolt and slaughter which have been put down by the strong hand in India of the law. Money is forthcoming to support a journalism which must obviously be all cost and no profit, young men exile themselves from their native land by openly joining the party of violence and in India itself repeated blows have been struck paralysing the hope and the effort to revive the activity of that broader and calmer Nationalism which, recognising modern conditions, still commands the allegiance of the bulk of the nation.

Its Growth

What is the precise nature, propaganda and strength of this party, which by so small an expenditure of energy has produced such surprising results? When the *Yugantar,* abandoning its habit of philosophic Revolutionism, first began to enter the field of practical politics, to sneer at passive resistance and gird at its chief exponents, no one thought that its change of attitude portended anything serious. Men read the paper for the amazing brilliance, grace and sustained force of its style, a new thing in Bengali journalism, and from the natural attraction men feel for strong writing and bold thought even when they do not agree with it. Afterwards the reckless fight of the *Yugantar* for existence attracted a more dangerous admiration and from that time the journal changed from a thing of literary interest into a political force. Even then it was taken as a practical guide only among a section of young men small in numbers and without means or influence. But things have changed since then. A void has been created by the conviction, deportation, self-imposed exile or silence of the great Nationalist speakers, writers, organisers, and the dangerous opinions and activities then created have rushed in to occupy the vacuum. The Nationalism we advocate is a thing difficult to grasp and follow, needing continual intellectual exposition to keep its hold on the mind, continual inspiration and encouragement to combat the impatience natural to humanity; its methods are comparatively new in politics and can only justify themselves to human conservatism by distinguished and sustained success. The preaching of the new revolutionary party is familiar to human imagination, supported by the records of some of the most inspiring episodes in history, in consonance with the impatience, violence and passion for concrete results which revolutionary epochs generate. The growing strength of this party is not difficult to explain; it is extremely difficult to combat. ...

ASSEMBLY BOMB CASE

Bhagat Singh

STATEMENT IN THE SESSION COURT

(Read in the Court on 6th June 1929, by Mr. Asaf Ali on behalf of Bhagat Singh and B.K. Dutt)

We stand charged with certain serious offences, and at this stage it is but right that we must explain our conduct.

In this connection, the following questions arise.

1. Were the bombs thrown into Chamber, and, if so, why?

2. Is the charge, as framed by the Lower Court, correct or otherwise?

To the first half of first question, our reply is in the affirmative, but since some of the so-called 'eye witnesses' have perjured themselves and since we are not denying our liability to that extent, let our statement about them be judged for what it is worth. By way of an illustration, we may point out that the evidence of Sergeant Terry regarding the seizure of the pistol from one of us is a deliberate falsehood, for neither of us had the pistol at the time we gave ourselves up. Other witnesses, too, who have deposed to having seen bombs being thrown by us have not scrupled to tell lies. This fact had its own moral for those who aim at judicial purity and fairplay. At the same time, we acknowledge the fairness of the Public Prosecutor and the judicial attitude of the Court so far.

VICEROY'S VIEWS ENDORSED

In our reply to the next half of the first question, we are constrained to go into some detail to offer a full and frank explanation of our motive and the circumstances leading up to what has now become a historic event.

When we were told by some of the police officers, who visited us in jail that Lord Irwin in his address to the joint session of the two houses described the event as an attack directed against no individual but against an institution itself, we readily recognized that the true significance of the incident had been correctly appreciated.

We are next to none in our love for humanity. Far from having any malice against any individual, we hold human life sacred beyond words.

We are neither perpetrators of dastardly outrages, and, therefore, a disgrace to the country, as the pseudo-socialist Dewan. Chaman Lai is reported to have described us, nor are we 'Lunatics' as The Tribune of Lahore and some others would have it believed.

PRACTICAL PROTEST

We humbly claim to be no more than serious students of the history and conditions of our country and her aspirations. We despise hypocrisy, our practical protest was against the institution, which since its birth, has eminently helped to display not only its worthlessness but its far-reaching power for mischief. The more we have been convinced that it exists only to demonstrate to world Indian's humiliation and helplessness, and it symbolizes the overriding domination of an irresponsible and autocratic rule. Time and again the national demand has been pressed by the people's representatives only to find the waste paper basket as its final destination.

ATTACK ON INSTITUTION

Solemn resolutions passed by the House have been contemptuously trampled under foot on the floor of the so-called Indian Parliament. Resolution regarding the repeal of the repressive and arbitrary measures have been treated with sublime contempt, and the government measures and proposals, rejected as unacceptable by the elected members of the legislatures, have been restored by mere stroke of the pen. In short, we have utterly failed to find any justification for the existence of an institution which, despite all its pomp and splendour, organized with the hard earned money of the sweating millions of India, is only a hollow show and a mischievous make-believe. Alike, have we failed to comprehend the mentality of the public leaders who help the government to squander public time and money on such a manifestly stage-managed exhibition of Indian's helpless subjection.

No Hope for Labour

We have been ruminating upon all these matters, as also upon the wholesale arrests of the leaders of the labour movement. When the introduction of the Trade Disputes Bill brought us into the Assembly to watch its progress, the course of the debate only served to confirm our conviction that the labouring millions of India had nothing to expect from an institution that stood as a menacing monument to the strangling of the exploiters and the serfdom of the helpless labourers. Finally, the insult of what we consider, an inhuman and barbarous measure was hurled on the devoted head of the representatives of the entire country, and the starving and struggling millions were deprived of their primary right and the sole means of improving their economic welfare. None who has felt like us for the dumb-driven drudges of labourers could possibly witness this spectacle with equanimity. None whose heart bleeds for them, who have given their life-blood in silence to the building up of the economic structure could repress the cry which this ruthless blow had wrung out of our hearts.

Bomb Needed

Consequently, bearing in mind the words of the late Mr. S.R. Das, once Law Member of the Governor-General's Executive Council, which appeared in the famous letter he had addressed to his son, to the effect that the 'Bomb was necessary to awaken England from her dreams', we dropped the bomb on the floor of the Assembly Chamber to register our protest on behalf of those who had no other means left to give expression to their heart-rending agony. Our sole purpose was 'to make the deaf hear' and to give the heedless a timely warning. Others have as keenly felt as we have done, and from under the seeming stillness of the sea of Indian humanity, a veritable storm is about to break out. We have only hoisted the 'danger-signal' to warn those who are speeding along without heeding the grave dangers ahead. We have only marked the end of an era of Utopian non-violence, of whose futility the rising generation has been convinced beyond the shadow of doubt.

IDEAL EXPLAINED

We have used the expression Utopian non-violence, in the foregoing paragraph which requires some explanation. Force when aggressively applied is 'violence' and is, therefore, morally unjustifiable, but when it is used in the furtherance of a legitimate cause, it has its moral justification. The elimination of force at all costs in Utopian, and the mew movement which has arisen in the country, and of that dawn we have given a warning, is inspired by the ideal which guided Guru Gobind Singh and Shivaji, Kamal Pasha and Riza Khan, Washington and Garibaldi, Lafayette and Lenin.

As both the alien Government and the Indian public leaders appeared to have shut their eyes to the existence of this movement, we felt it as our duty to sound a warning where it could not go unheard.

We have so far dealt with the motive behind the incident in question, and now we must define the extent of our intention.

NO PERSONAL GRUDGE

We bore no personal grudge or malice against anyone of those who received slight injuries or against any other person in the Assembly. On the contrary, we repeat that we hold human life sacred beyond words, and would sooner lay down our own lives in the service of humanity than injure anyone else. Unlike the mercenary soldiers of the imperialist armies who are disciplined to kill without compunction, we respect, and, in so far as it lies in our power, we attempt to save human life. And still we admit having deliberately thrown the bombs into the Assembly Chamber. Facts, however, speak for themselves and our intention would be judged from the result of the action without bringing in Utopian hypothetical circumstances and presumptions.

NO MIRACLE

Despite the evidence of the Government Expert, the bombs that were thrown in the Assembly Chamber resulted in slight damage to an empty bench and some slight abrasions in less than half a dozen cases, while government scientists and experts have ascribed this result to a miracle, we see nothing but a precisely scientific process in all this incident. Firstly, the two bombs exploded in vacant spaces within the wooden barriers of the desks and benches, secondly, even those who were within 2 feet of the explosion, for instance, Mr. P. Rau, Mr. Shanker Rao and Sir George Schuster were either not hurt or only slightly scratched. Bombs of the capacity deposed to by the Government Expert (though his estimate, being imaginary is exaggerated), loaded with an effective charge of potassium chlorate and sensitive (explosive) picrate would have smashed the barriers and laid many low within some yards of the explosion.

Again, had they been loaded with some other high explosive, with a charge of destructive pellets or darts, they would have sufficed to wipe out a majority of the Members of the Legislative Assembly. Still again we could have flung them into the official box which was occupied by some notable persons. And finally we could have ambushed Sir John Simon whose luckless Commission was loathed by all responsible people and who was sitting in the President's gallery at the time. All these things, however, were beyond our intention and bombs did no more than they were designed to do, and the miracle consisted in no more than the deliberate aim which landed them in safe places.

We then deliberately offered ourselves to bear the penalty for what we had done and to let the imperialist exploiters know that by crushing individuals, they cannot kill ideas. By crushing two insignificant units, a nation cannot be crushed. We wanted to emphasize the historical lesson that *lettres de cachets* and Bastilles could not crush the revolutionary movement in France. Gallows and the Siberian mines could not extinguish the Russian Revolution. Bloody Sunday, and Black and Tans failed to strangle the movement of Irish freedom.

Can ordinances and Safety Bills snuff out the flames of freedom in India? Conspiracy cases, trumped up or discovered and the incarcertion of all young men, who cherish the vision of a great ideal, cannot check the march of revolution. But a timely warning, if not unheeded, can help to prevent loss of life and general sufferings.

We took it upon ourselves to provide this warning and our duty is done. (Bhagat Singh was asked in the lower court what he meant by word 'Revolution'. In answer to that question, he said) 'Revolution' does not necessarily involve sanguinary strife nor is there any place in it for individual vendetta. It is not the cult of the bomb and the pistol. By

'Revolution' we mean that the present order of things, which is based on manifest injustice, must change. Producers or labourers in spite of being the most necessary element of society, are robbed by their exploiters of the fruits of their labour and deprived of their elementary rights. The peasant who grows corn for all, starves with his family, the weaver who supplies the world market with textile fabrics, has not enough to cover his own and his children's bodies, masons, smiths and carpenters who raise magnificent palaces, live like pariahs in the slums. The capitalists and exploiters, the parasites of society, squander millions on their whims. These terrible inequalities and forced disparity of chances are bound to lead to chaos. This state of affairs cannot last long, and it is obvious, that the present order of society in merry-making is on the brink of a volcano. The whole edifice of this civilization, if not saved in time, shall crumble. A radical change, therefore, is necessary and it is the duty of those who realize it to reorganize society on the socialistic basis. Unless this thing is done and the exploitation of man by man and of nations by nations is brought to an end, sufferings and carnage with which humanity is threatened today cannot be prevented. All talk of ending war and ushering in an era of universal peace is undisguised hypocrisy.

By 'Revolution', we mean the ultimate establishment of an order of society which may not be threatened by such breakdown, and in which the sovereignty of the proletariat should be recognized and a world federation should redeem humanity from the bondage of capitalism and misery of imperial wars.

This is our ideal, and with this ideology as our inspiration, we have given a fair and loud enough warning.

If, however, it goes unheeded and the present system of government continues to be an impediment in the way of the natural forces that are swelling up, a grim struggle will ensure involving the overthrow of all obstacles, and the establishment of the dictatorship of the proletariat to pave the way for the consummation of the ideal of revolution. Revolution is an inalienable right of mankind. Freedom is an imperishable birth right of all. Labour is the real sustainer of society. The sovereignty is the ultimate destiny of the workers. For these ideals, and for this faith, we shall welcome any suffering to which we may be condemned. At the altar of this revolution we have brought our youth as an incense, for no sacrifice is too great for so magnificent a cause. We are content, we await the advent of Revolution 'Long Live Revolution'.

STATEMENT BEFORE THE LAHORE
HIGH COURT BENCH

[Through this brilliant statement Bhagat Singh demolished the basis of the Sessions Court judgement and emphasised the importance of motive. The motive of action, he argued, should be the main consideration while judging the offence of an accused.]

MY LORDS,

We are neither lawyers nor masters of English language, nor holders of degrees. Therefore, please do not expect any oratorical speech from us. We therefore pray that instead of going into the language mistakes of our statement Your Lordships will try to understand the real sense of it. Leaving other points to our lawyers, I will confine myself to one point only. The point is very important in this case. The point is as to what were our intentions and to what extent we are guilty. This is a very complicated question and no one will be able to express before you that height to mental elevation which inspired us to think and act in a particular manner. We want that this should be kept in mind while assessing our intentions of our offence. According to the famous jurist Solomon, one should not be punished for his criminal offence if his aim is not against law. We had submitted a written statement in the Sessions Court. That statement explains our aim and, as such, explains our intentions also. But the learned judge dismissed it with one stroke of pen, saying that 'generally the operation of law is not affected by how or why one committed the offence. In this country the aim of the offence is very rarely mentioned in legal commentaries.' My Lords, our contention is that under the circumstances the learned judge ought to have judged us either by the result of our action or on the basis of the psychological part of our statement. But he did not take any of these factors into consideration.

The point to be considered is that the two bombs we threw in the Assembly did not harm anybody physically or economically. As such the punishment awarded to us is not only very harsh but revengeful also. Moreover, the motive knowing his psychology. And no one can do justice to anybody without taking his motive into consideration. If we ignore the motive, the biggest general of the wars will appear like ordinary murderers; revenue officers will look like thieves and cheats. Even judges will be accused of murder. This way the entire social system and the civilisation will be reduced to murders, thefts and cheating. If we ignore the motive, the government will have no right to expect sacrifice from its people and its officials. Ignore the motive and every religious preacher will be dubbed as a preacher of falsehoods, and every prophet will be charged of misguiding crores of simple and ignorant people. If we set aside the motive, then Jessus Christ will appear to be a man responsible for creating disturbances, breaking peace and preaching revolt, and will be considered to be a 'dangerous personality' in the language of the law. But we worship him. He commands great respect in our hearts and his image creates vibrations of spiritualism amongst us. Why? Because the inspiration behind his actions was that of a high ideal. The rulers of that age could not recognise that high idealism. They only saw his outward actions. Nineteen centuries have passed since then. Have we not progressed during this period? Shall we repeat that mistake again? It that be so, then we shall have to admit that all the sacrifices of the mankind and all the efforts of the great martyrs were useless and it would appear as if we are still at the same place where we stood twenty centuries back.

From the legal point of view also, the question of motive is of special importance. Take the example of General Dyer. He resorted to firing and killed hundreds of innocent and unarmed people. But the military court did not order him to be shot. It gave him lakhs of rupees as award. Take another example. Shri Kharag Bahadur Singh, a young Gurkha, killed a Marwari in Calcutta. If the motive be set aside, then Kharag Bahadur Singh ought to have been hanged. But he was awarded a mild sentence of a few years only. He was even released much before the expiry of his sentence. Was there any loophole in the law that he escaped capital punishment? Or, was the charge of murder not proved against him? Like us, he also accepted the full responsibility of his action, but he escaped death. He is free today. I ask Your Lordship, why was he not awarded capital punishment? His action was well calculated and well planned. From the motive end, his action was more serious and fatal than ours. He was awarded a mild punishment because his intentions were good. He saved the society from a dirty leach who had sucked the life-blood of so many pretty young girls. Kharag Singh was given a mild punishment just to uphold the formalities of the law. This principle (that the law does not take motive into consideration - ed.) is quite absurd. This is against the basic principles of the law which declares that 'the law is for man and not man for the law'. As such, why the same norms are not being applied to us also? It is quite clear that while convicting Kharag Singh his motive was kept in mind, otherwise a murderer can never escape the hangman's noose. Are we being deprived of the ordinary advantage of the law because our offence is against the government, or because our action has a political importance?

My Lords, under these circumstances, please permit us to assert that a government which seeks shelter behind such mean methods has no right to exist. If it is exists, it is for the time being only, and that too with the blood of thousands of people on its head. If the law does not see the motive there can be no justice, nor can there be stable peace.

Mixing of arsenic (poison) in the flour will not be considered to be a crime, provided its purpose is to kill rats. But if the purpose is to kill a man, it becomes a crime of murder. Therefore, such laws which do not stand the test of reason and which are against the principle of justice, should be abolished. Because of such unjust laws, many great intellectuals had to adopt the path of revolt. The facts regarding our case are very simple. We threw two bombs in the legislative Assembly on April 8, 1929. As a result of the explosion, a few persons received minor scratches. There was pandemonium in the chamber, hundreds of visitors and members of the Assembly ran out. Only my friend B.K. Dutt and myself remained seated in the visitors gallery and offered ourselves for arrest. We were tried for attempt to murder, and convicted for life. As mentioned above, as a result of the bomb explosion, only four or five persons were slightly injured and one bench got damaged. We offered ourselves for arrest without any resistance. The Sessions Judge admitted that we could have very easily escaped, had we had any intention like that. We accepted our offence and gave a statement explaining our position. We are not afraid of punishment. But we do not want that we should be wrongly understood. The judge removed a few paragraphs from our statement. This we consider to be harmful for our real position.

A proper study of the full text of our statement will make it clear that, according to us, our country is passing through a delicate phase.

We saw the coming catastrophe and thought it proper to give a timely warning with a loud voice, and we gave the warning in the manner we thought proper. We may be wrong. Our line of thinking and that of the learned judge may be different, but that does not mean that we be deprived of the permission to express our ideas, and wrong things be propagated in our name.

In our statement we explained in detail what we mean by 'Long Live Revolution' and 'Down With Imperialism'. That formed the crux of our ideas. That portion was removed from our statement. Generally a wrong meaning is attributed to the word revolution. That is not our understanding. Bombs and pistols do not make revolution. That is not our understanding. Bombs and pistols do not make revolution. The sword of revolution is sharpened on the whetting-stone of ideas. This is what we wanted to emphasise. By revolution we mean the end of the miseries of capitalist wars. It was not proper to pronounce judgement without understanding our aims and objects and the process of achieving them. To associate wrong ideas with our names is out and out injustice.

It was very necessary to give the timely warning that the unrest of the people is increasing and that the malady may take a serious turn, if not treated in time and properly. If our warning is not heeded, no human power will be able to stop it. We took this step to give proper direction to the storm. We are serious students of history. We believe that, had the ruling powers acted correctly at the proper time, there would have been no bloody revolutions in France and Russia. Several big powers of the world tried to check the storm of ideas and were sunk in the atmosphere of bloodshed. The ruling people cannot change the flow of the current. We wanted to give the first warning. Had we aimed at killing some important personalities, we would have failed in the attainment of our aim.

My Lords, this was the aim and the spirit behind our action, and the result of the action corroborates our statement. There is one more point which needs elucidation, and that is regarding the strength of the bombs. Had we had no idea of the strength of the bombs, there would have been no question of our throwing them in the presence of our respected national leader like Pandit Motilal Nehru, Shri Kelkar, Shri Jayaker and Shri Jinnah. How could we have risked the lives of our leaders? After all we are not mad and, had we been so, we would have certainly been sent to the lunatic asylum, instead of being put in jail. We had full knowledge about the strength of the bombs and that is why we acted with so much confidence. It was very easy to have thrown the bombs on the occupied benches, but it was difficult to have thrown them on unoccupied seats. Had we not of saner mind or had we been mentally unbalanced, the bombs would have fallen on occupied benches and not in empty places. Therefore I would say that we should be rewarded for the courage we showed in carefully selecting the empty places. Under these conditions, My Lords, we think we have not been understood, My Lords, we think we have not been understood properly. We have not come before you to get our sentences reduced. We have come here to clarify our position. We want that we should not be given any unjust treatment, nor should any unjust opinion be pronounced about us. The question of punishment is of secondary importance before us.

THE RIGHT OF WAY

Sarat Chandra Chattopadhyay

.

'What d'you mean?' cried Bharati in alarm. 'Did you really mean to kill Brojendra?'

Doctor nodded his head. 'Yes. If the police doesn't send him to jail in my absence, I'll have to kill him after I return.'

Bharati, who had been leaning against Doctor, now sat erect. Though she did not say anything, it was clear to Doctor that she had been greatly shocked. But he said nothing and picked up the oars so as to make the crossing.

After a while Bharati said softly, 'Suppose I had been Sumitra, would you've deserted me even then?'

'But you're not Sumitra; you're Bharati,' laughed Doctor. 'So I won't desert you. I'll entrust you with my work instead.'

'Please don't do that,' cried Bharati. 'I don't want to be associated with all these murderous activities. I can't work for your secret society any longer.'

'Then you'll also leave me in the lurch like the others,' said Doctor.

'How could you say such a thing?' said Bharati, terribly upset. 'Whatever you do, I can never leave you. I'll die before I do that. No, I'll continue to work for you until you choose to release me.'

She added after a pause, 'But I know that killing people isn't your mission in life. Rather it's making them learn how to live like men. I'll continue to help you fulfil that mission. That's why I had joined your organisation.'

Doctor stopped rowing for a minute and asked, 'And what is this mission?'

'It was not necessary for Pather Dabi to become a secret organisation. I've seen with my own eyes the miserable condition of the factory workers—their sinful lives, their evil habits, their inhuman condition. If I can reduce even a fraction of their misery, I shall consider my life well-spent. Tell me honestly, isn't this your work?'

Doctor did not reply immediately. He remained absorbed in his thoughts for a long, long while. Then suddenly he stopped rowing and said slowly, 'That's not your work, Bharati. Your duty lies elsewhere. That is Sumitra's job and I've entrusted it to her.'

The tide was rising, though it had still not reached them. In the still waters their small boat began to glide along slowly.

Doctor said calmly, as before, 'It'll be proper to tell you, Bharati, that I didn't establish Pather Dabi for the betterment of a few factory workers. It has a much higher aim. To achieve that aim it may even become necessary to sacrifice these people one day like so many sheep and goats.... You'd better not be associated with this work; you won't be able to tolerate it!'

Bharati was startled. 'How can you say that?' she cried. 'What d'you mean by sacrificing men?'

'They are no men,' he replied. 'They are no better than animals.'

Bharati was scared. 'Don't say such things even in jest,' she said. 'I confess I can't always clearly understand what you say. But I understand you much better than you think. Don't try to unnecessarily frighten me.'

'You're mistaken,' Doctor replied. 'I'm not unnecessarily frightening you. I'm serious. You mustn't waste your time trying to improve the lot of the factory workers. Nothing worthwhile can be achieved that way. Their true emancipation can come only through revolution. The aim of my Pather Dabi is to bring about such a revolution. You must remember that revolutions can't be achieved through peaceful means. Violence is essential for its success—this is both its curse as well as its boon! Look at Europe. It has happened in Hungary. It has taken place in Russia, not once but several times. The French Revolution of June 1848 is still a landmark in the history of revolutionary movements. That day the streets of Paris were drenched with the blood of peasants and workers! Even in present-day Japan the miseries of the factory workers is the same, Bharati. No Government has given in peacefully to the right of the people for self-determination.'

Bharati shuddered. 'I don't know all that,' she said. 'But d'you want such terrible things to happen in our country? Do you want to bathe the streets with the blood of those for whom we have been labouring ceaselessly day and night?'

Without a moment's hesitation Doctor replied, 'Certainly, I do. It has always been my dream to bring about human emancipation through such sacrifice. How will we wash away the sins of generations except with their blood? And if in the process I have to shed my own blood, I won't mind even that.'

'I know that,' replied Bharati. 'But have you set up this organisation just to create disturbances in the country? Don't you have any beter aim in life?'

'I haven't been able to find another,' replied Doctor, though I've travelled widely, read a lot, and thought deeply. But I've already told you, Bharati, violence is not necessarily evil. Peace! Peace! Peace! I'm fed up with this constant talk of peace! Do you know who are the people who've been preaching this falsehood for so long? They are the same people who've robbed the peace of others, who've usurped what was rightfully theirs. They are the preachers of the cult of peace! They've dinned this into the ears of the deprived, diseased and oppressed populace so that they now shudder at the very thought of unrest. They are convinced it's harmful, it's evil! Tell me, have you ever seen a cow die at the place where it is tethered? It prefers to die than to tear apart the tattered rope lest it should disturb its master's peace! It's the same with these poor people. That's what has been holding up, their progress. And if you too think the same way, then how'll it do? No, that won't do! However ancient and sacred may be the concept of peace, it can't be greater than man! We'll have to demolish everything today. No doubt it'll create an upheaval, may even hurt a few, but that's only natural, isn't it?'

'If that's so, then why give up the path of peace and adopt violence instead?'

'That's because the path of peace is obstructed by an ancient, sacred and accepted tradition of good conduct. Only the path of revolution is still open to us.'

'But tell me,' asked Bharati, 'was our endeavour to unite the factory workers with the purpose of calling a peaceful strike also not in their interest? After you go away, should we abandon that experiment as well?'

'No, but that's Sumitra's job, not yours. Your work is different. You see, Bharati, while there's something called a strike, there's no such thing as a peaceful, non-violent strike. No strike can ever be successful if it isn't backed by violence. One has to turn to it as a last resort!'

'Who? The workers?' asked Bharati in surprise.

'Yes,' replied Doctor. 'You may not know, but Sumitra knows the difference between the financial loss of the rich and the starvation of the poor. Day by day the helpless, unemployed worker is forced towards starvation. His wife and children cry of hunger ... their unending cries drive him insane ... he sees no other way of stopping their cries than by snatching the food of others. The rich wait for exactly such an opportunity. He has money, power and arms—in fact he has the power of the state behind him. He uses this power to crush the unarmed, famished strikers. The streets fill with blood, their blood, thanks to your ancient and sacred peace!'

'Then?' asked Bharati breathlessly.

'Then? And so once again the oppressed, vanquished, famished workers queue before heir murderers with begging bowls.'

'And after that?'

'Afterwards the workers again organise a strike in the hope of getting redressal. And so the cycle goes on.'

Bharati was momentarily filled with despondence. 'Then what do we gain from organising such strikes?' she asked slowly.

Doctor's eyes glowed in the darkness. 'Gain? You want to know what's the gain?' he asked. 'This'll bring about the revolution! That's the greatest gain! The strike ends in an apparent defeat for the impoverished, illiterate, famished workers, but this defeat leads to a sense of anger and hatred that erupts one day! This brings about the revolution! That's the gain! Nowhere in the world are revolutions brought about just for their own sake. It needs some long-standing grievance to sustain it. One is a fool if one doesn't realise this and instigates the workers to go on strike simply for an increase in their wages. That way he harms both the workers as well as the country.'

Suddenly Bharati said, 'We've come a long way downstream.'

Doctor laughed. 'I'm aware of that,' he said. 'I haven't forgotten our destination.'

'I now see why you want to get rid of me,' said Bharati. 'I'm weak, just like him. I mean nothing to you. Even now it's Sumitra-didi who matters to you. But I'll never accept that all our efforts were futile, that there's no other way of achieving emancipation except through violence. I can never believe that to help someone you've to hurt another, not even if you say it!'

'I know that.'

'But how can I leave your organisation? What shall I do then? And, if you don't come back … how'll I live then?'

'I realise that as well.'

'You know everything. Then what's the solution?'

No one spoke for a while. Then Bharati said quietly, 'I could never understand what you meant by a revolution, nor why was it so necessary. Still, whenever I hear you speak of it, my heart seems to bleed. You must surely have witnessed instances of terrible suffering and human misery. What else could've made you so uncompromising and determined? But can't you take me along with you when you go?'

Doctor laughed. 'Have you gone crazy?'

'Maybe I have.' After a while she added, 'It seems I'm a liability for you. That's why you're gradually easing me out from your group. But is there nothing I can do? Am I so very useless?'

'There's a lot you can do,' said Doctor. 'But you'll have to create the opportunities yourself.'

'I can't do that,' coaxed Bharati. 'You do it for me.'

Doctor remained silent for a while. His smiling face suddenly seemed to have turned grave, though Bharati could not see it in the darkness.

'There are so many institutions, big or small, that are doing good work in the country, like nursing the sick, performing acts of piety in the society, providing medical assistance to the ailing, rescuing those affected by floods and consoling them. They'll show you the path. But I'm a revolutionary. I've no love, no affection, no compassion; good and bad are both meaningless to me. Those acts of piety appear to me to be a child's play. The independence of India is my sole aim in life, its achievement my only dream; apart from this nothing holds any meaning for me! Don't try to detract me from my chosen path, Bharati.'

Bharati had continued to look at him steadfastly through the darkness. She now heaved a deep sigh and fell silent.

After a pause she added, 'As for me, I don't desire it any longer. It's true that I still love Apurbababu very much. It doesn't matter whether he's good or bad; I can never forget him. But at the same time I can't say that my life will be meaningless if I can't marry him and be his wife. It's not out of frustration or sorrow that I'm saying all this. Honestly, do guide me and give me your blessings. I too want to devote my life to the service of others just like you. I entreat you, do associate me in your work.'

Doctor gave no reply to her earnest request and continued to row the boat in silence. Bharati could not see his face in the darkness but his silence filled her with hope. When she spoke her voice was warm and hopeful. 'Then will you take me with you?' she asked. 'You're my only hope. Everything else seems shrouded in darkness.'

Doctor shook his head slowly. 'That's impossible,' he said. 'You know, Bharati, you remind me of Joan. Like you, her life too turned to ashes. My sole aim in life is to achieve the independence of India, but I've never made the mistake of thinking that there can be nothing greater in life. Independence is not an end in itself. Religion, peace, literature, happiness, are all greater than that. It's for their fullest development that freedom is essential; else of what use is it? Your heart, which is full of love, affection, compassion and sweetness, is far more valuable than freedom. It's far greater than anything I've ever strived for. I can't sacrifice it for the sake of independence!'

Bharati was filled with joy. This was an entirely different facet of Sabyasachi's personality that was now revealed to her. She said reverently, 'I feel that there's nothing that you don't know. But if this is so, why should you be engaged in conspiracy? Why go round setting up secret societies in different countries? Certainly no good can come out of that.'

'That's right,' said Doctor. 'But we've left the greatest good of man in the hands of God. We try to achieve only what's possible for ordinary mortals like us. Freedom of speech and freedom of movement—these are the only two things we seek for our people. Nothing more than that at present!'

'That's what everyone wants,' said Bharati. 'But does that call for intrigue and murder?'

As soon as she uttered these words, she felt ashamed. Because the accusation was not only harsh, but also untrue. 'Forgive me,' she said with repentance. 'I said that out of anger. I can't reconcile myself to the thought that you'll go away leaving me behind.'

'I know that,' smiled Doctor.

Both remained silent for a long while ...

I'm surprised how someone whose own life is on tenterhooks can indulge in jokes about others.'

The reason is very simple,' said Doctor in a calm voice. 'The matter was decided once for all the day I joined this revolutionary movement. I've nothing to worry about, nor anything to complain of. I know this much that if ever the police are able to catch me and don't kill me, they must either be incompetent or insane or lacking even the rope to hang me with.'

'That's exactly the reason why I want to accompany you,' replied Bharati. 'There's none who can kill you as long as I'm with you. I'll never allow it.' Her voice grew hoarse.

Doctor noticed it. He sighed silently and said, 'The tide is coming in. It shouldn't take us long to reach the other side now.'

'Dammit. I'm fed up with everything!'

After a minute or so, Bharati asked, 'Do you really believe you'll be able to drive away the British by force?'

'Yes, I believe it wholeheartedly,' Doctor replied without a moment's hesitation. 'If I didn't, I couldn't have continued with my mission.'

'That's the reason why you're slowly easing me out of your group, isn't it?' asked Bharati.

Doctor smiled. 'That's not entirely true,' he said softly. 'But at the same time, it's a fact that one derives strength only from one's convictions. Unless you've faith in your work, your doubts and hesitations will only serve to retard it. There are other types of work—beneficent and peaceful—in which you have faith. I'd suggest you do that instead.'

Bharati realised that it was out of his great affection for her that Doctor was trying to keep her away from his dangerous revolutionary activities. Her eyes filled with tears. Wiping them in the darkness, she said, 'Don't be angry with me, but you know how powerful the British are. They've got arms and equipment, they have a huge army. Compared to them, you're nothing! You're as insignificant as a pug mark when compared to the ocean. What can be your justification in locking horns with such a powerful adversary? Die if you must, but I tell you it's sheer madness! You'll ask, then is there no hope for the motherland? Should one do nothing for fear of dying? I don't say that. I've learnt that there can be nothing greater in life than to die for her sake. But has any country ever been free by committing suicide? However, don't misunderstand me. I'm not advocating this simply to avoid death.'

Doctor sighed, 'Undoubtedly.'

'What d'you mean by that?'

'I see I was wrong about you.' said Doctor. He added after a while, 'You see, Bharati, revolution doesn't mean just war and bloodshed. It means a rapid and radical transformation. I know that they have a well-equipped huge army. But my objective is not to wage a war against them. Who knows, those who are our enemies today may become our allies tomorrow Nilakant died trying to win them over. Poor Nilakant! Who remembers him today?'

Even in the darkness Bharati could make out the momentary excitement that the memory of an unknown youth who had died in the cause of his motherland in some foreign country, far away from his native shores, had brought about in the mind of this man who was normally composed and unruffled.

Suddenly he sat erect and said, 'What was it you said? Pug mark! Maybe you're right. But what is the size of the tiny spark that in course of time becomes a conflagration, consuming everything that stands in its way? When a city burns, it feeds itself. This is a universal law which no power can refute.'

'Your words terrify me,' said Bharati. 'You talk of setting the country ablaze, but d'you realise it'll be your own countrymen who'll perish in the holocaust. Don't you feel any pity for them?'

'No,' replied Doctor without any hesitation. 'Did you think I didn't mean it when I talked about their penance? How else shall we expiate for the sins committed by our forefathers over the ages? Justice is far more important than compassion, Bharati.'

Bharati felt miserable. 'You're merely repeating your old arguments,' she said. 'I can't conceive how cruel you can become when it comes to the question of India's independence. You can't think of anything other than bloodshed. But if bloodshed begets only bloodshed, where will it all end? Is human civilization incapable of providing any alternative to bloodshed? Nations may disappear but humanity, which is greater than everything, will persist. Can't men live in harmony with each other without bloodshed?'

'A great English poet once said, 'The East is East and the West is West, and never the twain shall meet.'

'Hang him!' said Bharati in exasperation. 'I don't care what he says. But you're a knowledgeable person. And so I ask you, as I've asked you many times in the past, tell me—aren't the British, the Europeans, also human beings? Then why can't we live in harmony and friendship with them? You know that I'm a Christian. I'm indebted to the British in many ways. I've seen with my own eyes their numerous good qualities. It pains me to think of them as evil. Please don't misunderstand me. I'm also a Bengali, just like you. I love my motherland and my people with all my heart, who knows whether I'll be able to meet you again. Before you go, you must answer this question of mine. You must advise me what I should do to rely on it as a guiding principle throughout my life.' Her voice broke down completely towards the end.

Doctor did not reply immediately and continued to row the boat in silence. Bharati felt that possibly he did not want to reply. She dipped her hand into the river, scooped up some water and proceeded to wash her eyes and face. Wiping it carefully, she was about to ask him another question when Doctor spoke. His voice was soft and mellow. There seemed to be no trace of anger or excitement in it—it was almost as if he were discussing some other topic, so easy was his manner. Bharati remembered their first encounter. She had taken him to be a timid and stupid school teacher. She remembered having controlled her laughter with difficulty at his faulty English and funny pronunciation. Later she had been angry with him for having fooled her. He now spoke in the same dispassionate and calm manner.

'There's a type of snake that feeds on others. Have you ever seen it?' he asked her.

'No, but I've read about them.'

'They can be seen in the zoo. When you visit Calcutta, ask Apurba to take you to the zoo and show them to you.'

'Now don't start that again, I warn you,' she said.

'No, seriously. They find it inconvenient to live amicably, but can do so most comfortably when one is devoured by the other. If you don't believe me, ask the zoo keeper.'

Bharati remained silent.

Doctor said, 'You profess their religion. You're indebted to them for various acts of kindness. You've seen their numerous good qualities. But have you seen their greed, their voracious appetite that seeks to devour everything? They now lord over this land of ours, but d'you remember when they first came to our country? Today they've enormous wealth. They own innumerable warships, factories, mansions, arms and ammunition with which to kill people. Even after meeting all their needs they are able to lend as much as three thousand crore rupees within a period of seventy years starting from 1810. Have you ever tried to know the source of this wealth? You claim to be a Bengali. The soil of Bengal, its air, its water, its people, are all dearer to you than your own self! Every year at least a million Bengalis die of malaria. Tell me, do you know how much a warship costs? With that amount of money one could wipe the tears from the eyes of a million mothers every year! Have you ever thought over these things? Have you tried to see the real picture of your motherland? We've lost our art and craft, our trade and commerce, our religion, our age-old wisdom. The rivers have dried up and turned into deserts. The farmer doesn't get two square meals a day. Our craftsmen work as labourers for the foreigners. Today we don't have water to drink or enough food to eat. The cattle—which was the greatest wealth a householder could have—are no more. Bharati, have you ever seen little children dying for want of milk?'

Bharati felt like crying out to him to stop, but only an indistinct sound escaped her lips.

When Sabyasachi resumed from where he had broken off, the calm and dispassionate tone was missing. He said, 'You're a Christian. I remember one day, out of curiosity, you had wanted to know about the true nature of European civilization. That day I didn't say anything, lest I should hurt you. But I'll explain it to you today. I don't know what's written in the books. I'm told all the references are favourable. But as a result of my long association with them, I know the reality is vastly different. Unscrupulous, naked selfishness and brute power form the bedrock of this civilization. In the name of civilization, they have exploited the weak and the powerless in every country. Look at the map of the world. No weak nation has been able to withstand the onslaught of their invasions, their insatiable hunger for greater acquisitions. Do you know the reason why the natives have been denied their rights, denied their due share of the wealth of the country? Their only fault was that they were weak, they lacked the ability to resist the foreigners. And yet they assert that they never act unjustly! They proclaim that it's for the ultimate good of the country that they've conquered it. They spread the myth of the white man's burden. These untruths they preach through their writings, their speeches, their missionaries, and their textbooks. This is their policy, the politics of the Christian civilization!'

FOUR CHAPTERS

Rabindranath Tagore

Ela was sitting in a lounge chair by the window, a cushion supporting her back, one knee over the other, busy writing. She had on a purple *sari* of homespun, tolerated as a useful working garment for domestic use. On her wrists were bangles of red-lacquered conchshell, round her neck a chain of gold. Her body, with its ivory sheen, was taut and trim in its shapeliness. She looked very young indeed, but her expression was one of grave maturity. Along one of the walls there was a narrow iron cot, with a green homespun counterpane over the bed. The floor was covered with a coarse cotton carpet. On a small table near her chair were an inkstand and a small brass bowl with a sprig of gardenia.

Darkness came on, and she was on the point of rising to light the lamp, when the curtain in the doorway was violently thrust aside, with a shout of 'Elie!' and Atin burst into the room like a gust of wind .... 'What made you keep me at a distance?'...

'Elie, you don't understand me simply because you won't. Don't go on saying that the unrealized is yet to come in my life. It has already come—it is you. And yet it's still unrealized. Shall I have to keep my window expectantly open forever? Through its emptiness only the wail of my yearning heart goes forth, "I want you, only you!" And no reply comes.'

'Oh, ungrateful! How can you say that you've had no reply? I also want you, you, you! And there's nothing I want more in all the world.

Only, our meeting happened at a time when it could not be auspiciously carried further.'

'Why, what harm would it have done to carry it on to union?'

'My life, indeed, would have been fulfilled, but what a trifle that is! You aren't like the others, but ever so much above them. And it's because I kept my distance that I was privileged to see this wonderful greatness of yours. I'm mortally afraid even to think of swathing you round with my smallness, of bringing you down to the pettinesses which make up my little household. There may be women who would have no compunction in smothering you under the numberless details of their lives. I know of so many tragedies which such women have brought about—monarchs of the forest stunted under a tangle of clinging creepers—as if their embraces are all-sufficient.'

'Elie! Only he who receives can say what is, or is not, all-sufficient.'

'I refuse to live in a false paradise, I know you, Ontu, better than you do yourself. Pent in the narrow cage of my love, you'd soon have begun to beat your wings. The little of satisfaction I have in me to offer, you'd have by now drained to the dregs. Then you'd have found out my utter destitution. That's why I gave up all my personal claims on you and surrendered you completely at the shrine of our country. There your gifts will not lack full scope.'

Atin's eyes flashed. He got up and began to pace up and down the room. Then, standing in front of Ela, he said: 'The time has come to talk to you straight and hard. What right have you, let me ask, to deliver me up to the country, or to any one else? Your offering to me could have been something beautiful—call it service, call it favour, as you will—and according to your mood I'd have come to you, proudly if you had allowed pride, humbly if such had been your pleasure. But you cut down your gift to paltriness. Your woman's glory you had to bestow, but that you cast aside and offered instead to place the country in my hands! That you can't do, positively cannot—no one can. The country cannot be passed from hand to hand like this.'

Ela winced at this blow to her self-assurance. 'What are you talking about?' she murmured.

'I'm saying that the realm of sweetness and light which has woman for its centre may appear small on an outward view, but, within, its depth is immeasurable. It's by no means a cage. But the place you've assigned me, calling it country—which after all is nothing but a country of your band's own make—whatever it may mean to others, it's nothing but a cage for me. My natural powers do not find full scope in it; they are becoming unhealthy and perverted. I'm ashamed of what I'm doing, but I find the way out blocked. You don't seem to realize how my wings have been clipped, my limbs shackled. I had the responsibility, as well as the capacity, to take my own true place in my country's service. You made me forget it.'

'What did I do to make you forget, Ontu?'

'I'll admit a thousand times that you can make me forget all else but you; had it not been so, I'd have doubted my own manliness.'

'Why then reproach me?'

'After making me forget myself, you should have taken me into your own realm, your own world. Instead of that you merely echoed the words of your band and showed me "the one and only way!" And, going round and round in the pursuit of my official duties over that cement road of yours, the whole current of my life is being stirred into muddiness.'

'Official duties?'

'Yes, the duty of pulling at the car of Juggernaut's. Our Supreme Counsellor decreed that our whole duty was to take hold of a thick rope and keep pulling with closed eyes. Thousands of boys caught hold, of the ropes. Some were crushed under the wheels, others crippled for life. Then came the order to turn back. The car began its return journey. But the broken bones did not become whole, and the cripples were swept out of the way on to the dust heaps. Independent thinking was knocked on the head from the very start and the boys came strutting up, ready and proud to be moulded into puppets. When they all began to dance to the same tune, at the wire-pulling of the Master, they were struck with admiration at their own performance. "Verily the dance of *Sakti* (Power)!"—thought they. But, whenever the Master slackens his pull, thousands of the puppet-boys fall out of the dance.'

'The boys themselves spoil it by trying to do their own steps, out of time.'

'They should have known from the first that live men cannot play the puppet for long. To ignore man's nature by trying to make him a puppet is folly. Had you respected me for my own individuality you would have drawn me not to your group, but to your heart!'

'Why, oh, why, Ontu, didn't you drive me away at the very beginning? Why did you make me guilty of doing you this injury?'

'That is what I've been trying to tell you. I desired union with you—a very simple desire, a most ungovernable desire. I found the usual way closed. I desperately entrusted my life to a crooked way. I have now come to know that it will lead me to my death. When at last I am dead to my real self, your outstretched arms will beseech me, by day and by night, to return to the equally dead emptiness of your bosom … I am talking like a fool, I know, a romantic fool. As if the getting of a shadow, without body or substance, is getting at all. As if your agony at our separation then, could pay the price of our frustrated union to-day!'

'The intoxication of words has got hold of you, now, Ontu!'

'Got hold of me now? It has always possessed me. Such a word-ridden creature has this Atin of yours always been! But I've lost all hope that you'll ever know him for what he really is—now that you've gone and made him one of the pawns in the game started by your precious hand.'

Ela slipped down from her chair and laid her head on Atin's feet. Atin drew her up beside him as he continued: 'With words have I decorated this slim, dainty body of yours in my own mind—my joy and my sorrow in one—what have I not called you! I'm surrounded by an invisible atmosphere, an atmosphere of words—they come down around me from the Elysium of literature to save me from the crowd. Ever aloof am I, and that your Master knows. Why, then, does he trust me, I wonder!'

'He trusts you for that very reason. To mingle with the crowd one has to come down to the crowd. But come down you cannot. That's why I, too, trust you. No woman ever so trusted any man. Had you been an ordinary man, then like an ordinary woman I'd have been afraid of you. But there's no place for fear in your company.' …

The daylight waned. The cicadas shrilled in the courtyard. The wheels of a distant cart creaked their agony.

Suddenly into his room came Ela, with steps, in a blind hurry, like that of a suicide taking the final plunge. As Atin jumped up, she threw herself on his breast, sobbing, 'Ontu, Ontu, I couldn't keep away any longer!'

Atin gently disengaged her arms and placing her before him, silently gazed at her tearful face, as he said ...

'Before I took this road there was much I wasn't aware of, much I didn't even suspect. Then I came to know the boys, one after another—boys the dust of whose feet I'd have taken, had not they been so much younger than I! What have they not seen since, what have they not suffered, what insults they have not borne—the whole story will never see the light of day. It was the torment of all this that drove me mad. Many times have I vowed to myself: I will not be vanquished by fear or torment; I will die striking my head against the heartless stone wall, but, snapping my fingers at it, I will ignore the wall.'

'Have you then changed your mind now?'

'Listen. One who openly fights a more powerful foe, even if his be a hopeless struggle, is in the same class as his opponent; his honour remains unsullied. I had imagined that at least that honour would be mine. But, as the days went by, I saw with my own eyes how even the most high-minded of the boys began to lose their manhood. What greater loss could there be? I knew for certain they'd only laugh at me, perhaps get angry with me, and yet I had to tell them that the worst of all defeats was to come down to the wrongdoer's level. It was for us, before we were knocked out, before we met our death, to prove ourselves the greater, as men—why else this play of pitting ourselves against immeasurably superior forces? Some of them understood me, but how few!'

'Why even then didn't you leave them?'

'How could I? The net of punishment was then closing round them. Every bit of their career had passed before my eyes. I had felt with them each heart-rending experience. So, however revolted my feelings, however strong my hate of the movement, I simply could not desert them in the moment of their greatest danger. One thing had become clear to me. To oppose overwhelming strength by brute force can but brutalize in the end one's very soul.'

'I must confess, Ontu, that lately the terrible tragedy of it has been revealed to me also. I had entered the lists at the call of glory but the shame of it is enveloping me more and more. Tell me, what can we do now?'

'Every man and woman is called upon to fight the great fight in the field of righteousness, where to die is to earn the highest heaven. But for us, the way to that battlefield is closed. We must now reap to the end the fruits of our past *karma*, our past deeds.'

'I understand you, Ontu, and yet the cynical way in which you talk of our patriotic movement hurts me deeply.'

'I'll confess to you for the first time today: what you call a patriot, that I am not. The patriotism of those who have no faith in that which is above patriotism is like a crocodile's back used as a ferry to cross the river. Meanness, unfaithfulness, mutual mistrust, secret machination, plotting for leadership—sooner or later these drag them into the mud at the bottom. That, the life of the country can be saved by killing its soul, is the monstrously false doctrine that nationalists all over the world are bellowing forth stridently. My heart groans to give it effective contradiction. I had it in me, perhaps, to express it in words burning with truth, words that would have remained great through the ages. But that has been denied me in this life. That is why the pain at my heart sometimes becomes so cruel.'

'Turn back yet, Ontu, turn back,' cried Ela, with a deep sigh.

'The way is closed.'

'But why?'

'Even if I'm on the wrong road, it has its own responsibilities to the bitter end.' ...

THE COUNTRY'S MISFORTUNE

Bal Gangadhar Tilak

The following is a summary of the leading article, entitled 'The Country's Misfortune', which appeared in the *Kesari*, dated May 12, 1908, and in respect of which the Bombay Government ordered Tilak's prosecution:

'We never imagined that the high-handedness of the white bureaucracy in this country would so soon drive some of the youthful patriots of Bengal to such acts of violence as they have recently committed. Their statements before the police bear witness to the fact that these men were not at all inspired by self-interest in what they did, but it was out of sheer exasperation at the autocratic doings of the bureaucracy that they have chosen this path. It is further evident that the same circumstances that have given birth to the anarchist cult in Russia have come into existence in this country, and are producing the same result.

'The British Government is, it is true, a mighty one, but all autocrats must bear in mind that there is after all a limit to human forbearance. All constitutional agitation for undoing the partition of Bengal having miserably failed, nothing could be more natural than that a few of the ardent spirits in Bengal should have lost their heads and resorted to excesses. It is true that long foreign domination has mostly quenched the spirit of the people, but it has not become altogether extinct. A knowledge of history and the rise of Japan has kindled in their minds a strong desire for Swarajya, and if there is no gradual fruition of that desire, some of them at all events will not hesitate to commit deeds of violence in a fit of exasperaion and despair.

'We, along with other newspapers, have frankly told Government that if they resorted to Russian methods of repression, Indians too shall have to imitate the Russian revolutionaries in their defence. To exercise every sort of oppression on the subjects, and at the same time to expect them to bear everything with meekness is to exhibit an utter ignorance of ordinary human nature. Such ignorance has been disclosed by the Anglo-Indian Press, which conveniently overlooking the fact that the present undesirable situation is the outcome of the unrestricted exercise of autocratic power by the white bureaucrats, has been indulging in all sorts of wild vapourings. Our rulers seem to desire that the indignation felt for their measures should never overstep certain prescribed bounds. The Muzaffarpur outrage will teach a lesson to Government on the vanity of this desire. Government can, of course, suppress such outrages with a high hand, but that will not effect a radical cure of the disease. So long as its germs remain in the body politic, it will break out at some place or other.

'The remedies, therefore, must be prescribed with due foresight. The fact must be recognised by Government that these excesses on the part of an inconsiderate few are due to the refusal of the Government to give due consideration to the suggestions for reform in the administration which the people have begun to dislike. They must, therefore, with true statesmanship, try to avoid bringing matters to a crisis.

'We, on our part, do not think that our duty ends with condemning the Muzaffarpur outrage. We regret the occurrence, but we are of opinion that so long as the causes which gave rise to it are allowed to remain, it will be impossible to prevent its repetition. It lies entirely in the hands of the Government to prevent the growth of nihilism in India. Reform in the administration is the only way to kill this new Upas tree, and if the powers that be are not disposed to resort to that remedy, nothing can be more unfortunate. If the authorities fail to read the sign of the times, what can we do?'

On June 25, Tilak, as editor and publisher of the *Kesari,* was produced before the Chief Presidency Magistrate, A. H. S. Aston. After Superintendent Sloane of the Bombay city police, who figured as complainant, had been sworn, and had identified the 'accused', Tilak's pleader asked that the case might be tried forthwith. But the Government pleader was not ready, and applied for an adjournment in order to call evidence. The hearing was postponed to June 29.

The Magistrate then took up Tilak's application for release on bail, and remarking that 'the offence in question is not bailable', rejected it. He added: 'I am of opinion, that there are reasonable grounds for believing that the accused has committed the offence of which he is charged.'

On July 2, Tilak's counsel, M. A. Jinnah, applied to the High Court urging that if the 'accused' was not released on bail, he would not be able to instruct properly those whose help he wanted to secure for his defence. Other grounds given by Jinnah were: Tilak had a good defence; he had been suffering from diabetes for sometime past and was under medical treatment when he was arrested; the official translation of the articles used in the proceedings before the Magistrate were incorrect and misleading; the Counsel would not be able to make a proper defence unless the 'accused' had himself an opportunity of explaining the correct meaning and spirit thereof to his counsel.

Jinnah also invoked the judgment of Justice Tyabji, and emphasised that since there was no doubt whatsoever that Tilak would be forthcoming to stand his trial, justice demanded that he should be enlarged on bail.

The application was opposed by the Government. In the written affidavit filed by the solicitor to Government he made a reference to Tilak's imprisonment in 1897 and his conditional release, and said that he had been informed by Government that if the 'accused' was released on bail, he would use his 'liberty to excite feelings of disaffection and hatred against Government and that it would be dangerous to release him'. The court was assured that the translation to be used at the trial of the case would be one made by the translator of the High Court itself.

After Jinnah had finished his arguments, the Advocate-General rose to argue the Government side of the case. But hardly had he uttered these two words, 'I appear ...,' than Justice Davar, who was presiding over the session, intervened and said: 'I will not trouble you, Mr. Advocate-General,' and delivered his judgment without hearing him. He said that he did not agree with the statement 'broadly made' that the only consideration, which ought to guide the court in deciding whether bail should or should not be granted, was the consideration that an accused would appear to take his trial. There were many circumstances that, in his opinion, should be weighed before coming to a conclusion. Unlike

Tyabji, he thought that nothing should be said before the trial that would in any way prejudice either the case for the prosecution or for the accused. He, therefore, rejected the application, and gave no reason for the rejection, for that, in his opinion, would prejudice the case one way or the other.

It would be interesting to recall that it was Davar who, as Tilak's counsel in 1897, four times argued the bail application and took his stand on the ground that the accused would not be able to instruct his counsel properly from inside the jail, and ultimately succeeded in securing his release. Then he had said: 'I ask your Lordship to exercise your discretion vested in you, and make an order which will show that the accused is not prejudged by the tribunals that administer justice and law.' Now he said that the Judge of the High Court had no doubt unlimited discretion, unfettered by any condition, and could release an accused person on bail pending trial. He argued that that was a judicial discretion, 'a discretion that must be judiciously exercised, and exercised with care and caution,' and therefore reached the conclusion that the bail application should be refused.

Meanwhile legal experts of the Government, both in Bombay and in Calcutta, who were assiduously preparing the prosecution, felt that the May 12 article might fail to secure conviction. A secretary of the Government of India suggested; 'It is most important that the case against Talk should be strengthened, for the present charge is a very weak one, and even if it end in conviction, which is improbable, we shall have an outcry from a large section of the radical party at home against a law under which an editor can be sent to jail for criticism which in England would be regarded as of quite a mild type. On the other hand the incitement to the use of bombs which appears in the article of June 9 would excite no sympathy in England among any section of politicians whose opinions count.' Now Tilak's prosecutors switched on their attention to that article which was entitled 'These Remedies Are Not Lasting', and which appeared in the *Kesari* dated June 9.

The Viceroy, Lord Minto, agreed that no effort should be spared to secure Tilak's prosecution. 'The present is not a time,' he said, 'to give a well-known agitator like Tilak the benefit of any leniency; and I certainly think we should call the serious attention of the Bombay Government to the possibility of proceeding against his press in respect to the article in the *Kesari* of the 9th June'.

The exchange of official notes that followed the recording of his opinion by the Viceroy makes interesting reading. Everybody seemed anxious to imprison Tilak for a long period. The Bombay Government were in favour of taking action under the Newspaper (Incitement to Offences) Act, but they suggested two possible objections. The first was that the 'offending article' was published only one day after the passing of that Act. The second possible objection was that action under the Newspaper Act 'would unfairly prejudice Tilak in his trial for sedition which is now pending before the High Court'.

These objections, however, did not damp the enthusiasm of the officers at the Secretariat level, and the same secretary of the Government of India again said in his note: 'I venture to think that it is most desirable that we should deal Tilak as shrewd a blow as we can. He is by far the ablest and most dangerous of the rebel party in this country, and his complete overthrow will stagger that party and show to all waverers the strength of the Government. It is not enough to imprison him when we can also suppress his newspaper. The *Kesari* has a circulation of 20,000 which is an enormous circulation for India. This is no time for rose-water administration, and I am confident that the great mass of moderate men will be glad to see Tilak completely overthrown. He ruined the National Congress at Surat and his methods have given great offence to the Moderate Party.'

But the Home Member of the Government of India brought about moderation in the official temper, and directed the Bombay Government to refrain from action under the Newspapers Act. 'It is no doubt a desirable thing,' he contended, 'to suppress both Tilak and his newspaper, but we should be careful that zeal does not out-turn discretion in a matter which has to be laid before Parliament and which will attract world wide attention'.

The Bombay Government therefore took two vital decisions: first, to frame a second charge based on the article of June 9; and secondly, not to hazard prosecution under the Newspapers Act, but to depend wholly on Sections 124-A and 153-A of the Indian Penal Code. The following is a substantial summary of the article:

'The Government of India has again entered upon a career of repression from this week. This demon of repression periodically possesses the Government, and one of such periods has now recurred. As liberty of the press and liberty of speech give birth to a nation and nourish it, our bureaucrats had long wished to extinguish both in India, and the bomb outrage afforded them an opportunity to carry out their design. But the question is, will these repressive measures succeed in their object? The officials first of all wish to see the bomb driven out of India, and this desire is both natural and laudable. But, the means they have adopted for this end being just the reverse of what should have been adopted, it is therefore plain that they have lost their senses. This mental aberration is a sign of impending ruin and one is grieved to think that worse days are in store both for the people and the authorities. The latter have raised the outcry that the cult of the bomb in Bengal is destructive of social order just like its prototype in Europe.

'But there is a vast difference between the two cults. While the cult in Europe is the outcome of the hatred of the self-aggrandising wealthy classes, the Bengal cult has got at its root an excess of the patriotic sentiment. The Bengal bomb-thrower has got more in common with the Portuguese patriots, who assassinated Don Carlos for suppressing their parliament, and with the hot-headed Russians who committed bomb outrages in desperation owing to the Tsar's refusal to convene the Duma than with anarchists pure and simple. The bomb in Portugal compelled the abandonment of the policy of repression in that country, while the mighty Tsar had to eat humble pie before the same engine of destruction. The cessation of the bomb outrages in the two aforesaid countries can never be ascribed to repressive measures. That consummation was due to the fact that the statesmen of both the countries recognised in the bomb new, rising aspirations of the people and made efforts to gratify these aspirations.

'The condition of Indians is worse than that of a cage bird. For while the latter is supplied with delicacies with a view that it may not feel the misery of its captivity, the Indians have been ruthlessly deprived of arms in order that they might never dream of freeing themselves from their bondage. The English have evidently emasculated the whole nation and reduced it to a state of impotence simply to enable even the lowest of their officials to exercise their high-handed sway with impunity. The English possess neither the magnanimity nor the power of the Moghuls who never disarmed the Indians. The Moghuls were able to keep up their Imperial status for over a century even after their forces had been annihilated during Aurangzeb's abortive campaigns in the Deccan. The British Government will not be able to outlive, even for a quarter of a century, a similar period of stress and strain. The disarmed condition of the people combined with the military strength of the Government had so long made the English masters of the situation. But the bomb has changed all this.

'Hitherto the Government had no means of knowing the degree of desperation to which some of their hot-headed subjects have been driven through exasperation at Government measures. The people only petitioned and their representations were regarded as mere froth worth no attention. They fretted and fumed in secret, but Government knew nothing about the matter. The bomb, however, has put a potent weapon into the hands of the people, and it has lessened the respect for the military prestige of the Government. England will not henceforward be able to carry on the administration of the country in a smooth manner unless Englishmen deign to take the people more into their confidence. Manufacture and possession of arms can be prevented by law and police supervision, but the same cannot be said about the bomb. It resembles more a magical charm than a visible object manufactured in a factory. The bomb required by hot-headed madcaps, bent on violence, does not require large quantities of materials for their manufacture, as was shown by the bomb factory unearthed at Calcutta.

'It appears that Government have failed to learn a lesson, from the discovery. No law possesses the power to keep the knowledge of the manufacture of bombs from those that are bent upon using them, for such knowledge is no longer regarded as a secret in Europe. It is still a secret in India, but if a policy of repression succeeds in adding to the number of hot-headed persons in the country, the knowledge will in no time spread to other parts of India from Bengal.

'The manufacture of the bomb has become such an easy matter that the police can be easily evaded. It was not so easy when the Explosives Act was passed in England, but recently it has been vastly simplified in consequence of new scientific discoveries. How far can legislation restrict the operations of the scientific expert? Government have been trying their hand at achieving impossibilities, which are sure to prove disadvantageous both to themselves and to the people. The new legislation will put a new weapon into the hands of the underlings of Government for the persecution of the innocent people. Government must act in such a way that no one should feel any necessity to have recourse to bombs.

They must see that no keen disappointment is caused to those men of high ability who are seeking the rights of Swarajya.

'But we fear that the new law about newspapers is likely to give a dangerous turn to the feeling of disappointment already prevailing in the country. The grant of the important rights of Swarajya is the only means to get rid of the bomb in India.'

The prosecution was now ready with its charges, which stated that Tilak 'brought or attempted to bring into hatred or contempt or excited or attempted to excite feelings of disaffection towards the Government established by law in British India', and 'promoted or attempted to promote feelings of enmity or hatred between different classes of His Majesty's subjects' by publishing the two articles. On the appointed date—June 29—the Chief Presidency Magistrate took up the Tilak case again, read the charges to the accused, recorded depositions, and committed Tilak to the Sessions.

July 13 was fixed for the hearing. In the meantime, the prosecution took a vital step to ensure conviction. On July 3, it applied for a special jury to be empanelled to try Tilak on the ground that the case was one of great importance and a special jury would be eminently fitted for it.

Tilak's counsel opposed the application. His argument was: 'This is a prosecution instituted by the Government for a political offence under the special sanction of the Government. It, therefore, comes with a force and recommendation naturally calculated to overwhelm the defendant. A special jury means that the majority shall consist of Europeans, judging from the list of jurors. This list shows that there are 242 Europeans against 156 Indians. In all probability, therefore, the majority in the jury would be Europeans. That was the case in the last Tilak trial, and that was the case in all sedition trials in this court. Europeans would not make fit jurymen on the present occasion as they would be handicapped on account of their inability to understand the language of the alleged incriminating articles. Lastly, it is impossible to close one's eyes to the fact that these political offences and press prosecution are really a struggle between the rulers and the ruled for political rights and privileges, which can be obtained from the rulers alone. Now Englishmen belong to the ruling class. There must exist some political and patriotic bias against Indian aspirations. Moreover Englishmen at the present moment are rather inflamed on account of the assassinations in Muzaffarpur. There is, therefore, a real danger that Englishmen would be unconsciously biased against the accused to his great prejudice. But if the prosecution insists, we are willing to yield provided it consents that the majority on the special jury consists of Indians conversant with the language in which the indicted articles are written, viz., Marathi.'

Davar, who presided over the sessions, rejected the defence arguments, and granted the prosecution application. Again, as in the case of the bail application, his reasons were hardly convincing. As he himself said at the outset, a special jury was necessarily summoned in all offences punishable with death; but the law—Section 276 of the Criminal Procedure Code—gave power to a Judge of the High Court to call a special jury in any other case also. In the Tilak case, he said, a special jury was necessary: 'There is no doubt whatever that the cases against Mr. Tilak are important cases from his own standpoint, and I feel in his own interest he should have the benefit of being tried by a jury selected from the citizens of Bombay, but from the higher class of citizens.'

Answering the other points raised by Tilak's counsel, Davar said: 'I hardly think that there is much substance in the arguments as to the knowledge of the language. Of course if it comes to a conflict, then the court must necessarily accept the translations of its authorised translators. I am quite sure that any member of the special jury will come in and take his oath to administer justice and will leave out all prejudices if he has any and all extraneous circumstances entirely out of his consideration.'

The 1897 trial was being repeated in every detail, and shrewd people began to forecast that Tilak would again be incarcerated for a long term.

SIRI RAM–REVOLUTIONIST

Edmund Candler

The goatherds of Zojpal would come and peep at Narasimha. Great was his reputation for occult power. He could project himself across the valley, they said, render himself invisible or dual, pass through a chink in the wall, and endure a month without food. The bowls of milk, the handfuls of grain, the little bundles of firewood they placed in front of the cave were often found untouched in the morning.

He would sit for hours, his eyes fixed on two pebbles at his feet, restraining his breath until the material world slipped away from him and his spirit floated in ether, looking down indifferently upon his shrunken body and his bowl and his staff and the grey sheep beside the stream as passing phenomena detached for the moment as the atoms cohere in the dance of matter and are reflected in the glass of illusion. Soon nothing objective would remain, and he would be drawn to the centre of light, conscious only of the rush and beat of wings as he was swept along with the eternal energy which informs all life.

Power and influence came out of these trances. The Swami owed much of his magnetism to them and the extraordinary hold he had upon the affections and imagination of his countrymen. Long ago before he visited Europe he had practised Yoga at Ujjain. Then he had studied the Vedanta philosophy nine years at Benares. Thus he became a kind of superman in his own country. Images of him carved in wood and stone and cast in metal were sold in the idol shops of Kashi, where he had a great name for piety and transcendental power.

When he went to Europe, the extreme forms of yoga asceticism which he had practised at Ujjain had left their print on his character and his face. He had a great deal of what is called in the jargon of the stance psychic force. He was of the stuff that founds sects among impressionable people, and in any other country than England he would have had disciples to apotheosize him. As it was, he became something of a lion. He addressed societies and sipped tea in fashionable boudoirs; romantic hostesses felt that he brought more of the mystery and repose of the East into their drawing-rooms than a shelf-ful of bronze Buddhas, and more than one emotional woman, English and Russian and American, embarrassed him with chelaship. A spirtualistic lady in Notting Hill literally knelt at his feet and offered herself to him wholly.

At Cambridge he lectured on Sanskrit and Indian philosophy. He spent two years on the Continent, and learnt to speak French and German and Russian and Italian fluently. He was six months at Göttingen. Then he went to the States and preached Vedantism. He was a figure in the West, and he found himself in danger of becoming the centre of a coterie of faddists, seekers after a new thing, women and degenerates, who would make him their Guru and call themselves Hindus. Esoteric was a word they were fond of using, though they would not have wasted an hour on the subtlest of philosophers if it had suddenly been made the State religion, or if they had been born under its orthodox sway. The Swami measured them and went his way.

In the end he took more from the West than he gave it. He never lost his transcendentalism, but his spirit became tempered like a sword, his ideals were crystallized. He remembered that the Vedas and all that they stood for were embodied in his own people. Gradually his flame-like energy became narrowed and concentrated into a cause. Nationalism became a religion with him.

The Swami was proud of his race and the stock to whom the eternal verities had been revealed, and in whose heart alone truth could germinate. When Narasimha's history became known, the Englishmen who had met him in the West could not associate the dreamer and mystic with the revolutionist who pulled the strings of the Bharat Red Flag Society. But the Swami was an anarchist because he believed that his people could not become regenerate until they were free, a much more dangerous doctrine than that they could not be free until they became regenerate. He had no scruples. He would sacrifice a thousand Siri Rams and foster a nursery of young murderers. And no service rendered to his people could lessen his hate of the English. The most disinterested reformers must go with the others; they were, in fact, more dangerous because they stemmed the tide, and he would devote them and the Hobbses, the 'martial-law-and-no-damned-nonsense wallahs', indifferently to the bomb. His father, the Lingayat, would not have hesitated between a black and white goat at the altar, and Narasimha had a good deal of the old Lingayat in him yet; only the crude religious fanaticism of the sect had been diverted into politics. Dean was right. The man had all the instincts of a wolf. 'To sacrifice a white goat to Kali', that is, to dedicate an Englishman to the altar of independence, the ironical catchword of young Bengal, had emanated from him.

He had despised the English even before the demon of anarchy had entered into his head. He hated their materialism and insensibility. Save for a scholar or two whom he respected, his associates had been mostly shallow dabblers in the occult, keyhole peepers, without power of abnegation or self-forgetfulness. The yogi would sweep aside the curtain while they fumbled with the woof, seeking an interstice in the hope that the light behind might steal through somehow upon their blind eyes. The best of England, the true tempered steel of the country, he did not meet and could never have understood. And Demos was an unclean beast he could not touch, projected obliquely across his vision like the ugly figures on the frieze of a temple wall that one passes by. The monster was symbolized for him sometimes in his memory by a country bumpkin in cap and gown, who had brushed up rudely against him in the Petty Cury at Cambridge and called him 'a damned nigger'.

He had more in common with the Gaelic American of the Western States.

On his return to India Narasimha was irresistible. He had studied man in two hemispheres, and to the open appeal of mystic and reformer was added the hidden one of the revolutionary. He was the superman who alone could unite and direct the dissipated energies of the national spirit. He captured the imagination of the people. He preached to young Bengal, and he based his message on the teachings of Krishna to Arjun in the Bhagavad Gita. It was an insidious appeal, this doctrine of *yoga* by action and death in the discharge of one's own *dharma,* rousing passion by the creed which preaches freedom from passion and denounces anger and fear and all manner of attachment, and giving secret murder the sanction of divine law.

From Bengal Narasimha carried the message north, preaching to a hardier and more dogged, if less subtle and impressionable, stock. Among the young men who were being put into the mould was Siri Ram. The Swami knew that he would come.

Sometimes when he was exhausted by *yoga* Narasimha would walk knee-deep through meadows of fritillary and iris and yellow spurge to the frozen stream where the striped lizards flicked in and out of the crevice between the rock and the snow. He would look down on the marg speckled with grey stones and sheep while the eagles swept under him, swerving from his feet by the turn of a point of a feather. Or he would go down the valley to the last outpost of the silver birches which hung over the Zojpat stream. Here he would sit in a sunny belt of thyme which fringed the shadow of a lonely tree like a fairy ring, or in a warm, close-cropped hollow bright with forget-me-not and marjoram and meadow rue and turreted with the yellow spires of the mullein. Fritillaries and tortoise-shells lighted on his bowl; the murmur of bees soothed him into a trance. The silence and the space carried his mind far away until he was without attachment, at rest in *brahm,* and all the colour and life that danced and quivered before his eyes became a vague, illusory, opalescent gleam cast upon the plane his spirit traversed.

Narasimha's flight to Zojpal had fulfilled the religious bent of his mind. He was life-wear; he needed peace. For the last few years politics had been the most Sisyphean task. And he had not practised *yoga* since Ujjain. Once more he sat on the antelope skin, head erect, immovable, his gaze fixed steadily on his feet, controlling the incoming and outgoing breath, free of attachment, closing the passage to each sense. When the herdsmen brought him his bowl in the evening he would be performing the *pranayam,* and he would look at them without speech, or rather over and through them, and they would depart in awe.

As darkness gathered he climbed the mountain-side to perform another exercise, an unspiritual one—to prepare his physical escape. Every night he dug with the axe-head of his staff at the foot of a great rock. The herdsmen would have been frightened if they had seen the sprite-like little man delving in the moonlight as if he had found a passage to the unseen. The Swami was loosening a pinnacle of the cliff which held back a mass of tumbled shale, and if dislodged would precipitate an avalanche upon the cave. . . .

II

REVOLUTION AND TERROR

MOTHER OF 1084

Mahashweta Devi

The colony that housed two hundred thousand people had not grown according to any plan. This was the first of the colonies in West Bengal where the residents had grabbed the land and settled down. In the beginning the landlord had a plot of land, a few garden plots, several pools and tanks, a few small villages.

After 1947, as more and more people moved in, the map of the region changed radically. The colony spread and spread till it had swallowed up the fields, the marshes, the coconut palm orchard, the cornfields, the villages.

The Opposition had always polled a majority of votes in the region. And the government had taken its revenge by denying the region the simple comforts of a decent road, a health centre, an adequate number of tubewells or a bus route. Those who had grown rich in the last two decades in the region itself had not cared to do anything for the area.

The CMDO has dug up the roads only recently in a spurt of developmental concern.

There is no longer any unrest or panic. No shops and markets suddenly pulling down shutters, no doors to houses being slammed shut, no rickshaw pullers, stray dogs and pedestrians running in a mad frenzy. Now you no longer hear exploding bombs, murderous shouts, the groans of the dying or the cheers of jubilant killers.

No black cars, helmeted policemen and gun-toting soldiers pursue some desperate lone young boy. Nor does one see bodies tied by rope to the wheels of police vans, still alive, being dragged and slammed against the asphalt.

One does not see blood on the streets, nor hear a mother's despairing lament these days. The lettering on the walls has been replaced by new slogans. Live Long, Comrade—Mazumdar! Revolutionary Comrade— we'll never forget you! The killers who killed our youth will never be forgiven! The victors proclaimed their triumph through new slogans that covered the old ones completely.

Adolescents no longer shout slogans even as they die. There is no sign anywhere of the two-and-a-half years' disorder that had disrupted the even tenor of daily life here.

Happy and peaceful households are back. Rice is hoarded freely again and sold freely in the blackmarket. The cinemas draw crowds day and night. People throng temples where godmen reign, seeking salvation.

The killers of yesteryear have changed their garb and move about fearlessly in their new identities. A chapter has ended. A new chapter of the great saga has begun.

Only where narrow lanes meet do memorial tablets stand as tireless avengers, like ugly scars on a clean body. But these tablets do not carry the names of Somu, Bijit, Partha or Laltu. There is no question of their carrying Brati's name. His name, their names, remain only in the hearts of a few. Perhaps.

Sujata sat in the house where Somu had once lived. She had already brought the ornaments from the bank vault. They were in her bag. At one time the ornaments had been allotted to Neepa, Bini, Tuli, and Brati's future bride.

She had already given Neepa and Bini their portions.

Tuli had put in a claim for the portion put aside for Brati's future bride.

She would probably leave a few for Neepa's daughter and Jyoti's son, and give the rest away to Tuli. Sujata herself never wore anything more than a slim bangle on her wrist, a pair of small earrings and a thin chain around her neck. She has never put on a coloured sari since Brati was born.

She looked tired, broken. Somu's mother sat before her, crying silently. Her frail, dark face was awash with tears. She had become thinner in the last one year. She wore a dirty coarse plain white sari.

It was a ramshackle house, with moss on the roof, cracked walls patched up with cardboard. Still, this was the only place where Sujata found some peace for herself. She felt as if she had come home.

The first time they had met, Somu's sister had broken into tears. But this time she only frowned. She had lost her father soon after Somu's death. Since then she had had to give tuition from morning till night in order to run the household. The fire of the cremation pyre burns up all the fat in the body. The fire of domestic responsibility had burned up Somu's sister. She bore a severe anger in her looks. Somu's dying had left her dead. He had been the only son in the family. Because he had to go to a good college their father had not provided money for his sister's education. She paid for her own education by tutoring children.

Somu's sister gave her a hostile look and went out without saying a word. Sujata could see that she had taken over the job of running the household. She hated the idea of an outsider coming in once a year to remind them of her dead brother. Sujata felt utterly helpless. She looked at her pleadingly. She wanted to ask her not to shut the door that allowed her to come and go once in a while. But she could not say the words. Somu's sister went out.

Somu's mother was weeping. Sujata waited in silence.

They tell me, don't cry, mother. He'll never come back. They tell me, why don't you think of the others? Think of Partha's mother. She lost Partha. And since then Partha's brother can't come home. He has to stay with his aunt or who knows where.

He isn't back yet?

No, didi. Those who died are lost anyway. But those who remain alive won't ever be able to come back home again. What kind of judgement is this, didi?

Somu's mother went on weeping.

The first time she had come here, a year after it had happened, Sujata had had her hesitations. Somu's mother had been widowed only a few months ago.

When she had come into the locality and asked for Somu's house the young men had looked at her with obvious surprise. At first they would not tell her. Finally someone pointed the house out—There.

Somu's mother kept staring, baffled, at Sujata's expensive white sari, aristocratic appearance, and sophisticated ageing face encircled with greying hair.

I'm Brati's mother.

As the words hit her, the woman had cried out—My Somu! and had raised a loud wail. She had clasped Sujata to herself—It was your son, didi, who came to warn them. He died for them. He knew Somu was back in his locality. He came and asked for Somu. He told me he had a message for Somu, and he would leave immediately. I stopped him, it's night, it's not safe to go through the colony. I asked him to stay the night and leave early in the morning. But there was no morning for them. That night, didi, in this little room of ours, Somu and Partha and Brati slept close to one another.

This room?

This room. There's no other room, really. My daughter went out with her sisters to sleep on the ledge outside. There's a fence to the ledge. The boys stayed inside. I sat at the window to keep watch.

Brati was here?

Yes, didi. My dead husband was a poor shopkeeper, he didn't have any capital. He had a stall selling exercise books, pencils, and slates. It had taken him a lot to raise this house. So the boys kept to the corner. Somu's father wouldn't sleep, he stayed awake to wake them up early in the morning.

They talked and talked and laughed and laughed as they lay on my torn mattress. Didi, Brati's laughing face floats before my eyes. Your son had a complexion of gold!

Brati used to come here often?

Very often. He used to come, and ask for water, for tea, and what a sweet way he had about it.

Brati used to come here. He had tea here, he chatted, he spent so much of his time here.

Sujata looked at Somu's mother, their room, the picture on the wall torn from a calendar, the cup with its handle broken, with new eyes.

Brati, blood of her blood, the child whose birth had endangered her life, the young man who had become so strange and impregnable to her, was coming back to Sujata again.

She could still see Brati in her dreams, putting on a blue shirt, combing his hair. Or looking at her.

Studying her face.

When, after a long, sleepless night, her eyes would shut in sheer exhaustion, Brati stood at the bottom of the stairs looking up into her eyes. Sujata pleaded, Brati, don't go away. Brati kept looking at her. Sujata called out to him, Brati, why don't you come up? Brati kept looking. He did not speak, his lips did not smile.

But here Brati would speak, laugh, ask Somu's mother to make some tea, to give him a glass of water.

Somu's mother was saying—I used to tell him, why do you waste your life like this, my child? You have everything. A well-known father, a mother so learned. He wouldn't say a word. He would only smile. His smile floats before my eyes, didi.

It hurt Sujata. Brati's smile, that wonderful smile.

She had thought that all the memories were hers alone. Why had she never known that Brati had left memories to Somu's mother, too?

Brati had been home that day. He sat in his room on the second floor writing who knows what. It was only later that Sujata discovered that he had been drafting slogans to be written on the walls. They took the papers away when they came to search his room. The papers were no longer in the house.

All that now remained in the house were books and exercise books, books received as prizes, gold medals, a snapshot with friends in Darjeeling, a pair of running shoes, a cup from a sports meet. All from Brati's days in school and college. Mementoes of a few years in Brati's life. They brought back memories to Sujata. Ma, I'll get a prize. Won't you be there? The day Brati went to the park nearby to become a member of the Boys' Club. The Independence Day parades when he marched so proudly with the boys, beating on the drums, playing on the bugles. The day he had come back with a cup from the football finals, and a fractured leg.

There was nothing from the days when he had begun to change— they had cleared away without a trace the books, papers, leaflets, sheets with revolutionary slogans, journals from that last one year. Sujata had been told that all these were burnt as a rule.

Brati was home the whole day. Sujata was quite surprised to see him when she came home from the bank. It was only later that she knew that he had been waiting all day for a call. He knew that Somu and his group would go back to their locality. A message had been sent, asking them not to go back. But Brati did not know then that the person who carried the message . . .

But I never make a mistake

So you'll make special payesh for me.

That's all I do these days for birthdays, anyway

Wait. Let's think. What can you make for me?

Don't ask for meat.

Why? Is Boss dining at home?

Yes.

Make whatever you like.

The phone rang as Sujata went downstairs. She saw Brati lifting the receiver as she left.

She came up. Looked. Brati had on a blue shirt and trousers, and was combing his hair.

What's the matter?

I have to go out. Could you give me some money?

Where are you going?

Some business. Could I have the money?

Here's the money. When will you be back?

I'll be back … back soon … Just a minute.

Brati dipped into the pockets of his trousers and rummaged through the contents. A piece of paper he tore up into pieces.

Which way are you going?

There was no special fear at the back of her mind when Sujata asked the natural question. For Calcutta was in a different state those days. For the older people, for people over forty, any place in Calcutta was safe. But for the younger people, Calcutta had too many banned localities.

Only recently Sujata had been going through a pile of old newspapers, and had discovered with a shock all that had been happening in Calcutta two and a half years ago.

Back in those days, she had only-felt something, everything, turning topsy turvy. When Brati was still alive and Sujata was yet to know that Brati belonged to the ranks of the doomed, she would read the papers and feel the shock of every bloody episode reported.

Nobody else in the house even looked at the papers at that time. They would say—all you see is gruesome descriptions of how many were killed, and how they were killed.

Since they were so repelled by the news, Sujata and Brati were the only ones who read the papers.

Sujata read the papers before she left for the bank. The city of Calcutta seemed wrong to her. It still had all its old landmarks—the

Maidan, the Victoria Memorial, the Metro cinema, the Gandhi statue, the Monument. Still, it was not Calcutta. She did not recognize, did not know, this Calcutta.

She had gone back to the old newspapers later, and discovered that the morning the telephone rang in her room, the gold rates had gone up as usual, the banks in Calcutta had had transactions worth crores of rupees, an elephant cub was flown from Dum Dum to Tokyo carrying the Indian Prime Minister's best wishes for the children of Japan, a festival of European films opened in Calcutta, the radical artists and intellectuals of Calcutta demonstrated against barbarities in Vietnam, on Red Road and before the American Centre on S.N. Banerjee Road.

Everything went on as usual, all that spelt normalcy in Calcutta's own terms, all that characterized Calcutta as India's most conscious city.

All this showed that things were quite normal in the city that day. Only, it was dangerous for Brati to go from Bhowanipur to South Jadavpur; in Barasat eight young men were first strangled and then shot dead before they could leave their locality. In east Calcutta, a group of young men seated the bloodstained corpse of a young boy who had grown up with them in a rickshaw, and escorted it with drums and a brass band, dancing alongside, like some divine idol being taken for immersion.

The radical citizens of Calcutta found nothing unnatural in the spectacle.

Exactly a year and three months later, the writers, artists and intellectuals of Calcutta turned West Bengal upside down out of sympathy with and support for the cause of Bangladesh. Surely they must have been thinking the right thoughts, and mothers like Sujata must have been on the wrong track altogether! If their radical consciences remained unaffected by a situation that did not allow the youth of West Bengal to move from one neighbourhood to another in the same city, they must have been right.

The deadly risks that the youth of West Bengal faced cannot have been important enough. If they had been important, wouldn't the artists, writers and intellectuals of this legendary city of processions have picked up their pens?

Somu had twenty-three wounds on his body. Bijit sixteen. Laltu's entrails had been pulled out and wrapped around his body. All this surely could not have smacked of barbarity, of bestiality. If it had, then the poets and writers of Calcutta would have spoken of the barbarities on this side of the border along with those on that side of the border. Since they didn't, since they could ignore the daily orgy of blood that stained Calcutta and concentrate on the brutal ceremony of death beyond the border, their vision must have been flawless. Sujata's vision was surely wrong. Surely. The poets, writers, intellectuals and artists are honoured members of society, recognized spokesmen for the country at large.

Who is Sujata? Only a mother. Who are those hundreds of thousands whose hearts, even now, are being gnawed by questions? Only mothers.

When Brati in his blue shirt patted his hair smooth in his usual manner before leaving the house for ever, Sujata had asked him: Where are you off to?

Brati had paused for a second. Then he had smiled and said: Alipur. If I am late, you'll know I'm staying the night at Ronu's place. Don't worry.

Brati already knew that something terrible had happened. The messenger who was supposed to inform Somu and his group had not carried the information to them. Without the message, Somu and his group had gone back to their locality as decided in the original plan.

Brati did not know, however, that their messenger, instead of warning Somu and his group, had alerted those who waited in the locality for them, that they were on their way.

Brati thought he would meet Somu and his group that night itself and bring them safely out of the locality. He did not have much hope of success, and yet he had thought he might just manage.

Yet his 'Don't worry' had sounded so disarmingly normal and casual that Sujata had not been worried at all.

It was safe to be with Ronu ...

WE NEVER WANTED ...

Tarit Kumar

We never wanted
to have four feet.
But you made us bend for every
need of ours.
So our hands became feet.
As you know,
For a bent man,
Two feet are not enough.

We never wanted
that fiendish nails
should grow on our toes,
and beneath our claws
you will writhe.

But you wanted
to put chains
around our necks.

You forgot—
Every four-footed animal
need not be a dog!

THE NIGHT OF THE FULL MOON

Saroj Dutta

Those who try to bind me—
With their flutes, herbs and rituals,
Those who hold me inside the choking basket
And break my poison fangs,
Those who wind me round their necks
And kill me now and then—
Warn them that the night of the full moon has arrived!

How often have I swayed my entranced hood
To the tune of their flutes.
How often have I sought for a pit to hide
My tired self.
How often have I roared in dumb rage,
Lashed out with my useless fangs,
Pounded my head against the earth!
They merely watched amused, and laughed.

In every marrow of my being today
A deep pain runs.
The sensitive skin slips away,
The fever of pain
Racks my body.

The two eyes are still—
Two drops of extracts of hatred!

The skin is shed at last.
I come out,
Afresh, smooth and dangerous!
And, in the revelry of their games
They have forgotten—
My sack of venom is full to the brim tonight.

THE ENEMY WITHIN

Bani Basu

'21st September 1987

'I had thought that if somehow you could manage to leave a certain time behind then the curtain would automatically come down on it. I had thought that no matter how time sustained its continuity, it would respect the drop of the curtain. Only intense grief can present its documents and make one understand that this notion is wrong in every respect. Time always keeps us floating in its endless flow. To it, all curtains are transparent. But when Time appears in the form of a human being, its blow is the hardest to bear! Only then can one rightly understand there is no basic difference between the day that has passed and the day that is to come. When you showed yourself again to me, Bibi, against the backdrop of a western Bengal sunset, after fourteen long years, only then did I fully understand what is Time. On the wide-spread, stark, and barren fields I saw row after row of men lying dismembered, as in the last phase of the battle at Kurukshetra, all those foot-soldiers who paid the price of other men's dreams, without knowing, alas, who was hiding his malice against whom. Bibi, I have sinned grossly. I crossed over to the land of safety, leaving my brothers to fight my battle. But even the greatest of sinners have something to say in self-defence. How many days have I followed you round just seeking an opportunity to speak and, not being able to speak, those words have churned around in my head. They have wanted to spurt out, at times without control, like blood from the mouth of a tuberculosis patient. I would not have asked for forgiveness. But why didn't I even get the chance to say even one word? I know that the sky and the winds are frowning at my question. After all this, all the dusty blinkers that I made others put on, after this weary, sordid chronicle, why should there be a question left to ask?

...The table-clock shows that it is two-thirty at night. They have just left—Bappa and Bacchu. Bacchu was standing with the green wall of the living room behind him, bent over, leaning on his crutch like a dried-up leaf, one hand holding on to the window-sill. He was standing there without a word. The sheer agony of having to stand made him tremble. Was this Bacchu? The Bacchu I knew? Whose hand didn't tremble even once when he obeyed my commands, who ran from danger to greater danger simply because I had asked him to do something. I said, 'Bacchu sit. Bappa sit down please.' Bappa just stared at me calmly and said, 'We haven't come to sit down, Antu-da. We only came to see you. Just once.' He didn't utter a single word more. He turned around and picked up Bacchu in his arms. Then clambered downstairs step by step. Bacchu's crutches went down casting geometrical shadows on the staircase walls. In that massive frame I could clearly see all my mistakes, crimes, and my penance.

'Bacchu, you mustn't forgive me either. Do we really ask for forgiveness because we think we will get it? It is just a way to admit guilt, to express pain. But still, I have something to say to you. No justification, believe me. The kind of inhuman torture all of you endured and, having done so, are more dead than alive, yet proud to be real men, braver than the bravest. Why couldn't I endure that torture? Why? I ask myself but don't find an answer. On the first two days I was treated like a prince, with luxury and respect. Then, all of a sudden, the fatherly faces changed. They became terrifying, demonic as they fired question after question at me. A pin, the whole of it, was shoved in below my navel. At the horrific possibility of what could follow, I screamed. I had no control left over myself. Off the rebound I found myself abroad, helped by the money of rich relatives. I did not know then what I had done to Bibi, what I had done to you. But I ought to have known. Bacchu, I am a coward, yes, but still a human being. Every wound on your body is a debt I owe to you. If I can even repay it, then, call me 'dada' Bacchu, once again, as you used to.'

Shirsha's letter was to his brother Soumya: 'Chhor-da, Atanu Sarkar is watching us all the time because of Antu-da. I knew this as soon as I saw his flat face. At first I couldn't understand how he had traced us so quickly. I now suspect that his vigil over our activities will never slacken. In the eyes of the law, we shall always be regarded as dangerous killers. They got to Antu-da, because they were following us. You have done well to pick up his diary. But why did you hide it from me? In case the idolater Bacchu forgives his idol, is that why?

'Chhor-da, our organisation was weak, we had nothing like a central leadership. We made a mistake in thinking that the ground for revolution was all set, that the ruling classes had lost the support of the masses. In a country where religious shortsightedness and psychologically ambiguous attitudes towards caste and creed, language and tradition, are so closely intertwined with poverty, what degree of relevance does pure Marxist-Leninist ideology have here? I don't want to go into the subtleties of this very learned debate. But do you know where our actual weakness lies? Do you know why all our efforts were reduced to a heart-rending tragedy? Revolution takes it for granted that the best among men are super-heroes, warriors. Revolution expects every man to be a man of fire, with boundless endurance. It claims the kind of power that can easily destroy. But the basic and supreme principle of creation is not to destroy, but to build. Those in whom the urge to build, to create, is strong are men of fine sensibilities. They do not themselves know how the crude and the coarse shatter them to pieces. If they are called to battle before they can restrain themselves, there is no hope of their passing the acid test of revolution. I don't know if you are aware, in the past ten years of the industrial history of the Middle East, Sumanta Sengupta is a revered name. It could have been the same, here as well. But penance, penance became more urgent. Because none of us gave him the chance to say a single word!

'And what should I say of myself? Anything I might have had to say dried up a long long while ago.

The sickness, the nausea, the pitiless pain
Have ceased with the fever that maddened my brain,
With the fever, called living, that burned in my brain ...'

Live the rest of your life the way you want to. And tell Didi to forgive him, even though he didn't ask for it. Forgive him, not for his sake, but for her own.'

AFTERWORD

The Naxalite movement was sparked off in 1967 by the killing of an infamous jotedar (landowner) in the obscure village of Naxalbari in North Bengal. This was an isolated act of desperation by local tribals. But in no time it triggered off a revolutionary movement that spread like wildfire to southern parts of the state and especially in Calcutta city, inspiring middle class urban youth who had turned restless with the non-performance and corruption of the existing system.

The movement gained maximum impetus in the early seventies. Students with Marxist leanings from such reputable institutions as Presidency College, Jadavpur University, Calcutta Medical College, etc., became Naxalites under the firebrand leadership of Charu Majumdar and Kanu Sanyal. Their signal slogans were 'China's Chairman is our Chairman' and 'Power flows from the barrel of a gun', announcing that they had lost faith in the then established political leadership which, according to them, was wrongly tilting towards parliamentary democracy and revisionism, thus betraying the Leninist ideology.

Hence the shifting of faith to Mao Zedong and the belief that the destruction and re-building of the existing establishment through violent revolution was the only way to stem the rot. They wanted to destroy and rebuild after the Chinese model. They promptly identified the class enemies, black-listed them and started small people's war groups. The result was known as 'red-terror'. They defiled the nation's heroes, decapitated statues, ransacked schools, colleges, universities, hospitals, and went on a killing spree. The victims were the theoretical class-enemies who turned out to be policemen, teachers, doctors, small tradesman, and the like.

This indiscriminate violence alienated a tacitly supportive public. They had been hoping against hope that these well-educated boys from a middle-class background would bring positive change to the political system after all, but were disgusted at the dastardly murders of police constables not on duty, teachers invigilating in examination halls, and small tradesman plying their trade. In their bid to end corruption and misuse of power, these self-styled sentinels of higher morality never even so much as touched the real culprits. The back-marketeers and other such murky operators were left untouched, so were political bigwigs masterminding these rackets. The justification that those being killed were symbols of the establishment couldn't hold water for long with the general public.

Retaliation came in the form of 'white terror' launched by the state machinery led by the United Front government in power at that time. Faced with the stark reality of the counter-attack from the establishment, the young rebels were found lacking in such basics as organisation and coordination.

There was also a growing disillusionment in the revolutionary ranks with the lack of direction of the movement's leaders. They seemed to have started working in extremely short-sighted and sometimes even devious ways, drifting away from the larger, fundamental goals of the movement. They were unable to provide viable strategies that would sustain it in the face of the crackdown from the establishment. The movement's ideological backbone was thus broken.

As the movement crumbled, many of the revolutionary mainstays turned informers, some just broke down while some fled the country leaving behind the very movement they had initiated. Young men were often captured with the help of double agents. They were ruthlessly tortured, maimed and/or killed. In the ensuing confusion the brilliant students who started the movement got mixed up with dangerous urban lumpen. The last nail was driven into the coffin when hundreds of youths were butchered by the police in Baranagar and Kashipur in August 1971. In this massacre the city witnessed the revolt once and for all.

The irony of this failed movement is that though it was started by farmers, the movement was taken over by urban intellectuals who could hardly establish any rapport with their rural counterparts. The experiment in this regard failed in Gopiballavpur in Medinipur district although a free zone had been created there temporarily. Neither the farmers nor the semi-urban mazdoors could be convinced that their salvation lay in capturing political power at gunpoint. Therefore no real people's army could be formed, no real war for liberation could be waged, and political power for the proletariat remained as distant a dream as ever.

In short it was a tragic waste. What started with noble aspirations and raised high hopes of widespread political reform, especially in the middle class, fizzled out within five years under the remote-control of fanatically capricious generals and a network of brigadiers severely lacking in tactical knowledge and nerve. The movement has long been over in West Bengal but it spawned other versions in Bihar, Orissa, and Andhra Pradesh.

Antarghat is concerned with the aftermath of the original movement. The curtain goes up about a decade later when everything can be seen and assessed in perspective. It turns out to be a tragedy of conscience for everybody concerned. The past decade haunts each and everyone. From the apparently calm exterior, no one can dream what terrible scars the erstwhile protagonists carry within. One can escape the police, flee the country, but not for ever. Destiny overtakes, if not by death, as least by searing self-reproach.

In the mid-sixties I had just started my career as a college lecturer. As a young teacher I was devoted to my job and to my students. Some of my best students went the Naxal way. I found them turn arrogant and lose their more likeable qualities. During examinations, they even encouraged outsiders to help the examinees copy out answers. When they failed, they could go so far as setting then murderous brethren on us.

In Shyampukur, where I lived, I saw the neighbourhood boys demanding money from people at gunpoint, killing and getting killed in turn. The episodes in *Antarghat* are all drawn from these experiences.

But it was not out of indignation alone that I wrote this book. It was out of immense sadness, that a whole bright generation could thus be misguided to a state of mental decrepitude, that so many class institutions could be laid waste, and the prevailing education system ruined. This fallout of Naxalism was apparent by 1987, the time I wrote the book. Today, we look on helplessly at hospitals that don't work, good education that is available only in exchange for a fortune, and corruption even more deep-rooted in every aspect of daily living than what the movement sought to eradicate. Where are the bright young people who made us dream of a better world? The brightest of them are in U.S.A., U.K., Germany, France, and the Middle East. Everywhere but in India. They are no longer concerned about their country which has been taken over by corrupt politicians, a spineless and selfish middle-class, and an indifferent upper class.

However, I did not mean the book to be a social discourse. It is a human drama, not of crime and punishment but surely of sin and retribution.

AUNI

Ashim Ray

'Didn't you say, Baba, that the Bengal Renaissance was all bogus?'

Perhaps Auni wants to use such words to convey something to me, but in our conversation we don't move our lips. The moment we try to talk all conversation comes to an end. Silence brings in an awareness of his closeness to me—that he is a part of my flesh and blood, and bones. And I do not want to destroy this invaluable moment of silence. Looking at his smile, a little hidden, but ever present, around his soft moustache I ask him in silence, 'But attacking Vidyasagar?[1] Whatever you might say, isn't it a bit too much?'

About a week ago when Auni's mother raised the issue of Vidyasagar, he had quipped, 'But how long do you want to use Vidyasagar as a popsicle to put us to sleep, Ma?' The same reply again peers through the smile around his tender moustache. I shake myself and stir up. I clear my throat in an attempt to break out from this silent magic. I ask him, 'How's your cough?'

Auni smiles hesitantly. Lifting his sad black eyes towards me, he says suddenly, 'There's a hell of a difference between today and 1948, when you had taken to the streets for armed revolution. At that time, you had no support; today the toiling masses of the world are with us.' I look back at my son in fear. I know my answer by rote. And it is only

---

[1] *Vidyasagar:* Reference to the attacks on statues of leaders of Bengal Renaissance like Ishwar Chandra Vidyasagar by the iconoclastic Naxalite youth.

inevitable that on hearing it Auni will not enter my room for the next few days. We have been playing such hide and seek in the darkness for the last one-year, no one being able to catch the other, possibly no one even trying to touch the other. Rather it is better if Auni sits in my room in silence for a while and my fatherly desires are satisfied. I yawn in an attempt to quieten myself, but my mind shrieks, 'Youth, Auni, youth. Your blood is boiling now. If I could only tame all these young men—their blood boiling—with sweets and pies! And then when your blood cools down, say when you reach your thirties, I'll let you go. Then you may judge with your mind and test your wit. Then you'll think twice before you believe in something. You'll see before you leap and you'll get entangled in the *maya* of this life which ensnares you like the tentacles of an octopus. Only these few years! If the youth of the country could leap over these ten or twelve years and become old! For, Bengal's youth will never come of age. Its banner of victory will never march step by step to reach the sunlit horizon. It always was, at least from the time of fighting the Britishers, a mere symbol of unfinished greatness. The courage of this unfinished greatness has dazzled my eyes, Auni. It has taken away my vision. I don't want to see again.'

It is as if Auni understands my feelings. From behind his thin moustache, his familiar sarcastic smile emerges. And I hear what he had said to his Ma, 'Actually, Baba cannot escape his own past. Because Baba is no longer a political element, he thinks it'll be the same as his time—the movement destroyed by police battering. He doesn't look around. He only dreams of what he had done in his time. The people have forgotten that; it's better to forget. It's no use worshipping the past. We've started our fight; we'll complete it'.

Auni's last words hurl themselves on my head like a hammer. It's true that I have withdrawn from politics, but I don't think I've lost the capacity to distinguish which slogan brings the blood to a boil or tightens the muscles for a new promise. There are strange words in the slogans that Auni uses. On the face of it, they sound emotional even melodramatic. But the strong determination of these words moves me. These words don't merely echo some new emotions, but they shake the middle-class Bengali existence by its very roots. If I didn't belong to this place and was not a middle-class Bengali, but a German or a Punjabi then I would have watched this new history of Bengal unfold from a distance and said with a typical, north Indian, yawn of indifference, 'Couldn't we call in the military?' But when the fire is so near, you can feel the heat. Here the circumstances have moved beyond judgement or analysis. The events have acquired a kind of detached self-sufficiency as they appear in the morning newspapers. They make me forget the history of revolutions or the geography that I had learnt in my youth, and to which I had clung for a long time like a straw in the eddies of my middle age. Often, I'm surprised at my own altered views. Since I can't make my son any older or maturer wouldn't it be better to send him abroad, at least to Delhi, Bombay or Ahmedabad? Such immature thoughts that come, like failing eyesight, obsess me at times. Then I feel there's no escape. I get immensely irritated at the failure of my fatherly duties. If this revolution would've come five years later I would've got Auni a job in the Corporation's lighting department after my retirement, even though it would mean cringing and currying favour with Bose Babu. Like many other offices it's a long tradition in our office to give the son placement after his father's retirement. Today, futuristic problems like what would be the face of our country in another five years seem to bother me less than the harrowing question, 'Will I be able to keep my son alive?' Auni will possibly get up now. Our internal dialogue cannot go on for long. At least Auni does not like it even if I do. He feels restless. So do I. To start a real conversation I now open my mouth, 'Rupnarayanpur is a nice place, isn't it, Auni?'

'Too boring, extremely isolated. There's nothing to do but sleep. Besides it was not possible to stay on any longer. There was pressure on *Dadu*. You did ask me to stay on but that would've been inconvenient for them.'

I couldn't send my son abroad. So I sent him to Rupnarayanpur, near the Bihar border, where a distantly related *jyathamoshai* was the stationmaster. About two months ago, when a bomb ripped apart a police van in the street before our house and killed a policeman, the police arrived after three hours, possibly with a deep belief that the accused would wait and munch popcorn nearby. They arrested Auni along with other boys of the locality. Auni came back after two days. The police had made him their football in the lockup. The small finger of his left hand was broken. The police became frequent visitors to our home and my wife developed her nervous problems. In the middle of the night, Nihar would scream at the slightest noise even when the door creaked because of high wind. Out of desperation I wrote to my *jyathamoshai*—the stationmaster. He is a decent man devoted to a Guruji. He feels restless in his loneliness. He was willing to accommodate Auni when he received my letter.

'Actually I'm a coward. We need to conquer death. Unlike Sugato, I'm incapable of that. That's my problem. But Baba, you make me laugh. Do you think men are animals, that if they are fed and petted their problems will be solved?'

Auni destroyed the silent magic of friendship that we had created till now. When we talk it becomes amply clear that the two of us—father and son—are traversing two parallel lines. Silence creates a warm, confidential atmosphere, which emerges out of a sense of time—mornings, evenings and nights—spent together in closeness. This blunts all feelings of enmity. In fact there are many hidden possibilities in silence—possibilities of coexisting and living together slowly crept in our blood. Yet now there was no escape. Auni's painful remark forces me to answer back.

'Auni, are you going to create a made-in-Bengal revolution?' Unknowingly the words escape my lips. I pick up the pencil from the table and make it dance on my fingertips to lighten the impact of my words.

'What do you mean?' The movement of Auni's neck reflects the determination of those young boys of Bengal who have taken up the sword. But I don't heed the warning. In utter impatience I scream, 'What else but made-in-Bengal? Where have you seen that targeting the individual hastens the process of revolution? Show me just one country - Russia, China, Cuba, Vietnam?'

'Baba, forget what you had learnt. A new revolution is happening, new measures of judgement are being set. I had given you material on this for your reading. Have you read them carefully?'

Auni's calm patient voice makes me all the more restless. It mocks, as it were, my whole existence. My political thoughts and feelings, judgement and analysis are thrown to the wind.

'Oh, I've read all that, but they're all a bunch of advice! It's all a set of assumptions! It has been assumed that the entire population has arisen, and peasants all over the villages, fields and haystacks are inspired by class-hatred. Actually speaking, you've created a world of romanticism and desired ideal, but a revolution is practical, a revolution stands on material situations.'

Having said this I thought that I had said something great. I congratulate myself silently on my analytical capacity and look at Auni.

But Auni hardly pays any heed. The words do not seem to affect him. They seem like the many mundane things he hears.

'Actually you didn't concentrate on the literature I gave you.'

At this, I take Auni as my rival as though I have no responsibility towards him. The old self-confidence that our close relationship of twenty years can never be destroyed by all this sound and fury around us suddenly disappears. I completely forget my evening's promise to keep peace.

I say, 'I've told you—that this revolution—was a necessity. Really, when everybody is making a career in the name of revolution, then your infinite self sacrifice …'

Auni stands up in protest, with one hand up in the air. He says quietly, 'Don't utter this rubbish. It's a cliche. Everyone says this. Do you also have to say it? Does revolution mean writing a newspaper editorial or is it a cocktail party? There is death in revolution, sacrifice is inevitable. Today, people have conquered death, in the way Sugato has overcome death. Revolution is inevitable.'

Of course he does not utter those words. But silently I hear them all. He talks about the revolution in this vein with his Ma. With me his talks never progress very far. It ends after a while. With me Auni has discovered a certain technique. Whenever my analytical mind becomes restless, Auni grows quiet. And then I can decipher the correct answers from his silent lips.

Looking at his sharp handsome brown face, with his hands raised up, I suddenly feel tired. I almost shriek, 'Just wait a little Auni. Don't destroy yourselves by jumping into this fire. One must keep the fire burning year after year.'

A slight smile plays on Auni's lips. I hear Auni's reply clearly. 'Just as you've kept the fire alive these twenty-two years!' But I am not the person to give up. I say, 'I am not making excuses for our weaknesses or frailties. In fact, a definite resolution should have been reached after Independence when we took to the streets shouting 'This Freedom is Fake'. That moment could have been a turning point in Indian history. Had it been so, in India, at least in Bengal, the youth wouldn't have had to make this sacrifice today …' I still remember the day. We were on the streets marching in a procession to break open the jail gates while on the other side girls in sunglasses thronged the Eden Gardens to watch a cricket match. Well, we were the ones to be bashed up by the police.

Auni's face lit up with a calm smile. That confident smile almost slapped me on my face. He said, 'But now? Don't you see what's happening now? Calcutta is about to be a liberated zone. There is no place for middle-class sentimentalism. Don't you get the smell of gunpowder when you step down into the streets, Baba? The revolution has arrived.'

I stiffen immediately. I remember the days 25 years ago when we had taken up arms against the police. The footfalls of revolution had jingled in our blood every moment. And then when the tide of the movement ebbed away within two years we felt the mockery of it all in our bones. A close associate of mine rushed for a high post in an advertising firm, I stood cringing in front of the deputy mayor of Calcutta, another distantly related uncle of mine. After that, there grew the trend to justify everything in the name of Marxism. Pages of history unfolded before us in our youth—the history of total self-deceit. Compared to that isn't Auni's revolution far more defined and dear? More meaningful? Is it really a repetition, or is it a rebirth?

Auni watches me without batting an eyelid, and then moves towards my bookshelf, to the dust covered books on Marx, Lenin, Stalin, Mao-Dze-Tung. Dusting the books unmindfully, with an old duster, he suddenly stops. I look through the corner of my eyes to see which book he is looking at—Lenin or Mao-Dze-Tung.

'Baba, don't you think there's no relation between these books and your present cringing existence with its entrenched corruption for the sake of making some money? These books are not meant for this museum. There's no link between the frothy type of revolution and this dead, self-repetitive, mechanical cycle of life. Through his death in the twenty-first year of his life Sugato has achieved what you've not been able to achieve in your fifty years of revolution. Through his sacrifice he has helped to light up the fire of revolution. What have you done with your analytical powers or your dust covered books on Marxism?'

Auni is now looking beyond the window at the western horizon. Maybe because I am aging I love to watch this western sky. I stand transfixed. The late autumn's purplish sky in the west has an orange tinge. Looking at it I look back at my own past. Like their slogans, these words coming out of Auni's silent lips ruffle my consciousness. Have I really been transformed to an antique in my Marxist museum? Politics indeed is that principle that drives men to a definite goal. In the ebb of the revolution have we not lost our goal and got into a quagmire and built houses on such murky soil? Have we not become a pathetic tribe of petty bourgeois in our effort to overcome that degeneration? What else could we have done? My analytical sense sharpens immediately. We could have inspired the people towards mass suicide throughout the country, failing which we could have become martyrs!

I pick up the pencil and make it dance to cover my restlessness. Auni laughs. He looks at me. There is no sarcasm in this laughter—it's the bright laugh of a fun-loving youth. I also join in the laughter. I feel that the blood flow of my body has come down to normal.

When Auni had just joined college two years back, one day I was surprised to see a line written at the back of his exercise book—'I want to sit on the grass of Bengal.' 'Whose poem is this?' I had asked. Hesitantly Auni had said, 'Jibanananda Das. Haven't you heard his name?' On admitting my ignorance he had said with his head bowed, 'Beautiful Bengal is the title of the book. Excellent poetry.' At that time, I had thought that Auni was into writing poetry. I don't understand much of poetry, but was satisfied with the thought that such poems are not dangerous. But in the last two years Auni's face changed along with the change in the beauty of Bengal. His loud, open laughter stopped. He used to play cricket in a small plot of land bordering an open drain nearby, which was littered with garbage and cowdung. That too stopped. Gradually his face became serious. And at times he would sit quietly with inverted eyes. This continued for a while. Suddenly one day, I got a call from the police station. I didn't know that the O.C (officer-in-charge) was my classmate. I used to avoid this locality since at one time I was politically associated with that area. I couldn't recognize him now. He had developed such a serious face with age that recognition was difficult. Conversing on various subjects while having tea, he suddenly commented, 'Keep an eye on your son. He's mixing with the wrong people.' I didn't probe further. I escaped without sipping the last of the tea. Possibly to pacify me, before I left, my classmate said, 'Of course I admit that there is the socio-economic factor. You've also been in politics. Certainly now you understand that violence doesn't pay.' I didn't say anything but it spoilt my mood. The leaders of our country are filling up the newspaper columns with their views on the pros and cons of violence. What could I, a mere Corporation lighting inspector, say? I seek consolation in such reasoning.

In this autumn evening that situation of last summer is now like a dream. The bomb explosion in our locality and Auni's experience in jail made him even more desperate to cling on to his politics. He left home altogether. Suddenly he would arrive and then as suddenly disappear after meeting his mother. There was a spontaneous throbbing relationship with his mother that I did not share with Auni. His mother used to shout at him, use strong words and then again lovingly embrace him. It was a pulsating experience—alive at every moment. His mother was not afraid of him. Instead she would make fun of him. Dejectedly sitting in the next room, I would try to analyze this feminine urge to find an answer to everything through immediate physical contact. And then a strange thing happened. My home was attacked by the very same political party that I had worked for—the same party under whose flag I had worked for in my youth and with whom I am still inextricably associated on account of old friendships. The boys of the same party came last Tuesday evening to search for Auni. They carried sticks, iron rods, and knives of different sizes and pipe-guns. They came shaking up the whole locality, exploding bombs; boys whose elder brothers or uncles I had joined once to bring about a political revolution. I was dumbstruck looking at the faces of these killers. I did not know a single boy, they did not know me either. I was not at all prepared for this strange melodrama. Hearing the commotion outside I looked through the window and lost my wits. They hurled strong abuses at me. One of them came forward and said, 'So you've got yourself a nice potbelly with all that bribe.' Someone else said, 'Slit it, man'. Their incessant kicks soon pulled down a part of the door. At that moment I suddenly remembered that Auni had come to see his mother and was inside. I immediately jumped like a Kandiyan dancer and held on to the broken door facing a raised sword. It seemed that I stood without my body. The cruel commotion and the steady gaze of the lined up attackers were beyond my sight or hearing. Suddenly it seemed that from some previous birth a face had emerged from among that cruel crowd. A heavy commanding voice said, 'Not here, not here. Whatever you do will be outside the house, not in this house.' After that

I remember nothing. Possibly, I had lost consciousness. Regaining my senses I saw my wife sprinkling water on me. Auni was not at home.

Suddenly, I wake up from my world of thought at the sound of Auni's cough. Auni has got up. Staying on longer could be dangerous for him. 'It isn't that we don't have any doubts'. These words alert me. I look at my son like a hunger driven beggar suddenly discovering a plate of rice. Auni continues to himself in a low voice, 'You say what everyone else says, that a revolution comes with the participation of the majority of people—poor people—of the country! But what could we do? Someone has to awaken them, show them the way. You yourself saw that your path makes ministers, not a revolution.'

I do not say anything. In our evening of silent conversation this is a rare moment of clear and straightforward outspokenness. Whenever we speak I mouth platitudes in favour of my past and present convictions while Auni gives vent to his sarcasm. I keep looking anxiously at Auni's sharp, handsome face as though I am looking at him for the last time. He says slowly, 'Having come this far if I show any weakness my comrades won't forgive me.'

'I'll send you to Delhi,' I shout like a madman.

Auni looks at me for a while in deep sympathy. Looking at his calm gaze I feel as if I am Auni's child. I acknowledge the natural defeat of my paternity.

Auni said, 'You'll not be able to save me, Baba. I'm the target of the police on the roads. If I come home, men from other parties will come and kill me. And if I think of taking up a job then my comrades won't let me go. Don't try for me, Baba.' Auni gets up. I close my eyes. When I open them I find that Auni has left.

For the next few days I neither look up the newspapers nor listen to the radio. I avoid any political discussions. I did not lag behind from doing what people generally do under such circumstances, i.e. drinking. But I was acutely self-conscious. Such melodrama as to drink to drown one's sorrow was beyond my being. Lots of people preach to me about the responsibilities of a guardian; some relatives come and reprimand me for my political past.

These do not touch me, because there is no escape from that future which is like the inexorable fate. A well wisher of mine advises me to inform the police about my son so that his life may be spared. But I do not want such an escape. Such an attempt may bring temporary relief but I am certain that in the long run Auni cannot be saved. Rather it would snap all his ties with me. Besides, these youths with swords in their hands, are indeed our posterity. The victory flag of those innumerable youths who are no longer with us is in the hands of Auni. There is nothing that I can say if Auni and his friends take to the path of suicide. It is clear to me that I am not in the position to preach. If I must practice what I preach then I have to be out there in the battlefields. The questions raised by Auni must be answered instead of burying them with the hatchet. I do not have that courage, and I do not know whether anyone else has it. So in spite of my eyes I am blind, and deaf in spite of my ears.

I received the phone call at dawn. The police have given the permission to release Auni's body from the morgue. I was prepared for the phone and I remember everything clearly. There was no tremor in my voice when I asked the first question, 'Did Auni throw a bomb at the police?' and without waiting for an answer asked my second question, 'Did he die of police firing?'

I was devoid of all feelings. To me this was not just Auni's death. This was the death of my dream of socialism, the death of my Lenin, Stalin, Mao-Dze-Tung. I was taken by surprise when they shouted, 'Auni the thief! Auni the thief! Has anyone come for him?' I get up in a hurry. I always thought that no one could ever distort the name Anirban Mukherjee. It would be difficult to give such aliases like 'Hauray or 'Gulay'. I cannot but appreciate this magical power of changing names. My companion who is a forensic expert comes forward, examines Auni's wound and says, 'Shot at from very close'. But can anyone say anything when he confronts his own dead body? I turn my neck and look outside the window. A short, *neem* tree plastered with cowdung cakes stands under the early winter sun. Below, on a strip of yellow land two *shalik* birds fight with each other. I remember the lines seen a long time ago in Auni's exercise book, 'I want to sit on the grass of Bengal.'

Translated by Simita Ray

NEPAL

A REFUGEE

Samrat Upadhyay

Pitamber Crossed the Bridge to Kupondole and found the gift shop where he'd been told Kabita worked. But the man behind the counter said she'd quit after just a few days. 'She wasn't right in the head, you know,' the man said, 'after all that happened to her.'

'Where did she go?'

'I don't know. I tried to convince her to stay on, but she just stopped coming.'

Pitamber left the shop and stood on the sidewalk, squinting at the sun and noting the intense heat, strange for autumn. This morning he'd woken restless, with a hollowness in his stomach, and thought about the letter he'd received a fortnight ago from his childhood friend Jaikanth. The feeling remained with him throughout the day as he searched for this woman named Kabita, whose story Jaikanth had described to him. 'She's in Kathmandu with her daughter, and I know what a kind man you are, Pitamber. Please do what you can to help her. She's suffered immensely.'

Now Pitamber made his way to his flat in Dharahara, where his wife, Shailaja, was cooking French toast in the kitchen. She turned to smile at him as he came in. 'Any luck?'

He said no and mopped his forehead with a handkerchief. 'Why hasn't she contacted us? Jaikanth said he gave her our address. It's been nearly two weeks.'

'Maybe other people are already helping her. Didn't Jaikanth mention other people she knew here?'

He nodded, then told her what the man in the gift shop had said. 'I hope she's found another job,' he told Shailaja, then said that his stomach had been mildly upset all day.

'It must be hunger,' she said. 'Why don't you go wash your face and I'll give you some French toast. Sumit should be home any minute now.'

He went to the bathroom, washed his face, took several deep breaths, then went to find Jaikanth's letter. He read it again, and paused as he did: 'They killed him in front of her, Pitamber. Can you imagine what that must have been like?' Jaikanth hadn't explained the details of the killing, but over the past two weeks Pitamber had formed a picture in his mind: three Maobadi rebels, barely past their teens (they were always so young in the news), storming into her house, dragging her husband out to the yard, slitting his throat with a knife. The four-year-old daughter probably inside the house, perhaps sound asleep, perhaps with a nasty cold. And after the men leave, a woman standing there, her palm over her mouth.

The woman's face was never clear, but Pitamber's mind always flashed with these details: the sun's rays glinting on washed pots drying on the porch, one rebel raising his finger to warn the neighbors peeking from the windows of their houses, the men's footprints on the rice paddies through which they escape.

He massaged his temples. Surely she still needed help now. It was clear that Jaikanth was expecting him to house the woman and her daughter for a while, and Pitamber was willing to do this, even though his was only a three-room flat in a small house. He wanted to help her, mostly out of compassion, but partly out of obligation to an old friend of his family, a friend from the village where he grew up.

When Sumit, his twelve-year-old son, returned from school, they drank tea and ate French toast, then Pitamber and the boy settled down to play chess. Pitamber had bought the set two months ago, after the first set, a cheap one with plastic pieces, disappeared from their flat. Pitamber suspected that one of Sumit's friends from the neighborhood, who had a reputation for lifting small objects from the surrounding houses, had swiped it, but he didn't pursue the matter. Sumit had shown remarkable skill in the game, so this time Pitamber bought a marble set with finely carved pieces. It had cost him nine hundred rupees at a tourist shop in Basantapur. His stomach dropped when the shopkeeper first told him the price, but he'd rationalized the purchase, convincing himself that his son would become a master someday. 'We should enrol him in the neighborhood chess club,' he'd said to Shailaja the other day. 'He can play with older kids and learn more quickly.' But Shailaja was hesitant. 'He might be intimidated. There'll be kids his age better at the game, and you know how he is.' She had a point. Sumit was a sensitive kid; he berated himself whenever he lost to his father. Perhaps he should gain more confidence before joining any clubs.

The two played chess that evening for nearly an hour. Sumit made a couple of silly mistakes and slapped his forehead each time. Pitamber deliberately muddled his moves to compensate for Sumit's errors, careful to pretend that the mistakes were genuine. Toward the end of the game, Sumit captured his remaining knight and paralyzed Pitamber's king. 'You're getting much better,' Pitamber told his son, and suggested the three of them go for a walk.

The air had gotten considerably cooler and more pleasant, but Pitamber soon grew annoyed by the crowds on the pavement and the cars and trucks spewing fumes and blasting their horns beside them. The three walked toward the stadium, and Sumit spotted a large billboard advertising a Hindi action movie. 'I want to see that,' he said, and he held out his arms as if he were carrying a machine gun. *'Bhut bhut bhut bhut.'* He mock-shot some pedestrians, and Pitamber scolded him. The boy had been watching too many of these movies on video. Shailaja was too lenient with him, and on weekends, when he and Pitamber were not playing chess, Sumit remained glued to the television despite Pitamber's pleas for him to turn it off. He even recognized all the actors and actresses and knew their silly songs by heart.

Chess was better for him. It taught him to think, to strategize, to assess his own strengths and weaknesses. It was a good game for a future statesman or a philosopher. The idea of his son's becoming someone important brought a smile to Pitamber's face, and he ruffled the boy's hair.

After dinner that evening, Pitamber went to his bedroom to read the day's paper. In Rolpa, dozens of policemen had been shot by the

Maobadis. In Baglung, two rebels had been beaten to death by villagers, who now feared reprisal. The cold, passive language of the news reports disgusted Pitamber, and he set down the paper. It was hard to believe that this country was becoming a place where people killed each other over differences in ideas about how to govern it. At his office the other day, a colleague openly sympathized with the rebels and said that the Maobadis had no choice. 'Think about it,' the man had said. 'For years we suffered under the kings, then we got so-called democracy, but nothing got better. Most of our country lives in mind-boggling poverty. These Maobadis are only fighting for the poor. It's a simple thing that they're doing.'

'Simple?' Pitamber had said. 'Your Maobadis are killing the very people they claim they're fighting for—innocent villagers.'

'They're casualties of the revolution,' the man said. 'They are martyrs. But the revolution has to go on.'

Pitamber took a deep breath and said, 'It's easy for you to blather on about revolutions from your comfortable chair.'

The discussion ended with him walking away from his colleague. Later Pitamber barely acknowledged him when they passed in the hallway, even though he knew that what the man said was not entirely untrue: poor people in the country were fed up with how little their conditions had changed, democracy or no democracy.

Pitamber again went to find Jaikanth's letter and reread it, this time stopping at the three names and addresses of the contacts Kabita already had in the city. Through one of these people, Pitamber had learned about the gift shop where she had worked. He had tried reaching another of the contacts but had been told the man was out of town. Pitamber reached for the phone and called the number again. The man answered this time, but said he didn't know the whereabouts of Kabita. 'She hasn't been in touch, but I believe she has a distant relative who is a sadhu in the Pashupatinath temple. You might try him.'

Early the next morning, after some searching, Pitamber found the communal house for ascetics near the Pashupatinath temple, where Kabita's relative, Ramsharan, lived. When Pitamber announced whom he was looking for, a small old man with soft eyes and full lips said, 'That's me.' He told Pitamber that Kabita was renting a flat in Baghbazar and gave him directions. 'She hasn't come to see me,' the man said. 'And I'm too old to walk around the city. But I did go to her flat once when she first came to Kathmandu.' Ramsharan shook his head sadly. 'What can we do? God creates, God destroys. We can only sing his praises.'

Pitamber thanked him and left, mildly annoyed by the sadhu's sanctimonious words. It was already nine o'clock, and Pitamber would be late for work. But he felt so close to finding Kabita that he decided he'd risk his new supervisor's irritation. Thus far Pitamber was in Mr. Shrestha's good graces at the municipal branch office in Naxal where he worked—maybe the man would tolerate one day of tardiness.

Kabita's flat was located above a shoe store, and the smell of leather hung in the staircase as Pitamber climbed to the third floor. He knocked on the door. After a few moments, a small woman with sunken eyes opened it. She couldn't have been more than twenty-five or so, and she had on the standard white dhoti that widows wore.

'Kabitaji?'

She nodded. A girl appeared by her side, and Pitamber could hear the sound of a kerosene stove burning inside. He introduced himself, said Jaikanth had written to him about her. 'Oh, yes,' she said without much expression.

'I don't want to bother you,' Pitamber said. 'But could we talk?'

She let him in. It was a one-room flat, with a bed in one corner and cooking equipment in another. There were no drapes on the windows, and Pitamber noticed two girls at the window of the neighboring house looking in at them and whispering. 'How old is she?' he asked, gesturing toward the girl. He reached into his pocket, took out a lollipop, and extended it to her. She took it shyly.

'She'll be five next month.'

'And how are things for you?'

For a moment she looked at him as if he were a complete fool. Then she said, 'All right.'

'I was saddened to hear what happened,' he said, searching for something more comforting to say. 'People in this country have simply gone mad.'

'It was God's will,' she said. 'My only worry is for her.' She placed her hand on her daughter's head, and the girl reached under the bed and pulled out a doll with yellow hair and blue eyes.

Pitamber said what a nice-looking doll it was and asked the girl her name.

'Priya,' she said, staring at her feet.

'What a pretty name. I have a son who's a bit older than you. He's named Sumit.'

'Did you do namaste to him?' Kabita suddenly reprimanded her daughter, who halfheartedly joined her palms together for Pitamber.

He again expressed his sorrow, then said that he was willing to offer any help he could. 'I heard you had a job, but quit.'

'It's hard to work with her around,' she said, gesturing toward her daughter. Kabita said she'd taken Priya with her to the gift shop in Kupondole, but after two days the owner said that he couldn't have a child running around a shop frequented by tourists. The owner of the shoe shop below the flat offered to look after her while Kabita worked, but every evening when she returned, she found Priya bawling. 'I've thought about returning to my village,' she said, 'but those men are still there.'

It took him a moment to understand that the men she referred to were the Maobadis. 'Listen,' he said. 'There's no reason for you to be all alone in this city. I am here, my family is here. Why don't you come and stay with us while you look for a job? We'll see if we can find a school for your daughter. And once things fall into place, you can move into a flat of your own.'

She shook her head. 'I couldn't burden you like that.'

'It's no burden! What are you talking about? Listen, we don't have much space, but we can certainly manage. How about you talk to your landlord? Or better, I'll talk to him, explain the situation, and maybe he'll return the money you gave him for the rest of the month.'

'I wouldn't know how to repay you for this.'

'Nonsense.'

Kabita's landlord was argumentative when Pitamber went to see him the next evening after work. 'With anyone else I'd require at least two months' notice, but with her, because of her situation, I can let her go at the end of the month. But not before.'

Pitamber tried to reason with him, said he should consider all that Kabita had endured, that she couldn't possibly afford to let go of almost a month's rent.

But the landlord wouldn't budge. 'I also have my own household expenses to think of. Where am I going to find another tenant on such short notice?'

Pitamber looked around the man's room, lowered his voice, and said, 'Listen, muji, you better let her go. Otherwise people will think you're a Maobadi yourself. Why else would you give her such a hard time? A good question, isn't it?' His own words surprised him, how quickly he said them.

The landlord stared at him. 'Are you threatening me?'

Pitamber straightened his back, deciding to finish what he'd started. 'Take it how you want to take it. I'm just saying your being stubborn makes you suspicious.'

'What kind of a world is this? All I'm asking for is a month's rent that's due to me.'

'But in a situation like this, you shouldn't be thinking only about the money.'

The landlord looked angry but defeated. 'All right, how about a week's rent? At least she can give me that much.'

'How much?'

'Two hundred rupees.'

Pitamber had anticipated something like this and was prepared for it. He didn't want to part with the money, but it was a small price to pay given Kabita's circumstances. He took out his wallet and gave him the money. 'She'll move out tomorrow.'

'Don't tell her or anyone else about our conversation today. I don't want people to get the wrong idea about me.'

'Rest assured,' Pitamber said. As he walked back to Kabita's flat, a few houses away, he felt a bit remorseful about how menacing he'd been, but it had to be done, he supposed. People needed to be reminded of what was important when dealing with those who'd suffered.

The next evening, Kabita and Priya moved into Pitamber's flat. She had only one large suitcase, a thin, folding mattress with a blanket, and a couple of bags, so it was easy to fit everything in a taxi. Kabita wanted to repay the money Pitamber had given to the landlord, as well as the taxi fare, but Pitamber wouldn't hear of it.

Initially, Shailaja said he'd been hasty when he told her that he'd invited Kabita to live with them. 'She might not feel comfortable living with strangers like this,' she said. 'And we don't have much space.' But Pitamber said that he'd feel awful if Kabita was forced to return to the village, and that this arrangement was only temporary. Shailaja finally agreed. 'You've always been like this,' she said, stroking his hair. 'You can't bear to see anyone suffering.'

Now she offered Priya and Kabita tea and snacks, and they chatted about her village and how expensive it was to live in Kathmandu. Shailaja said that a seamstress who sewed her blouses in New Road was looking for help. 'Do you know how to run a sewing machine?' Kabita shook her head. 'I'm sure that wouldn't be a problem,' Shailaja said. 'She actually taught me. I used to work for her until about a year ago, before my fingers began to swell and I could no longer run the machine.'

'But what will I do with her when I work?' Kabita asked, gesturing toward Priya.

'I'll look after her until we find a school for her. All right?'

Pitamber was glad Shailaja showed no signs of her earlier doubts about this arrangement, but even then he'd known that once she met Kabita, her heart would take over. He had always admired Shailaja's generous spirit, and in moments like these he considered himself lucky to have her as his wife.

At Shailaja's offer, Kabita lowered her eyes, as if overwhelmed.

Shailaja went to prepare dinner, and Priya began to cling to her mother, who scolded her and said that she needed to help with the cooking.

'Come here, daughter. Why don't you and I play chess with this brilliant fellow here,' Pitamber said, pointing to Sumit, who so far had shown little interest in the girl.

'I don't want to play with her,' Sumit mumbled.

'And why's that?'

'She's too young.'

'What if I help her?'

'Then it'll take me five seconds instead of one to beat her.'

'Did you hear that, Shailaja?' Pitamber said loudly. 'I think your son is getting arrogant. I think it's time he challenged some real players at the chess club.'

The sound of spinach frying in oil filled the flat, and he heard his wife chatting with Kabita.

'Come, daughter, I'll teach you how to play chess,' Pitamber said, and Priya came to his side.

He set up the pieces and began teaching her the rules. But she was more interested in admiring the pieces than anything else, and after a while he sighed and gave up. Sumit, who was sitting next to them doing his homework, laughed. 'She's too young, buwa. I told you.'

'Why don't you two play a game that she'll find more interesting?'

'But I'm doing my homework.'

'Do you like to listen to stories?' Pitamber asked Priya.

Shyly chewing the hem of her dress, she nodded.

'Then I'll read to you. Come.' He searched in their bookcase for one of Sumit's old children's books and found one about a cat and a rabbit. Priya sat on his lap, and he began reading. Her eyes followed his finger as it moved across the page. Soon Sumit abandoned his homework and sat next to them, and Pitamber felt a strange happiness come over him, as if somehow his family was expanding. He and Shailaja had both wanted a daughter after Sumit, but despite years of trying, Shailaja hadn't gotten pregnant again. In time, they'd become grateful for at least having had a son.

After dinner, they settled down to watch television. Shailaja turned on some comedy show, and soon Pitamber lost interest. Surreptitiously, he watched Kabita, whose eyes were steadily focused on the screen in front of her. What was going through her head right then? he wondered. Did she think about the killers? If she did, what kinds of things did she think? Kabita appeared to sense him watching her, for she quickly glanced at him. He felt something transpire between them, something he couldn't quite define.

He and Shailaja had decided that Kabita and Priya would sleep in Sumit's bed and Sumit would sleep on a mattress on the floor of their room. But when everyone began getting ready for bed, Sumit balked. 'I want to sleep in my own bed,' he said to his parents. 'I don't want to sleep with you two.' At twelve years old, he'd already begun acting like a teenager, Pitamber thought and sighed. Kabita said, 'Why should Sumit babu relinquish his bed? We can easily spread our mattress right here.' She pointed to the living room floor. Pitamber tried to reason with his son, saying he should at least let the guests spread their mattress on his floor, but Sumit stormed off to his room and closed the door. 'I don't know what's wrong with your son,' Pitamber told Shailaja, who retorted, 'Yes, when he doesn't obey he's my son, but when he wins at chess, he's yours.'

'This is how it is in our house,' Pitamber said to Kabita, trying to smile, and quickly helped her set up her mattress on the living room floor.

Later, in their room, Shailaja said, 'Poor thing. With everything that's happened, she's still maintaining a good attitude.'

'She seems to be a strong woman,' Pitamber said.

'That kind of tragedy—I mean, what did she do to deserve it? And here we are—we still believe in God.'

Shailaja regularly worshiped at the city temples, and her words surprised him. 'I'm not sure I believe in God anymore,' he said.

'You shouldn't say that.'

'But you just said it.'

'I didn't say I don't believe in God. I meant that we must believe in God no matter what. You know that.'

'So adept at twisting your own words,' Pitamber muttered.

After a moment she said, 'I want to do a puja at the Maitidevi temple.'

'Why?'

Her face was very serious. 'Why do people do puja? To ask for God's protection.'

'Nobody is threatening us,' he said. Then, noting his harsh tone, he said, 'Okay, go ahead and do it, that's no problem. I was just asking why.'

'There doesn't need to be a why when praying to God,' she said, and turned off the light.

The seamstress was more than happy to hire Kabita. 'These Maobadis! They should all be burned alive for everyone to see,' Ratnakumari said to Shailaja and Pitamber when they went to her.

A routine was soon established. Kabita would leave for the seamstress's house early in the morning, around seven. Pitamber would entertain Priya, who inevitably cried and whined after her mother left, while Shailaja cooked the morning meal. Soon it was time for Sumit to go to school, then for Pitamber to head to work. Kabita returned home at around one or two, depending on how busy things were with Ratnakumari. Pitamber left his office at five. In the evening, after dinner, they all sat around the flat, talking or reading or watching television.

Over the days, Pitamber and Shailaja learned more about Kabita. Both her parents had died of illnesses soon after she got married. Her in-laws lived in another village, in Gorkha, which was also subject to attacks by the Maobadis, so she couldn't go there after her husband was killed. She had a sister who worked as a hotel maid in the Indian state of Bihar. Kabita had very little contact with her—they'd never been particularly close—and most likely she wasn't aware of all that had happened to her sister. No one knew for sure why her husband was killed, Kabita said, for he was only a schoolteacher and had no political affiliations. Whenever she mentioned her husband, she grew restless.

'It won't always be this painful to think about,' Shailaja frequently consoled her. 'You have to focus on your new life here, and your daughter's.'

Kabita usually nodded, looking at the floor. Sometimes she pulled her daughter to her side. In these moments Pitamber found it hard to look at Kabita and Priya without something roiling in his stomach, without vividly recalling the photographs of the Maobadi leaders that had recently appeared in the newspapers. The confounding thing was that these men looked so ordinary, like the men he worked with, the men he saw in tea shops across the city.

As it turned out, a school for Priya was hard to come by. She was too young for kindergarten, and preschools were very expensive. 'I have no problem looking after her,' Shailaja insisted to Kabita. 'Look, she's already taken a liking to me.' It was true. Priya now clung to Shailaja as much as she did to her own mother. 'Auntie,' she called Shailaja, and followed her around the house.

Sumit seemed to be the only one having difficulties adjusting to Kabita and Priya in the flat. He hardly said anything to Kabita and never played with Priya. Once Pitamber saw him push the girl away as she was attempting to get something from the floor near him. Pitamber took him to his bedroom and said, 'You should treat her like your younger sister. You should be nice to her.'

'Don't call her my sister,' Sumit said sullenly.

'Why not?'

'They're not part of our family.'

'Well, while they're here we have to treat them that way, understand?'

'When are they going to leave?'

'Soon. Now go play with Priya for a while.'

But Sumit stayed in his room alone and shut the door. When Pitamber told Shailaja about his talk with Sumit, she said, 'This is normal for someone his age. He'll get used to them.'

One morning, right after he reached work, Pitamber heard that Mr Shrestha had called in sick. Because of the man's grouchy demeanor and strict rules, the employees treated this day as if it were a holiday. Some signed in and went home, others sat around and chatted and made personal phone calls. Mr Shrestha hadn't said anything to Pitamber the morning he arrived late after searching for Kabita, but Pitamber hadn't risked being late since then. Today, though, he and his colleague Neupane decided to go to a restaurant nearby. There, over samosas and jalebis, Pitamber told Neupane about Kabita.

'You're doing the right thing, Pitamberji,' Neupane said. 'I'd have done the same.'

'Can you believe they'd murder a schoolteacher?' Pitamber said.

'Well, the police and the army are just as cruel. Haven't you heard how they raped and killed those two teenage girls, then accused them of being Maobadis?'

Pitamber grew silent, then he said, 'Do you suppose Kabita thinks about revenge?'

'Revenge?' Neupane raised his eyebrows. 'Do you expect a young widow to go searching in the hills for those men?'

Pitamber gazed out the window. People were walking, laughing, swinging shopping bags, hailing taxis. Across the street, a teenage boy appeared to be teaching another boy some karate moves.

'God will punish them, Pitamberji. God is watching all of this.'

He turned to Neupane. 'I don't really like thinking about God anymore.'

Neupane laughed. 'But where would we be without God, eh? Seriously, though, she has a new life, and she should let the past go. And you should stop thinking about it all so much.' When Pitamber said nothing, Neupane added, 'Thinking about revenge just puts us on their level.'

They left the restaurant and started walking back to the office, but, preoccupied and irritated, Pitamber soon decided that he'd rather go home. Neupane slapped him on the back and said, 'Pitamberji, you need to relax. Everything is fine. Your job is fine, and everything is going well with your family. So stop all this obsessing.'

Pitamber nodded. 'You're right, Neupaneji,' he said, but he still wanted to go home, so he said goodbye to Neupane and headed off. Clouds were gathering in the sky, and he recalled the morning's weather report forecasting rain. At least the rain would be a distraction.

On the way home, he had to pass by New Road, and he decided to pay a visit to Kabita. Four women worked at the seamstress's shop, all busy running the machines. A steady and fast *click-click-click* filled the room, which overflowed with pieces of cloth and unfinished dresses. Kabita sat in the back, her eyes focused on the needle as her fingers slid the cloth underneath it. He went and stood in front of her, but she seemed unaware of his presence until he said her name. She looked up, gasped, and the stitch on the cloth went askew. 'Tch,' she said to the machine, then to Pitamber, 'Dai?'

'I got the day off,' he said. 'I thought I'd drop by to see how you were doing.'

She managed a smile. The other women in the shop glanced in their direction. 'Dai,' she said loudly, introducing him to them above the clatter, and they nodded, went back to work.

'Everything going well?'

She nodded.

'Where's Ratnakumariji?' 'She's gone to run some errands.' 'Have you had tea?'

She shook her head. 'There's no time for tea. I have too much work to do.' And she set her hand on the wheel of her machine.

'How about I bring tea to the four of you, then?'

'Dai, you don't have to. There's a boy from the tea shop who comes here sometimes.'

'It'd be my pleasure. Besides, maybe the boy won't come today.'

The tea shop was just around the corner, and the boy who was rinsing the glasses there offered to take the tea to the women, but Pitamber insisted on doing it himself. Awkwardly carrying a container with five glasses of tea back to the shop, he shouted, 'Chai garam,' imitating the men who sold tea at Indian railway stations, and Kabita seemed a bit embarrassed. 'I'll just have a little tea and be on my way. Not to worry,' he said to her. He sat and chatted with them for a while, asking the other women about their lives, how long they'd been working for Ratnakumari. Kabita remained quiet for most of the conversation, offering only a brief yes or no when he directed a question at her. When Ratnakumari came in and saw Pitamber, she teased him that he was bothering her workers. He sensed that she was not entirely joking, so, somewhat self-conscious, he quickly finished his tea and left.

Pitamber made his way through the dense crowd of New Road, where in a side alley he saw a crowd gathered in front of a wall. He went to them, peeked over their shoulders, and saw, pasted on the wall, large photos of the Maobadis who had been listed as 'Wanted' by the government. People were talking excitedly, and a man next to Pitamber said, 'They should all be tied together and burned in one big pyre.'

Some murmured in agreement, but a voice from behind Pitamber said, 'What are you saying? Our revolution has arrived! These are our heroes.'

'Heroes?' Pitamber swiveled around. 'Who said that?'

Someone pointed to a boy of about nineteen, and Pitamber lurched toward him and grabbed his shirt collar. 'What did you say?' He could feel the pulse in his own throat as he slapped the boy hard on the right cheek. Encouraged by his slap, other men now crowded around the boy, shoving him, punching him, shaking him. 'I wasn't being serious,' the boy screamed. 'I didn't mean it!' He began pleading for mercy.

His throat still pulsing, Pitamber walked away. He couldn't believe how fast his hand had flown, how thoughtlessly he'd struck the boy. He knew he ought to go back and try to rescue him, but things were already beyond his control now, and the crowd could easily turn its anger on him. He moved rapidly through the market, pushing his way past the shoppers. What did he do that for? For a teenager's stupid joke. And now the boy was probably all bloodied and injured, perhaps left with a broken arm. Pitamber's head was beginning to throb, and he wished he'd gone right home from the restaurant instead of stopping by Kabita's work.

At home Shailaja was feeding Priya, and Pitamber asked them how their day had gone, then said that he felt the need to lie down.

'You came home because you didn't feel well?' Shailaja asked, and he didn't answer her, just continued on to their bedroom and lay down, trying to slow his breathing and forget what had happened in the alley. But he could still hear the boy's panicked pleas.

A little while later, Shailaja came to him and placed her hand on his forehead. 'Doesn't feel like you have fever. Are you nauseous?'

'Not really. Just a bit of a headache. I'm sure I'll be fine.'

She stayed beside him, and the warmth of her body comforted him. He told her that he'd stopped by Kabita's work. 'I think I might have embarrassed her,' he said.

'She probably liked that you went to visit her.'

Pitamber wanted to tell her what happened next, but he knew it would upset her, and she'd be shocked that he'd hit anyone, let alone a boy. 'How is Priya?' he asked instead, his eyes closed.

'If I feed her, she'll eat anything. But with her mother, she makes all kinds of excuses.'

Pitamber laughed and pressed his hands to his closed eyes. Little stars burst in the darkness there, and for a moment he felt soothed. 'She's so happy with you. If we'd had a daughter, I bet she'd have been like her.'

'No point in thinking about that now. Come, I'll rub your forehead.'

He let her, and her soft fingers felt good on his head.

A while later he woke with a start to sounds of boys arguing outside in the yard. He went to the window, looked out, and saw Sumit tussling with some boys from the neighborhood. 'Stop that!' Pitamber shouted. He put on his slippers and hurried downstairs. As soon as they saw him, the other boys ran away, and he grabbed Sumit by the shoulder. 'Why were you fighting? What's wrong with you?'

'They were saying things about Kabita auntie,' Sumit muttered, looking down.

'What things?' Pitamber's eyes searched for the boys, but he remembered the earlier incident in Indrachowk and immediately controlled himself. 'Look at you,' he said to Sumit. 'Your shirt is torn.' Pitamber grabbed his arm and walked him back inside and upstairs.

Shailaja inspected her son's face, and thankfully he didn't have any bruises. She too scolded him, then said, 'What did they say to get you so bothered?'

'They were saying bad things about her, about …' He looked at Pitamber, then said, 'I don't want to live in this house anymore.'

Shailaja and Pitamber looked at each other. Finally Shailaja told Sumit, 'If they say something bad, just ignore them, okay?'

Sumit glared at her and stormed off to his room. Pitamber shook his head and said, 'I have no idea what's going through his mind. Now I have a bigger headache.'

'Maybe he's having problems at school,' Shailaja said. 'I'll go talk to his headmaster.'

Shailaja eventually coaxed Sumit out of his room for dinner, and they all sat down to eat. Kabita, who'd gotten home late from work, said, 'Dai, my work friends were saying you seem like a fun person.'

'Hmm, I don't exactly feel like a fun person right now.'

'After dinner, you should go back to sleep,' Shailaja said. 'Then you'll feel better.'

Everyone ate quietly, and about halfway through the meal, Sumit stood and returned to his room. Pitamber was about, to follow him, but Shailaja told him to let him be. She then began talking about how the Dashain and Tihar festivals would be more fun this year with Kabita and Priya around. 'Now Sumit will have a little sister to do bhai puja with, and Kabita, you can put tika on him.' She gestured toward Pitamber.

'I could, but it's only been a few months since my husband died,' she said.

'Of course, of course,' Shailaja said. 'I guess it wouldn't be appropriate.'

'What harm would it do? Doing tika doesn't mean you're no longer in mourning,' Pitamber said to Kabita.

'That decision is up to her, isn't it?' Shailaja said.

'I don't know,' Kabita said. 'It might anger God.'

Pitamber grew flushed and said, 'Why bring God into it? You are starting a new life. Your God should be pleased about it.'

'These days the mere mention of God sets you off, doesn't it?' Shailaja said.

Pitamber said to Kabita, 'It's your decision. Do what you want to do.' Then he stood and went back to bed.

The next morning, a Saturday, Pitamber woke up and went to the living room, where Shailaja was arranging a basket of incense, rice, nuts, and red, orange, and yellow powder. He remembered that today was the day she planned to go to the Maitidevi temple. Despite himself, a groan escaped his lips, and Shailaja, now spooning some curd into a container, said, 'You don't have to go if you don't want to.'

'I'll go, I'll go,' he said.

In the taxi on the way there, Sumit sullenly stared out the window, and Pitamber tried to lighten his mood. 'Hey, champion, what happened to your chess game? You don't play these days.'

'I don't feel like it anymore,' Sumit said.

Pitamber looked sideways at Shailaja, but she was busy rearranging the items in her basket.

'If you stop practicing, how will you become a great player?' Pitamber prodded.

'I don't want to be a great chess player.'

'Why not? What do you want to be, a hoodlum, and fight with everyone?' He tried to control his irritation.

'No, I don't want to be a hoodlum,' Sumit said. 'Anyway, who are you to speak? You're the one who brought a second wife in our house.'

Shailaja looked sharply at Sumit, then at Kabita. Pitamber pinched Sumit's left ear, pulling his head toward him. 'Say that again?'

Sumit shouted, 'Why don't you and Kabita auntie go live somewhere else?'

Pitamber felt his left hand tighten into a fist, make a wide arc, and hit his son on the head. Sumit slumped in his seat, his body limp. The taxi driver braked, then continued. Shailaja gasped something like, 'What? What?' and Kabita pressed her hand to her mouth. Pitamber shook his son, said, 'Sumit, Sumit?'

Letting the puja basket fall to the floor, Shailaja climbed over Pitamber's lap to her son's side. She too shook Sumit, whose eyes were closed. She pressed her ear against his chest, then said, 'I can't hear his heart.' Pitamber tried to listen, but he couldn't tell whether the pounding he heard was the rapid beating of his own heart. A wave of panic washed over him, but he managed to tell Shailaja, 'He's all right, he's fine.' He felt around Sumit's throat with his fingers—there seemed to be a pulse there.

It was the taxi driver who finally said, 'Drive to the hospital, hajur?'

Fortunately Bir Hospital was only a stone's throw away, and as they headed inside, a doctor who was on his way to work rushed over to look at Sumit, who was beginning to stir and open his eyes. The doctor fingered the purplish swelling on Sumit's right temple, then guided them into the emergency room. There, he examined Sumit more thoroughly and said, 'Nothing serious. Looks like he went unconscious for a few minutes. Did he fall or something?'

Everyone exchanged looks, and the doctor said, 'Who hit your son? Did you hit him to discipline him?'

Pitamber knew he ought to step forward and confess, but admitting he'd hit Sumit would further complicate things, so he shook his head and miserably kept quiet.

The doctor said, 'Do you know that we've had people die in here from head concussions? Do you parents think before you act?' He looked as if he were about to say something more, but a nurse came to him saying a man had just arrived who'd been injured in a bomb blast. 'Take him home and make him rest,' the doctor said to Pitamber before he left. 'If this type of thing happens again, I'll have to call the police.'

The nurse stayed and applied a compress to Sumit's temple, gave him some painkillers, then discharged him.

'We're obviously not going to the temple,' Shailaja said as they left the hospital, and during the taxi ride back home, no one spoke. Shailaja didn't look at Pitamber. Sumit lay with his head on her lap, and she murmured to him while stroking his hair. Pitamber glanced at Kabita in the front seat, holding Priya close to her chest, and suddenly he wished he could disappear.

At home Shailaja put Sumit to bed and went to the kitchen to make some soup. Pitamber went to his son's room and sat by his side. He wanted to apologize, to say that he didn't mean to hit him (he'd certainly never hit Sumit before), but as he watched Sumit lying there, his eyes on the ceiling, Pitamber found himself unable to say anything. He had always detested those who hit their children. 'Son,' Pitamber finally said, and without meeting his eyes Sumit said, 'All my friends tease me about her.'

Shailaja appeared in the doorway holding a bowl of soup, and without looking at Pitamber, she asked him to leave so she could feed her son. Pitamber went to the living room, where Kabita was trying to mollify her daughter, who was clinging to her, asking her what had happened to

Sumit. 'Maybe she's hungry,' Pitamber said, and Kabita, her eyes cast down, said, 'Maybe.'

For three days Shailaja didn't sleep with Pitamber in their bedroom; instead, she slept beside Sumit. A heavy silence had permeated the flat, and Pitamber felt constantly ostracized and increasingly guilty. 'I didn't mean to hit him,' he repeated to Shailaja a few times, but she merely tightened her jaw and refused to look at him. Kabita too seemed wary of him. She averted her eyes whenever he was nearby and instinctively touched her daughter in a gesture of protection. Whenever Pitamber tried to talk to Kabita, she came up with a reason to rush off. It was Sumit who at last broke the silence in the flat one evening, when, after two days of staying home from school, he announced that he was ready for the chess club.

'The chess club?' Shailaja said. 'No chess for you, after all that happened.'

'But I want to go.' They were sitting around the living room. Shailaja was sewing a garland for another attempt at puja the next day.

Pitamber said gently, 'Son, don't feel that you have to.'

'But I want to. I miss playing.'

For a while no one said anything, then Shailaja said, 'Son, it's your choice. Don't feel forced to do anything.'

'I want to go now,' Sumit said. 'Buwa, can we go now?'

Pitamber looked at Shailaja, who said, 'What's the point of staring at me? It's Sumit who wants to go, not me.'

'Okay,' Pitamber said to Sumit. 'And if you don't like it, you don't have to go anymore.' A few months ago, Pitamber had stopped by the club and inquired about its schedule, so he knew it would be open at this time. He had to seize this opportunity—finally here was a break in the gloom and doom of the flat, and Sumit would get a chance to hone his skills with some accomplished players. 'All right, let's go,' he said to his son.

It turned out that Sumit loved the chess club, and every day after school, he and Pitamber walked to the small brick building, where on the ground floor children and adults of all ages, their eyes intently focused, sat around small tables before chess boards and strategized about how to beat their opponents. After his first time there, Sumit asked Pitamber to wait outside. 'I can't concentrate with you in the room,' he said, and Pitamber reluctantly obeyed. From outside, he tried to peek through the window and watch his son, but the glass was too dirty and all he could see were blurred figures inside. 'He plays well,' said Kamal, the man who managed the club, 'but he lacks confidence. He needs more encouragement.'

That evening as they walked home, Pitamber said to Sumit, 'Kamal Sir was saying that you're a marvelous player.'

'Really?'

'Of course. You're a natural. You only need a little practice, that's all.' He put his hand on his son's shoulder.

Pitamber had sensed it coming—in the past few days Kabita had often mentioned that she and Priya had stayed with them for too long. Still, it surprised him when a week later Kabita announced that she was moving out the next evening, that she and Priya would move in with one of her coworkers, a young woman who lived with her widowed mother and was looking for ways to cut down on their rent. 'I can't possibly burden you any longer,' she said. In her new flat, her friend's mother would look after Priya while Kabita worked. 'I am so grateful for all you gave me,' she said to Pitamber and Shailaja.

'I was hoping we'd put tika during Dashain and Tihar,' Shailaja said.

'That we'll do, Shailaja didi, I promise. I'll come back for it.'

The next evening, Pitamber hurried home after dropping off Sumit at the chess club. Shailaja and Kabita were struggling to get Kabita's belongings down the stairs. 'Why didn't you wait for me?' Pitamber said as he grabbed the suitcase and the bedding from them.

'The taxi will be here any minute, dai,' Kabita said, smiling. She looked the happiest he'd ever seen her look.

Downstairs, he hauled her things into the trunk of the waiting taxi and said, 'Now remember that we're always here for you if things don't work out there.' But he knew she wouldn't return—she was too proud to ask for help again. He squatted in front of Priya. 'Daughter, you be a good girl to your mother, okay?' She nodded, then opened her palm. He reached into his shirt pocket and handed her a lollipop.

'She has no shame,' Kabita said, laughing.

'Don't forget us, you two,' Shailaja said as the two stepped into the taxi. Pitamber squeezed Shailaja's shoulder as they watched the car drive away. They trudged back up to the empty flat, and Shailaja immediately headed into the kitchen. He stood inside the door and called, 'Shailaja, how long are you going to remain like this?'

She didn't answer, and he heard her start to cry. He went to her and slid his arms around her. 'Don't do this to me,' he said.

'I thought he was dead,' she said between sobs. 'I swear, I thought our son had died that day.'

He held her tighter.

'You'd never raised your hand against him. Or me.'

'I know, I know.' He knew that he had no excuse. And maybe he should have seen it coming, given how he'd lost control and slapped that boy in the crowd. 'I don't know what came over me,' he said.

She squirmed out of his grasp and faced him. 'If you do it again, I'll leave you.'

He nodded and embraced her again.

The country was soon plunged into mayhem. Maobadis threw bombs at the village homes of several high officials; army men shot at a group of villagers they suspected were aiding the rebels. Rumors spread about rebels stalking the countryside, carrying the severed heads of villagers who refused to give them money. Families abandoned their homes and moved to India. Every day, newspapers announced atrocity after atrocity. Pitamber refused to read the papers or watch the news on television anymore. At the office he began to keep to himself, declining Neupane's occasional offer to go out for a cup of tea or snacks.

Sometimes Pitamber wondered whether Kabita's wounds had begun to heal. Now and then he had the impulse to visit her at her work, and once he actually went, but he couldn't bring himself to walk inside the shop, afraid that his old, dark feelings would resurface.

Every day he went to work, came straight home, and waited for Sumit to return from school so they could play a game of chess before he went to the club. Pitamber found a number of books on the game at a discount store, and he studied them intensely. He taught himself how to anticipate an opponent's moves, how to consider the outcome of his own options and strategize accordingly. And ignoring Sumit's impatient sighs, he often spent long minutes planning his next move.

One evening after work, he ran into Kabita near a busy intersection of New Road. Smiling, she told him that Priya had begun attending a school near where they lived, and that Ratnakumari had asked her to manage a new shop she was opening in Patan. He expressed his pleasure at the good news, then reminded her that he and Shailaja expected her and Priya to visit their home during Dashain, which was only a month away.

'Of course I will, dai,' she said.

DISPATCHES FROM THE PEOPLE'S WAR IN NEPAL

Li Onesto

Our entourage—a People's Army squad, my translator Pravat and me, and a couple of others—are heading for another village today and there will be many goodbyes. The cultural team that has been travelling with us is going off in another direction and several other people who have been with us over the last couple of days are returning to their villages.

The travel today is much easier—we only go for about six hours, mainly in daylight. After we reach our shelter we have a hearty meal of *dal bhat,* curry potatoes, and mutton. Then a teacher from the area comes to be interviewed. I have already met many teachers in the countryside who are involved in this revolution. It seems like village teachers frequently end up 'educating' their students in more than reading and writing.

This teacher has a gentle face that contrasts with his strong, stout body. His voice is soft, but his presence fills the room even when he is silent. Like many of those who have been tortured by the police, he is deadly serious when he talks about their brutality and surrenders no smiles as he recounts his story.

He tells me he started working with the Party in his village shortly after the government adopted the parliamentary system in 1991. Then, in 1996, in the first year of the revolution, the police came to his house, arrested him, and dragged him to a police post two hours away. He says the police beat him the whole time and threatened to kill him on the spot. He was thrown in jail and then for a whole week the police tortured him, trying to get him to give information about the Party and its work. He says, 'I never told them anything, even though I thought they might kill me. After a week they continued to interrogate me. But still, I refused to tell them anything. I only told them I was a sympathizer in the village but nothing more. The police charged me with breaking the 'peace and security' law and I was finally released after paying a high bail of 10,000 rupees' (10,000 rupees is about $180, a huge sum of money for the majority of people in Nepal where the per capita yearly income is around $210).

When this teacher is done with his story I tell him that he has given me some insight into one of the reasons the government is having a hard time crushing this revolution. Like many others who support the Maoists, his resolute belief in what he is fighting for gave him the strength to defy the police and refuse to give them any information, even in the face of death.

'What I am doing in the People's War is part of the world revolution,' he says. 'I thought that all the people in the United States were rich. But after meeting you, seeing how you have come from so far away to learn of our struggle, and after hearing about the struggle of people in the US, it makes me even stronger in my revolutionary determination to stand up to the enemy. I see you as an actual physical example of proletarian internationalism and this inspires me. In our People's War many people are being martyred and compared to this, what I have done is little. Now I am no longer underground and do legal work openly. But the Party's work encompasses both legal and underground work and in the future, if I have to, I will go underground again. Now the police are watching me and looking for a chance to arrest and torture me again. And I pledge that if that happens again, I will never give away any Party secrets to the enemy.' ...

Pravat, my translator, also used to be a teacher in his village. He tells me he taught high school kids during the day and farmed his land before and after class—from dawn to 10:00 am and 3:00 pm to sunset. He had a small plot of land, a two-story house, and several buffaloes, goats, and chickens. He was not rich, but his land and animals provided food and clothes for his family. Soon after the People's War started he had to give this all up.

A short, slender man in his forties, Pravat has been underground now for over two and a half years. One night, as we sit outside under a full moon, he tells me how he went from being a simple peasant farmer and schoolteacher to an underground full-time Party member. The first thing he tells me is how proud he is of his wife. She is also a full-timer in the Party and has been underground since the first day of the Initiation, when she participated in an armed action. She is now a leader in the revolutionary women's organization.

After his wife went underground, Pravat continued to live in their house, taking care of his young son and daughter by himself. But about six months later, the police came and arrested him. They bound his hands and dragged him to a police post quite a distance away. They threatened and questioned him, trying to link him to an incident that had just happened in the area. This was during the monsoon season, and at night they left him tied up standing outside in the pouring rain, wearing only his shorts, a tee-shirt, and rubber thong sandals.

Eventually, Pravat was released, but the police filed several charges against him, including 'public disturbance' and 'treason,' so he was forced to go underground. Later they filed more charges against him, including a false charge for murder, which he knew nothing about. Now it is very dangerous for him to go anywhere near the area where he and his family used to live.

Pravat's house now stands empty. After he left, the police came looking for him and when they found no one at home, they wrecked everything, smashing the cupboards, beds, and other furniture. The two children now live with a relative in another area and see their parents every three or four months for a day, or only a couple of hours. The children have to be careful—they cannot talk about their parents, so they call the relatives they stay with 'mama' and 'papa,' and they call their real parents 'auntie' and 'uncle.'

Pravat says his children know that their parents are fighting in the People's War and his son already talks about how he wants to learn how to use a gun so he can join the revolution. Pravat and his wife work under different conditions and in different areas so they don't see each other often and sometimes only for short visits. But they seem to have a deep bond.

I am struck by the reserved and matter-of-fact way Pravat has of telling the most hair-raising stories. But even when we are joking around there is a serious edge—a side to Pravat that is always tense, alert to the danger in his life, and solid on the commitment he has made to this revolution.

...

Everywhere I go, it seems the women are particularly enthusiastic about this revolution. I see it in the eyes of the old women who have suffered many years under the thumb of feudal relations—and who now want to fight for a new kind of society. I hear it in the words of young women who never went to school, who tell how excited they were the first time they carried out an armed action. I feel it in the determination and spirit of the women who have lost husbands, sons, and daughters, but continue to shelter and aid the guerrillas at the risk of their own lives.

These women really believe that the fight against women's oppression is woven into the fabric of this People's War. So when the armed struggle started in 1996, it was like opening a prison gate—thousands of women rushed forward to claim an equal place in the war. Some had to defy fathers and brothers. Some had to leave backward-thinking husbands. Others ran away from arranged marriages where parents had decided their fate. They all had to rebel against feudal traditions that treat women as inferior and make women feel like their ideas don't matter.

In Kathmandu I interviewed Rekha Sharma, the president of the All Nepal Women's Association (Revolutionary) who described the situation for women in Nepal:

In the rural areas women are oppressed by the family, mother-in-law, husband —and some women are killed because of dowries. This problem exists all over the country, in the city and countryside. The thinking in society is that women are brought into the home to serve the husband and to have children, that this is all they're good for. To solve these kinds of problems we try to educate women, to show that it's not because of their mother-in-law, husband, etc., but that it is the social structure that is protected by the state and that we need complete change, revolution, We educate women to this fact.

Rekha also told me about the widespread trafficking of women. Every year, 5,000-7,000 females between the age of ten and 18 are 'exported' to India and forced to work as prostitutes. These young women are literally sold for the price of cows and goats by their own fathers, brothers and uncles. Sometimes they are tricked into going with the promise of a 'good job.' Estimates of the number of girls and women working in

India as prostitutes range from 40,000 to 200,000. Nepalese women are also kidnapped and taken to countries in the Gulf area to work in brothels. Every year hundreds of women return to Nepal after being forced into prostitution in another country, and many of them come back HIV-positive.

Early marriage, early pregnancy, and multiple pregnancies take a toll on women's mental and physical health. And there is a lot of pressure for a woman to produce a son to inherit the family's property, even if this endangers her health. In fact, Nepal has one of the highest maternal mortality rates in the world—539 per 100,000. Women who do not produce sons are frequently abandoned, socially ostracized, and many times their husbands take a second wife.

Women in Nepal also face extremely oppressive anti-abortion laws. It is illegal to have an abortion here—abortion is classified as homicide and punishable by law, even if the pregnancy is a threat to the woman's health or life or is the result of rape or incest. Many women are in prison, serving sentences of up to 20 years, for having an abortion. These strict anti-abortion laws have also given rise to illegal, unsafe, and induced abortions which, according to news reports in Nepal, account for more than half of the country's maternal deaths. I read about one doctor who toured hospitals throughout Nepal and discovered that huge numbers of women were in hospital because of complications related to an illegal abortion. In the Maternal Hospital in Kathmandu, 61 per cent of gynae-obstetric cases he observed were abortion-related.

The most simple and routine parts of the day here in the countryside are being affected by the People's War in terms of the division of labor between men and women. In feudal society, women are saddled with prescribed roles that keep them in a subordinate position—taking care of children, cooking, washing clothes, etc. But in the guerrilla zones, this seems to be changing. For example, it was very common, as we travelled, for the men in the squad to do a lot of the day-to-day cooking.

Sometimes we get to a village and right away, men from the squad start gathering firewood and preparing the meal. When we sit down to eat they serve the food and then wash the dishes after we finish. Sometimes women in the squad and women in the village will be sitting around doing something else while all this is going on. As I observe all this, I think about how unusual and *radical* this scene is in a semi-feudal country like Nepal. One woman told me:

'There have been many changes in people's thinking since the Initiation. Fathers and brothers are now involved in things like cooking, getting water, washing dishes. There is also a change in the women's thinking. Before, women were not permitted to do things like make the roof of the house or plow the fields. But now where the People's War is going on, it is easy for women to do this. Before, women didn't make baskets and mats according to tradition and women used to think they weren't good enough to do this work. But when we dared to do it we found it was easy. So if we dare, we can do anything—there's no distinction between men and women. There are two changes [with regard to the roles of women]—ideologically and in practice.

'There are two things that have led to women doing 'men's work.' First there is necessity—some of the men have to go underground and so then the women have to plow the fields, make roofs and do other 'men's work.' For example, in my father's village all the men had to leave because of the police. The police raided and looted things like food, grain, and ghee [cooking butter]. So the women started to plow the land and make house roofs. The second thing is women becoming ideologically convinced to do such work.

'Before the Initiation few women dared to do 'men's work,' but after the Initiation there is no type of work women don't dare do. Also, men can do any type of 'women's work' and they don't hesitate to do it. Before men didn't think this way, but with the Initiation their ideology changed.'

I also notice other ways this revolution seems to be changing the way men and women relate to each other. For example, living and travelling with the guerrillas, I am somewhat surprised by the way the women and men are completely relaxed around each other. There is no 'sexual tension' and I don't feel nervous or unsafe like women in the US often feel when they are alone with men they don't know very well. Sometimes we find ourselves in a situation, like in a cowshed or on the floor of a peasant's home, where we all have to sleep together like sardines in a can. But I never feel uncomfortable in these situations.

In all the guerrilla zones I visit, it seems that the women still have primary responsibility for taking care of the children. But this is also starting to change slowly. I have met many women Party members with small children, and other people are always taking turns caring for the children. In the 'revolutionary community,' everyone is considered an 'auntie' and 'uncle' to the children of martyrs or kids whose parents are absent because of their revolutionary responsibilities.

There is not yet organized collective childcare. But several party leaders told me they are trying to figure out how to set this up so women can play a bigger role in the revolution. When base areas are formed where the guerrillas will have (relatively) more stable control, it will be easier for them to organize and maintain things like collective childcare. But at this point, most of the women involved in the revolution full-time have to take their infants with them wherever they go. They do this while nursing and then, when the baby gets older, they find a relative to take care of the child.

For many women, the People's War offers an immediate escape from an oppressive situation where they can't go to school, may be forced into an arranged marriage, and are expected to spend the rest of their lives devoted to husbands, in-laws, and children. Many women find a new life in the revolution—women who have been abandoned by their husbands, who have been socially shunned because they were raped, or women whose family could not afford to pay a dowry for them.

The women who have joined the revolution feel strongly that the present government will not and cannot do anything about the inequality women face. And they are inspired by a revolution that puts forward the vision of a society in which women participate equally in all aspects of life.

One woman organizer in Rukum tells me:

There are various reasons I became a revolutionary. First, there is inequality between sons and daughters—like in terms of property, daughters have no rights. Women get neglected compared to men, by parents, husbands, and other family members. Nepalese women are suppressed by the feudalistic system and some women go to India to become prostitutes. This women's oppression is the main reason why I was inspired to become a revolutionary.

I also heard stories of the obstacles women encountered when they wanted to join the revolution. One leader in the revolutionary women's organization tells me:

My father's brother was the head of our household and at first he wouldn't give me permission to join the women's organization. I rebelled against this and for six months I lived somewhere else. When I went back to the house the family members would not accept me because of what I was doing. The women's organization, including me, went to my uncle and tried to convince him, talking to him about women's rights, and we did this many times. He did not speak out against the women's organization but he still didn't want me to participate. He wanted me to stay home and do all the work in the house.

Another woman in Rolpa says:

At a young age my family arranged a marriage for me. I went to live in my husband's family house when I was 15 and lived there for eight years. My husband was one or two years younger than me but after two years he was sent to India to work and didn't come back. I went with my brother to India to try and find him and we brought him back. But then, within a month, he went back to India and never returned. I am 27 now. Two years ago I left my first husband's house and married my second husband—a love marriage, not arranged. When we got married he was a squad member and he is now a platoon member. In the war period it is easier not to have children, especially for full-timers. And even after the revolution it will be better to have fewer children than more.

In Rukum I talk with the chairman of the District Committee of the women's organization. She is a Party District Committee member and her husband has been in jail for the last two years. She tells me:

After the Initiation more and more women became involved in armed struggle, in volunteer groups, militias, and squads. In this area, there are eight women's militias with five to seven members and there are also women in militias made up of both men and women. Women are involved at different levels of the Party, up to district Party committee members. In the whole district there are about 500 local committees of the women's organization, eight area committees, and one district committee. They are all active and they participate in the revolutionary united front.

The People's Army has a policy that each guerrilla squad (which consists of nine to eleven members) must recruit at least two women. Women guerrillas work as combatants, do propaganda work, and farm the land. Women not directly involved in fighting work as organizers, propagandists, cultural activists, and nurses. They do logistics, spy on the enemy, provide shelter for Party cadres and guerrillas, and visit families of martyrs and those in jail.

When I think about how these women grew up, suppressed by all kinds of feudal traditions, I realize how hard it must have been for them to join this revolution—often in defiance of their families. The sight of young peasant women carrying rifles, khukuries, and grenades is one of the strongest images I carry with me as I travel through these guerrilla zones …

In our evaluation meeting, people ask me what I have gotten out of this trip. I tell them how I have learned a lot about the role of the youth, women, and the oppressed nationalities. I talk about how the families of those killed by the police seem determined to win, even in the face of vicious repression. And I tell them that I see that they are trying to wage a revolution that is not only about destruction of the present society, but also about what they see as revolutionary *construction* of a new way of life. I have seen how they are trying to develop the seeds of a new society, how people are breaking with feudal traditions and social relations and creating a new economy and culture.

I also tell people that I have learned a lot about how they have advanced the military theory and practice of waging their People's War—in just a short period of only three years. They have gone from primitive fighter groups to squads, platoons, and larger task forces. They have developed from small attacks to more developed military raids and ambushes.

We talk about how the situation is at a very critical point right now. The government is compelled to step up their efforts to crush the People's War, exactly because the revolution has continued to grow. The government is especially worried about the development of power vacuums in areas where government officials have fled and the police are afraid to come in. The police posts are being centralized in many areas, which will mean that the guerrillas will be confronted with larger groups of police. So far, the national police have been the ones sent against the People's War, but there has been talk in the government about sending in the Royal Nepal Army. All this will require a leap in the military capacity of the People's Army - in the size of military groups (from platoons to companies and even larger); in the level of military actions; and in the quantity and quality of weapons. I think that in the near future there will be some major moves by the government against the People's War and this would demand a big leap in the capacity of the People's Army as well as the whole party leadership, mass organizations, etc. This would also make it more urgent for there to be international awareness of the situation.

Before we leave this last village, people gather outside for a final farewell. People remind me that I am the first foreign journalist to be allowed this kind of access in the guerrilla zones, and they reiterate how important it is now for me to make their story known to the world.

We leave at noon and, a bit later, arrive at the village school where about 100 people have gathered. The local villagers heard that we were going to come through here on our way out and they want to greet me. The local party leader presents me with some farewell words and gifts. Then we shake hands with everyone and many step forward with garlands of flowers to put around our necks.

On our way out of the Rolpa/Sallyan districts, the people I am with point to a tall, pointed mountain peak, not too far away. It is where the government's Jhimpe Communications Tower used to be before the People's Army raided it, injuring two police and seizing a number of rifles and ammunition. As the sun begins its descent over this scene, this seems a fitting image for my exit and I mark the sight, sound and feel of this moment in my memory.

As we leave Rolpa, I turn to look back up at the towering countryside and I think about all the dreams of the peasants, deep in the crevices of this incredible terrain. Geologists have reported that every year the Himalayan range pushes further up towards the sky. Now, in the foothills of these majestic mountains at the top of the world, another force is radically changing the landscape.

WAITING FOR THE WAR
TO END

Sushma Joshi

I see the black smoke of bodies
charred and burning up my dreams, the red tears
of my dismembered country—
Nepal, you used to be a canvas, green and radiant,
now painted darkly with the brush of human despair
and the sticky patina of blood, hope
disemboweled by rusty khukuris and AK-47s
and old helicopters given for free by friendly countries
wanting only security, but do they see—
do they see the dead bodies? We have
become a nation where the mountains and the fields
and especially the rivers are flooded, flooded, flooded—
over and over with the sacrifice of human corpses—
and once again the soul is at large, like modernity
torn forever, mixed with too much hate and ideology
once again we come back to this time and place
back to this impasse, back to this place of power
where the struggle is less for the future than it is
for the bloody now, so here we are, all of us,
here and now and breathing still, waiting for the war to end

THE PEOPLE'S WAR

Pankaj Mishra

In Kathmandu this March, I met a Nepalese businessman who said he knew what had provoked Crown Prince Dipendra, supposed incarnation of Vishnu and former pupil at Eton, to mass murder. On the night of 1 June 2001, Dipendra appeared in the drawing-room of the royal palace in Kathmandu, dressed in combat fatigues, apparently out of it on Famous Grouse and hashish, and armed with assault rifles and pistols. In a few frenzied minutes, he killed his parents, King Birendra and Queen Aishwarya, a brother, a sister and five other relatives before putting a pistol to his head. Anointed king as he lay unconscious in hospital, he died two days later, passing his title to his uncle Gyanendra.

Dipendra's obsession with guns at Eton, where he was admired by Lord Camoys as a 'damn good shot', his heavy drinking, which attracted the malice of the *Sun*, his addiction to hashish and his fondness for the films of Arnold Schwarzenegger—all this outlines a philistinism, and a potential for violence, commonplace among scions of Third World dynasties (Suharto, Nehru-Gandhi, Bhutto). And it is not so hard to believe the semi-official explanation for his actions: that his parents disapproved of his fiancee. However, the businessman, who claimed to know the royal family, had a more elaborate and intriguing theory.

We sat in a rooftop cafe in Thamel, Kathmandu's tourist centre, a few hundred feet from the royal palace. March, the businessman said, was a good season for tourists in Nepal. 'But look,' he continued, pointing to the alleys below us, where the bookshops, trekking agencies, cybercafes, bakeries, malls and restaurants were empty. In recent years, the tourist industry has been damaged by news in the international press about the Maoist guerrillas, who model themselves on the Shining Path in Peru, and whose 'people's war' has claimed more than 11,000 lives since 1996. Even fewer tourists have ventured to Nepal since 1 February this year, when King Gyanendra, citing the threat presented by the Maoists, grounded all flights, cut off phone and internet lines, arrested opposition politicians and imposed censorship on the media.

A portly man wearing a cotton tunic, tight trousers and a cloth cap, the businessman had the prejudices of his class, the tiny minority of affluent Nepalese whose wealth comes largely from tourism and foreign aid; and that morning—the spring sun growing warm and burning off the smog over the Kathmandu Valley; the vendors of carpets, Gurkha knives, pirate DVDs and Tibetan prayer flags sullenly eyeing a stray tourist in tie-dye clothes—he aired them freely.

He said that Maoists had bombed the private school he sent his children to; he worried that his servants might join the guerrillas, who controlled 80 per cent of the countryside and were growing strong in the Kathmandu Valley. He said that he was all for democracy—he had been among the protesters demanding a new constitution in the spring of 1990—but peace and stability were more important. What the country needed now, he declared, was a strong and principled ruler, someone who could crush the Maoists. He said that he missed Dipendra: he was the man Nepal needed at this hour of crisis.

According to him, Dipendra's three years as a schoolboy in Britain had radicalised him. Just as Pandit Nehru had discovered the poverty of India after his stints at Harrow and Cambridge, so Dipendra had developed a new political awareness in England. He had begun to look, with mounting horror and concern, at his homeland. Returning to Nepal, he had realised that it would take more than tourism to create a strong middle class, accelerate economic growth, build democratic institutions and lift the ninth poorest country in the world to the ranks of modern democratic nations. As it turned out, he had been thwarted at every step by conservative elements in the royal palace. He had watched multi-party democracy, introduced in 1991, grow corrupt and feeble while enriching an elite of politicians and bureaucrats; equally helplessly, he had watched the new rulers of Nepal fail to tackle the Maoists. Frustration in politics rather than love, the businessman claimed, had driven Dipendra to alcohol, drugs, guns and, finally, to regicide.

It's often hard to know what to believe in Nepal, the only Hindu kingdom in the world, where conspiracy and rumour have long fuelled a particularly secretive kind of court politics. Independent newspapers and magazines have been widely available only since 1990, and though intellectually lively, the press has little influence over a largely illiterate population easily swayed by rumour. In December 2000, news that a Bollywood actor had insulted Nepal incited riots and attacks on Indians and Indian-owned shops across the country. Little is known about Dipendra, apart from his time at Eton, where his fellow pupils nicknamed him 'Dippy'. There is even greater mystery surrounding Pushpa Kamal Dahal, or Prachanda, the middle-aged, articulate leader of the Maoists, who has been in hiding for the last two decades.

King Gyanendra appeared on national television to blame the palace massacre on a 'sudden discharge by an automatic weapon'. A popular conspiracy theory, in turn, blamed it on the new king himself, who was allegedly involved in smuggling artefacts out of Nepal, and on his son, Paras, much disliked in Nepal for his habit of brandishing guns in public and dangerous driving—he has run over at least three people in recent years, killing one. More confusingly, the Maoists claimed that they had an 'undeclared working unity' with King Birendra, and accused Gyanendra, and Indian and American imperialists, of his murder.

This atmosphere of secrecy and intrigue seems to have grown murkier since February, when Gyanendra adopted the Bush administration's rhetoric about 'terrorism' and assumed supreme power. Flights to Nepal were resumed after only a few days, and the king claimed to have lifted the emergency on 30 April, but most civil rights are still suspended today. When I arrived in Kathmandu, fear hung heavy over the street crossings, where soldiers peeped out from behind machine-gun emplacements. Men in ill-fitting Western suits, with the furtive manner of inept spies, lurked in the lobby of my hotel. Journalists spoke of threatening phone calls from senior army officers who tended to finger as Maoists anyone who didn't support the king. Many of the people I wanted to meet turned out to be in prison or in exile. Appointments with underground activists, arduously made, were cancelled at the last minute, or people simply didn't turn up.

Sitting in her gloomy office, a human rights activist described the routine torture and extra-judicial killing of suspected Maoists, which had risen to a startling average of eight a day. Nothing was known about the more than 1200 people the army had taken from their homes since the beginning of the 'people's war'—the highest number of unexplained disappearances in the world. She spoke of the 'massive impunity' enjoyed by the army, which was accountable only to the king. She claimed that the governments of India, the US and the UK had failed to understand the root causes of the Maoist phenomenon and had decided, out of fear and ignorance, to supply weapons to the Royal National Army: 20,000 M-16 rifles from the US. 20,000 rifles from India, helicopters from the UK.

She said that the 'international community' had chosen the wrong side in a conflict that in any case was not likely to be resolved by violence. Though recently expanded, and mobilised against the Maoists in 2001, the army was no more than 85,000 strong, and could not hold the countryside, where, among the high mountains, ravines and rivers— almost perfect terrain for guerrillas—it faced a formidable enemy.

She spoke with something close to despair. Much of her work— particularly risky at present—depended on international support. But few people outside Nepal cared or knew enough about its human rights record, and the proof lay in her office, which was austerely furnished, with none of the emblems of Western philanthropy—new computers, armed guards, shiny four-wheel drives in the parking lot—that I had seen in December in Afghanistan.

'People are passing their days here,' she said as I left her office, and the remark, puzzling at first, became clearer as I spent more time in Kathmandu. In the streets where all demonstrations were banned, and any protest was quickly quashed by the police, a bizarre feeling of normality prevailed, best symbolised by the vibrant billboards advertising mobile phones (banned since 1 February). Adverts in which companies affirmed faith in King Gyanendra appeared daily in the heavily censored newspapers, alongside news of Maoist bombings of police stations, unverified reports of rifts between Maoist leaders, promotional articles about Mercedes Benz cars and Tag Heuer watches, and reports of parties and fashion shows and concerts in Kathmandu.

Thamel opened for business every day, but its alleys remained empty of tourists. Months of Maoist-enforced blockades and strikes were also beginning to scare away the few foreign investors who had been deceived by the affluence of Kathmandu into thinking that Nepal was a big market for luxury consumer goods. Interviewed in a local newspaper, a Dutch investor described the Nepalese as an 'extremely corrupt, greedy, triple-faced, myopic, slow, inexperienced and uneducated people, and declared that he was taking his hair-replacement business to Latvia. Western diplomats and United Nations officials – darting in their SUVs from one walled compound to another -speculated about a possible assault on the capital by guerrillas.

But it is the middle-class Nepalese, denounced by the Maoists as 'comprador capitalists', who appear to live most precariously, their hopes and anxieties echoed in the newspapers by royalist journalists who affirm daily that Nepal needs a strong ruler and Gyanendra is best placed to defend the country, by means of a spell of autocratic rule, from both Maoist 'terrorists' and corrupt politicians.

Often while listening to them, I would remember the businessman I had met in Thamel and what he had told me about Dipendra; and I would wonder how the crown prince, if he had indeed been sensitised to social and economic distress during his three years in Thatcher's England, had seen his strange inheritance, a country where almost half of the 26 million people earned less than $100 a year and had no access to electricity, running water or sanitation; a country whose small economy, parasitic on foreign aid and tourism, had to be boosted by the remittances of Nepalese workers abroad, and where political forces seen as anachronisms elsewhere—monarchy and Communism—fought for supremacy.

Histories of South Asia rarely describe Nepal, except as a recipient of religions and ideologies—Buddhism, Hinduism, Communism—from India; even today, the country's 60 ethnic and caste communities are regarded as little more than a picturesque backdrop to some of the world's highest mountains. This is partly because Western imperialists overlooked Nepal when they radically remade Asia in the 19th and 20th centuries.[1]

---

[1] For an accessible account of the beginnings of modern Nepal, see John Whelpton's *A History of Nepal, Cambridge*, 2005. Some recent scholarship on the Maoists is collected in *Himalayan 'People's War': Nepal's Maoist Rebellion*, ed. Micheal Hutt, Hurst and Co., 2004. The Nepalese novelist Manjushree Thapa provides an

While a British-educated middle class emerged in India and began to aspire to self-rule, Nepal remained a country of peasants, nomads and traders, controlled by a few clans and families. Previously dependent on China, its high-caste Hindu ruling class courted the British as they expanded across India in the 19th century. As in the so-called princely states of India, the British were keen to support despotic regimes in Nepal, and even reward them with territory; it was one way of staving off potentially destabilising change in a strategically important buffer state to Tibet and China. The country was also a source of cheap mercenaries. Tens of thousands of soldiers recruited by the British from the western hills of Nepal fought during the Indian Mutiny, the Boxer Rebellion in China, and in the two world wars. The Gurkhas also helped the British suppress political dissenters in India, and then, more violently, Communist anti-colonialists in Malaya in the 1950s.

As the movement for political independence grew in India, Nepal came to be even more strongly controlled by Hindu kings and the elites they created by giving land grants to members of the high castes, Bahun and Chhetri, which make up less than 30 per cent of the population. The end of the British Empire in Asia didn't lead to rapid change in Nepal, or end its status as a client state. Indian-made goods flooded Nepalese markets, stifling local industry and deepening the country's dependence on India. In the 1950s and 1960s, as the Cold War intensified, Nepal was the forward base of the CIA's operations against China.

American economists and advisers trying to make the world safe for capitalism came to Nepal with plans for 'modernisation' and 'development' then seen as strong defences against the growth of Communism in poor countries. In the Rapti valley, west of Kathmandu, where, ironically, the Maoists found their first loyal supporters in the 1990s, the US government spent about $50 million 'improving household food production and consumption, improving income-generating opportunities for poor farmers, landless labourers, occupational castes and women'.

Modernisation and development, as defined by Western experts during the Cold War, were always compatible with, and often best

---

engaging personal account of Nepal's recent turbulent years in *Forget Kathmandu: An Elegy for Democracy*, Penguin India, Delhi, 2005.

expedited by, despotic rule. Few among the so-called international community protested when, after a brief experiment with parliamentary democracy in the 1950s, King Mahendra, Dipendra's grandfather, banned all political parties. A new constitution in 1962 instituted a partyless 'Panchayat' system of 'guided democracy' in which advisers chosen or controlled by the king rubber-stamped his decisions. The representatives of the Panchayat, largely from the upper castes, helped themselves to the foreign aid that made up most of the state budget, and did little to alleviate poverty in rural areas. The king also declared Nepal a Hindu state and sought to impose on its ethnic and linguistic communities a new national identity by promoting the Nepali language.

Such hectic nation-building could have lulled Nepal's many ethnic and linguistic communities into a patriotic daze had the project of modernisation and development not failed, or benefited so exclusively and egregiously an already privileged elite. During the years of autocratic rule (1962-90), a few roads were built in the countryside, infant mortality was halved, and the literacy rate went up from 5 per cent in 1952 to 40 per cent in 1991. But Nepal's population also grew rapidly, further increasing pressure on the country's scarce arable land; and the gap between the city and the countryside widened fast.

What leads the sensitive prince to drugs and alcohol often forces the pauper to migrate. Millions of Nepalese have swelled the armies of cheap mobile labour that drive the global economy, serving in Indian brothels, Thai and Malaysian sweatshops, the mansions of oil sheikhs in the Gulf and, most recently, the war zones of Iraq. Many more have migrated internally, often from the hills to the subtropical Tarai region on the long border with India. The Tarai produces most of the country's food and cash crops, and accommodates half of its population. On its flat alluvial land, where malaria was only recently eradicated, the Buddha was born 2500 years ago; it is also where a generation of displaced Nepalese began to dream of revolution.

In Chitwan, one of the more densely populated districts in the Tarai, I met Mukti Raj Dahal, the father of the underground Maoist leader, Prachanda. Dahal was one of the millions of Nepalese to migrate to the Tarai in the 1950s. His son was then eight years old. He had travelled on to India, doing menial jobs in many cities, before returning to Chitwan, which American advisers and the Nepalese government were then developing as a 'model district' with education and health facilities. In

Chitwan, Dahal bought some land and managed to give his eight children an education of sorts. Though he is tormented by stomach and spinal ailments, he exuded calm as he sat on the verandah of his two-roomed brick house, wearing a blue T-shirt and shorts under a black cap, a Brahminical caste mark on his forehead.

He had the serenity of a man at the end of his life. And, given the circumstances, he had not done too badly. I had spent much of that day on the road from Kathmandu to the Tarai, shuffling past long queues of Tata trucks from India, through a fog of dust and thick diesel smoke, ragged settlements occasionally appearing beside the road: shops made of wooden planks, selling food fried in peanut oil and tea in sticky clouded glasses, mud houses with thatched roofs—a pre-industrial bareness in which only the gleaming automatic guns of young soldiers and the tangle of barbed wire behind which they sat spoke of the world beyond Nepal.

The jittery soldiers who approached the car with fingers on their triggers were very young, hard to associate with stories I had heard in Kathmandu—stories no newspaper would touch—of the army marching men out of overcrowded prisons and executing them. My companion, a Nepalese journalist, was nervous. He knew that the soldiers in the countryside attacked anyone they suspected of being a Maoist, and journalists were no exception. Many of the soldiers barely knew what a journalist was.

There are few places in Nepal untouched by violence—murder, torture, arbitrary arrest—and most people live perpetually in fear of both the army and the Maoists, without expectation of justice or recompense. Dahal, however, appeared to have made a private peace with his surroundings. He told me that he spent much of his day at the local temple, listening to recitals of the *Ramayana*. He said that he still believed the king had good intentions. He appeared both bemused by, and admiring of, his famous son, whom he had last seen at the funeral of his wife in 1996. The ideas of equality and justice, he thought, had always appealed to Prachanda, who was a sensitive man, someone who shared his food with poor people in the village. He couldn't tell me how his son had got interested in Mao or Marx in such a place as Chitwan, which had no bookshop or library. But he did know that Prachanda had got involved with Communists when he couldn't find a good job with the government and had to teach at a primary school in his native hills of Pokhara.

In his speeches, which claim inspiration from Mao and seek to mobilise the peasants in the countryside against the urban elite, Prachanda comes across as an ideologue of another era: he's an embarrassment to the Chinese regime, which is engaged in the un-Maoist task of enriching Chinese coastal cities at the expense of the hinterland, and feels compelled to accuse Nepalese Maoists of besmirching the Chairman's good name.

In the few interviews he has given, Prachanda avoids answering questions about his background and motivation, which have to be divined from details given by Dahal: the haphazard schooling, the useless degree, the ill-paid teaching job in a village school, all of which seem to lead inexorably to a conflict with, and resentment of, unjust authority.

The 'modernisation' and 'development' of Nepal during the 1950s and 1960s created millions of men like Prachanda, lured away from their subsistence economies and abandoned on the threshold of a world in which they found they had, and could have, no place. Nepal's agricultural economy offered few of them the jobs or the dignity they felt was their due, and they were too aware of the possibilities thwarted by an unequal, stratified society to reconcile themselves to a life of menial labour in unknown lands, and an old age spent in religious stupor. Educated, but with no prospects, many young men like Prachanda must have been more than ready to embrace radical ideas about the ways that an entrenched urban elite could be challenged and even overthrown if peasants in the countryside were organised.

Growing up in Nepal in the 1960s, Prachanda watched these ideas grow in the Naxalbari movement in India. Communist activists lived and worked secretly in parts of Nepal during the Panchayat era—in the 1950s, a famous Communist leader called M.B. Singh travelled in the midwestern hills and acquired followers among the Magars, one of Nepal's more prominent ethnic groups now supporting the Maoists. But Prachanda says that the 'historic Naxalbari movement' of India was the 'greatest influence' on the Communists of Nepal.

In the late 1960s, thousands of students, many of them middle-class and upper-caste, joined an armed peasant uprising led by an extremist faction of the Communist Party of India (Marxist) in West Bengal and

Bihar. Known as Naxalites, after the Naxalbari district where the revolt first erupted in 1967, they attacked 'class enemies'—big landlords, policemen, bureaucrats—and 'liberated' territories which they hoped would form bases for an eventual assault on the cities, as had happened in China. The Indian government responded brutally, killing and torturing thousands. Driven underground, the Naxalite movement splintered, and remained dormant for many years.

In the 1990s, when India began to move towards a free market, the Naxalite movement revived in some of the poorest and most populous Indian states. Part of the reason for this is that successive Indian governments have steadily reduced subsidies for agriculture, public health, education and poverty-eradication, exposing large sections of the population to disease, debt, hunger and starvation. Almost three thousand farmers committed suicide in the southern state of Andhra Pradesh after the government, advised by McKinsey, cut agricultural subsidies in an attempt to initiate farmers into the world of unregulated markets. In recent years, Naxalite movements, which have long organised landless, low-caste peasants in Bihar and Andhra Pradesh, have grown quickly in parts of Uttar Pradesh and Madhya Pradesh—where an enfeebled Indian state is increasingly absent—to the extent that police and intelligence officials in India now speak anxiously of an unbroken belt of Communist-dominated territory from Nepal to South India.

The Naxalite uprising in the late 1960s invigorated the few Communists in Nepal, who, like the members of the Nepali Congress, the main underground political organisation, sought guidance and encouragement from India. In 1971, some Nepalese Communists living across the border from Naxalbari declared a 'people's war against the monarchy. They killed seven 'class enemies' before being suppressed by the king. As fractious as their Indian counterparts, the Nepalese Communist parties split and split again over petty doctrinal or personality issues. In 1991, after the restoration of multi-party democracy, several of them contested elections, and even did well: a Communist coalition became the biggest opposition party, and briefly held power in 1994. In the early 1990s, however, few people in Nepal could have predicted the swift rise of Prachanda and the obscure faction he led.

The Maoists under Prachanda resolved as early as 1986 to follow Mao's strategy of capturing state power through a 'people's war'. They did not start the war until the mid-1990s, however, when disillusionment with parliamentary democracy created for them a potentially wide popular base in the countryside. Still, hardly anyone noticed when on 4 February 1996 the Maoists presented the government with a list of 40 demands, which included abrogating existing treaties with India, stripping the monarchy of all power and privileges, drafting a new constitution by means of a constituent assembly, nationalising private property, declaring Nepal a secular nation and ending all foreign aid. These demands were not likely to be met; and as though aware of this, the Maoists began their 'people's war' by attacking police stations in six districts four days before the deadline.

For the next five years, the Maoists forced their way into the national consciousness with their increasingly bold tactics. They financed themselves by collecting 'taxes' from farmers, and they exacted 'donations' from many businessmen in the Kathmandu Valley. They indoctrinated schoolchildren; they formed people's governments in the areas they controlled and dispensed rough justice to criminals and 'class enemies'. But much of the new power and charisma of the Maoists came from their ability to launch audacious attacks on the police and the army.

The military wing of the Maoists initially consisted of a few ill-trained men armed with antique rifles and homemade weapons. But they chose their first target cannily: the police, almost the only representatives of the central government in much of Nepal. Poorly armed, often with little more than sticks and .303 Lee Enfield rifles, the police retreated swiftly before the Maoists, who also attacked roads, bridges, dams, administrative offices, power plants—anything they felt might aid the counter-insurgency efforts of the government.

In recent years, the Maoists have grown militarily strong, mostly through conscription in the countryside, and regular training—allegedly provided by Indian Naxalites. They have acquired better weapons by looting police stations and buying from the arms bazaars of India; they have also learned how to make roadside explosives, pipe and 'pressure cooker' bombs. In November 2001, the Maoists launched 48 attacks on the army and the police in a single day, forcing the Nepalese government to impose a state of emergency. More than 5000 people died in the next 15 months, the bloodiest period in Nepal's modern history.

But violence is only a part of the Maoists' overall strategy. In an interview in 2000, Prachanda criticised Indian Communist groups for their lack of vision and spoke of the importance of developing 'base areas'. Since 1996, the Maoists have spread out from their traditional home in the midwestern hills of Rolpa and Rukum districts. Their cadres—estimated to number as many as 100,000—travel to deprived areas, addressing, and often recruiting from, the large and growing mass of people deeply unhappy with Nepal's new democratic dispensation.

Some measure of democracy was inevitable in Nepal by the 1980s. In previous decades, the state's half-hearted efforts at development had produced many low-level bureaucrats, small businessmen, teachers, students and unemployed graduates. This new class resented the continuing dominance of upper-caste clans and families. The conflict between the old elite and its challengers was aggravated by a series of economic crises in the late 1980s. In 1985-86, Nepal had negotiated a loan with the IMF and World Bank. The bank's euphemistically named (and free-market oriented) 'structural adjustment programme', which was then causing havoc in Latin American economies, forced the Nepalese government to cut farm subsidies and jobs in the public sector. GDP grew as a result but the gains were cancelled out by inflation of up to 10 per cent and a trade and transit embargo imposed by India in 1989, which caused severe fuel shortages and price rises.

The protesters who filled the streets of Kathmandu in the spring of 1990 were convinced that the decaying Panchayat system could not deal with the shocks of the new world and needed to be reformed. In acceding to demands for multi-party democracy, the king appeared to acknowledge the strength of the new educated class and to recognise that the old political system needed a degree of popular legitimacy if it was to survive. It's clear now that what happened in 1990 was less a revolution than a reconfiguration of power, sanctified by elections, among the old royalist oligarchy and an emerging urban middle class. Many courtiers and sycophants of the king managed to reinvent themselves as parliamentary politicians, often joining the Nepali Congress, the political party that ruled Nepal for all but one of the next 13 years. There were few ideological differences between the Nepali Congress and the main opposition party, the radical-sounding Communist Party of Nepal (United Marxist-Leninist), both of which continued to be led by upper-caste men motivated largely by a desire for money and power. Elections were held frequently, and a procession of governments—13 in as many years—made Nepalese democracy appear vibrant. But the majority of the population, especially its ethnic communities, went largely unrepresented.

In 1992, when democracy still promised much, and Maoism was no more than another rumour in the streets of Kathmandu, Andrew Nickson, a British expert on Latin America, wrote prophetically:

The future prospects of Maoism in Nepal will … depend largely on the extent to which the newly elected Nepali Congress government addresses the historic neglect and discrimination of the small rural communities which still make up the overwhelming bulk of the population of the country. As in the case of Peru, this would require a radical reallocation of government expenditures towards rural areas in the form of agricultural extension services and primary healthcare provision.

Needless to say, this didn't happen. In 2002, Dalits, low-caste Hindus, had an annual per capita income of only $40, compared to a national average of $210; fewer than 10 per cent of Dalits were literate. The upper-caste men who dominated the new democratic regime were competing among themselves to siphon off the money pouring into Nepal from foreign donors. A fresh convert to the ideology of the free market, the Nepalese government dedicated itself to creating wealth in urban areas. Trying to boost private investment in Kathmandu, it neglected agriculture, on which more than 80 per cent of the population depend for a living. Not surprisingly, absolute poverty continued to increase in the late 1990s, even as Kathmandu Valley benefited from the growth in the tourist, garment and carpet industries, and filled up with new hotels, resorts and villas.

In such circumstances, many people are likely to be attracted to violent, extra-parliamentary groups. The Maoists in Nepal had their first ready constituency among rural youths, more than 100,000 of whom fail their high school examination every year. Unemployed and adrift, many of these young man worked for other political parties in the countryside before becoming disillusioned and joining the Maoists.

Mohan was one of the young men who joined a newly legitimate political party after 1990 and then found himself remote from the spoils of power. He then worked with the Maoists for almost five years, living in jungles, once travelling to the easternmost corner of Nepal, before deciding to leave them. He couldn't return to his village, which lay in the Maoist-dominated region of Rolpa, and had gone to India for a while. He was now trying to lie low in Kathmandu, and although he didn't say so, he seemed to be 'passing his days' and making a living through odd jobs, like so many other people in the city.

We had arranged to meet in Boudhanath, Kathmandu's major Buddhist site. Sitting in the square around the white stupa, among monks in swirling crimson robes and often with white faces, Mohan spoke of 'feudal forces' and the 'bourgeoisie': their corruption had paved the way for the Maoists, whom he described as 'anarchists'. He used the foreign words with a Nepalese inflection. He said that he had picked them up while accompanying a Maoist propagandist on tour; and it occurred to me, as he described his background, that he still used them despite having left the Maoists because he had no other vocabulary with which to describe his experience of deprivation and disappointment.

He was born and brought up in a family of Magar shepherds in a corner of Rolpa district that had no proper roads, schools or hospitals. Educated at a school in Palpa, a walk of several miles from his village, he had joined the Nepali Congress in 1992, when still in his late teens, and become a personal aids to a prominent local politician. There were many such young men. They received no money for their services, but slept in the politician's house, ate the food prepared for his family, and travelled with him to Kathmandu. Mohan said that it was a good time, the early years of democracy. He liked being in Kathmandu, especially with someone who had a bit of power. But he couldn't fail to notice that the politician returned less and less often to his constituency in the hills and often refused to meet people who came to his door asking for jobs, money and medical help. He was surprised to hear that the politician was building a new house for himself in Kathmandu. Soon, he felt he was not needed, and one day the politician's wife told him to eat elsewhere.

Clashes between Nepali Congress activists and the Maoists were common in his area; he felt that he could be useful to the Maoists with his knowledge of politics. He was also attracted to the idea of ethnic autonomy that the Maoists espoused. He had seen in his time with the politician how the upper-caste-dominated government in Kathmandu possessed an unjust share of the country's wealth and resources. Many people he knew had already joined the Maoists, and in 1995, one of his friends introduced him to the Maoist 'squad commander' in the region.

As he spoke, I wondered if this was the whole truth, if he hadn't joined the Maoists for the same reason he had joined the Nepali Congress, the reason many young men like him in India joined political parties: for food and shelter. In any case, he joined the Maoists at a bad time: it was in 1995 that the Nepalese government launched Operation Romeo.

This scorched-earth campaign is described as an instance of 'state terror' in a report by INSEC (Informal Sector Service Centre), Nepal's most reliable human rights group. The police, according to the report, invaded villages in the Rolpa and Rukum districts, killing and torturing young men and raping women. When I mentioned this to Mohan, be said that things weren't as bad as they were made out to be by the 'bourgeois' intelligentsia in Kathmandu, who, he thought, were soft on the Maoists. He said the Maoists were simply another opportunistic political group; this was why he had left them. They were interested in mobilising ethnic communities only to the extent that this would help them capture 'state power'; they weren't really interested in giving them autonomy. He had also been repelled by their cruelty. He had heard about—if not actually seen—instances of Maoists punishing people who refused to pay taxes, defied their alcohol ban or were suspected of being police informers. Using rocks and hammers, they often broke all the bones in their victims' bodies before skinning them alive and cutting off their tongues, ears, lips and noses.

Many of these stories appear in reports by Nepalese and international human rights groups. The Maoist leaders were, I often heard in Kathmandu, riding a tiger, unable to prevent their angry and frustrated cadres from committing torture and murder. Criminals had infiltrated their movement, and some Maoists now made a living from extortion and kidnapping. When confronted with these excesses, Maoist leaders deny or deplore them. They probably realise that that they are losing many of their original supporters, who are as tired of the organisation's growing extremism as of the years of indecisive fighting. Nevertheless, these leaders can often seem constrained in their political thinking by revolutionary methods and rhetoric created in another time and place.

Prachanda, for instance, is convinced that 'a new wave of revolution, world revolution is beginning, because imperialism is facing a great crisis.'

When the subject is not world revolution but the specific situation of Nepal, he can be shrewdly perceptive. A police officer in India told me that many of the Indian Communists he interviewed confessed to learning much from the Maoists in Nepal, who were not as rigidly doctrinal as Communists in India and Afghanistan. As Prachanda put it:

The situation in Nepal is not classical, not traditional. In the Terai region we find landlords with some lands, and we have to seize the lands and distribute them among the poor peasants. But in the whole mountainous regions, that is not the case. There are smallholdings, and no big landlords ... How to develop production, how to raise production is the main problem here. The small pieces of land mean the peasants have low productivity. With collective farming it will be more scientific and things can be done to raise production.

It is not clear how much collective farming exists, or what non-military use the Maoists make of the taxes they collect. In fact, there is little reliable information about what goes on in the countryside. Few journalists venture out of their urban bases, and the Maoists aren't the only obstacle. Most of the very few roads outside Kathmandu are a series of large potholes, and then there are the nervous soldiers at checkpoints. And once you move away from the highway, no soldiers or policemen appear for miles on end. In Shakti Khor, a village in the Tarai region populated by one of the poorest communities in Nepal, a few men quietly informed us that Maoist guerrillas were hiding in the nearby forest, where no security forces ever ventured and from where the Maoists often escaped to India. At a small co-operative shop selling honey, mustard oil, turmeric and herbal medicines, two men in their mid-twenties appeared very keen to put in a good word for the Maoists—who the previous night had painted red anti-monarchy slogans on the clean walls.

In the other Maoist-dominated regions I visited, people seemed too afraid to talk. At Deurali Bazaar, a village at the end of a long and treacherous drive in the hills near Pokhara, a newly constructed bamboo gate was wrapped with a red cloth painted with a hammer and sickle and the names of Maoists either dead or in prison. The scene in the square appeared normal at first—women scrubbing children at a municipal tap, young men drinking tea, an old tailor hunched over an antique sewing-machine, his walking stick leaning against his chair—but the presence of the Maoists, if unacknowledged, was unmistakable. When I tried to talk to the men at the teashop, they walked away fast, one of them knocking over the tailor's stick. The shopkeeper said that he knew nothing about Maoists. He didn't know who had built the bamboo gate; it had simply appeared one morning.

When I got back to Pokhara that evening, the news was of three teenage students killed as they tried to stop an army car on the highway. The previous day I had seen newspaper reports in which the army described the students as 'terrorists' and claimed to have found documents linking them to the Maoists. But it now seemed clear that they were just collecting donations for Holi, the Hindu festival of colours. There were eyewitnesses to the shooting. The parents of the victims had exhumed their corpses from the shallow graves in which the army had quickly buried them and discovered that two of them had been wearing their school uniforms. Like much else in Nepal, this would not appear in the newspapers.

The bloody stalemate in Nepal may last for a long time. The army is too small and poorly equipped at present decisively to defeat the Maoists. In some areas it has recently tried arming upper-caste villagers and inciting them to take action against the Maoists. In the southern district of Kapilavastu, vigilante groups organised by a local landlord and armed by the government claim to have killed more than fifty Maoists in February. Such tactics are not only likely to lead to a civil war but also to increase support for the Maoists in areas where the government is either absent or disliked.

Though unlikely at present, talks may offer a way forward. The Maoists have shown themselves willing to negotiate and even to compromise: in July 2001 they dropped their demand that Napal cease to be a monarchy. More recently, Prachanda hinted at a flexible stance when he called for a united front of mainstream political parties against the monarch. He probably fears that the guerrilla force might self-destruct if its leaders fail to lead their more extreme cadres in the direction of moderate politics. But any Maoist concessions to bourgeois democracy are unlikely to please Gyanendra, who clearly wants to use the current chaos to help him hold on to his power.

If he periodically evokes the prospect of terrorists taking over Nepal, Gyanendra can count on the support of India, the US and the UK. In late 2001, the US ambassador to Napal, Michael Malinowski, a veteran of the CIA-sponsored anti-Soviet jihad in Afghanistan, said that 'these terrorists, under the guise of Maoism or the so-called "people's war", are fundamentally the same as terrorists elsewhere—be they members of the Shining Path, Abu Sayaf, the Khmer Rouge or al-Qaida.' The then Hindu nationalist government in Delhi, just as eager to name new enemies, also described the Maoists as 'terrorists'.

The present Indian government has a more nuanced view of Nepal. But it is worried about India's own Communist rebels and their links with the Nepalese Maoists, and it believes that, as Malinowski put it, 'all kinds of bad guys could use Nepal as a base, like in Afghanistan.' Responding to fears that the army in Nepal was running out of ammunition, India resumed its arms supply this year, partly hoping to contain the Maoists and wanting too to maintain its influence over Nepal in the face of growing competition from the US.

There is no evidence that bad guys, as defined by the Bush administration, have flocked to Nepal; the Maoists are far from achieving a military victory; and the Communists in India are unlikely to extend their influence beyond the poverty-stricken districts they presently control. The rise of an armed Communist movement in a strategically important country nevertheless disturbs many political elites, who believe that Communism died in 1989 and that history has arrived at the terminus of liberal-capitalist democracy.

A European diplomat in Kathmandu told me that although Western countries hoped the political parties and the king would put up a joint front against the Maoists, they knew they might at some point have to support the king and his army if he alone was left to protect the country from the Maoists and keep alive the prospects for democracy. I did not feel that I could ask him about the nature of a democracy that is protected by an autocrat. Perhaps he meant nothing more by the word 'democracy' than regular elections: the kind of democracy whose failure to contain violence or to limit systemic poverty and inequality does not matter so long as elections are held, even if, as in Afghanistan and Iraq, under a form of martial law, and in which the turnout of voters does nothing but empower and legitimise a native elite willing to push the priorities of its Western patrons.

Such a form of democracy, which is slowly coming into being in Pakistan, could be revived again in Nepal, as the king repairs his relationship with the mainstream political parties. It is possible, too, that the excesses of the Maoists will cause them to self-destruct. Certainly the international revolution Prachanda speaks of will prove a fantasy. Yet it's hard to wish away the rage and despair of people who, arriving late in the modern world, have known its primary ideology, democracy, only as another delusion—the disenchanted millions who will increasingly seek, through other means than elections, the dignity and justice that they feel is owed to them.

I AM A TERRORIST

Tenzin Tsundue

I am a Terrorist
I like to kill.

I have a horn,
two fangs
and a dragon fly tail.

Chased away from my home,
hiding from fear,
saving my life,
doors slammed on my face,

when patience is tested,
pushed against the wall,
battered, justice constantly denied,
from that dead end
I have returned.

I am the humiliation
you gulped down
with faltened nose.
I am the shame
you burried in darkness.

I am a terrorist
shoot me down.

Cowardice and fear
I left behind
in the valley
among the meowly cats
and lapping dogs.

I am a bullet
I do not think

from the tin shell
I leap for that thrilling
2-second life
and die among the dead.

I am the life
you left behind.

III

IDENTITY AND TERROR

SRI LANKA

IN THE GARDEN SECRETLY

Jean Arasanayagam

Dusk. In this terrain which grows slowly familiar to me, my feet in their dusty boots take exploratory steps. My hands do not let go of their firm grip on the T-56 rifle. I am wary. An eerie silence pervades the landscape. The sky is fringed with palmyrah fronds which look like dark wings. An abandoned village, once full of houses which are now only empty shells, bombed out. The palmyrah fences surrounding the ruins are ripped asunder, as if gigantic hands had torn them apart in a fit of rage. The armoured tanks had gone through them to avoid the pressure mines laid on the paths and roads. Such are the routes which invading armies take. The enormous wheels had crushed the fences that protected the privacy of lives of those who had once dwelt behind them, effaced the rituals and lives of whole families who had belonged to this village for generations, people whom we never knew and never would know.

All around me is complete silence. There are no human voices. The palmyrah fronds rustle in the slight breeze. A crow caws, a jarring sound. In the distance, there are other bird calls, which intensify my loneliness. And my sense of fear too … the fear of the unknown.

A house in front of me attracts my attention. The once-blue walls are shattered, the paint has peeled off and blistered. The roof has caved in. It is surrounded by trees, the branches of which are laden with ripening mangoes. There are also tamarind trees covered with golden yellow flowers, the ground below is strewn with fallen fruit. Bougainvillaeas spill cascades of sunset colours: pink shading into orange, white, purple, magenta, bright red. A lone jasmine bush is covered with white blooms. There is not a soul in sight. In the distance, I can hear the voices of my comrades making their own discoveries. We are all still alert. Terrorists may still remain hidden in pockets. We constantly look up at the trees—that's where snipers wait and watch.

I walk closer to the house. Blue walls are unusual. Perhaps it is a church. No, it can't be a church. It doesn't look like the usual church architecture. Some of the churches in this area are centuries old, I know, dating from Portuguese and Dutch times. American missionaries too had built churches, as well as schools and colleges. There were many conversions to Christianity. In the past, students from the south travelled north to study in these famous seats of learning. My grandfather had come to the north to study under the great scholars of his day.

I want to be by myself. Ever since I have come north, I have been plagued by this need to understand what I am doing here. The others in my company are elated, overcome by the euphoria of victory. They sing as our crowded trucks lurch along the broken roads, swerve past the huge potholes. Those on foot move warily for there are lots of casualties from the landmines planted everywhere by the guerrillas in anticipation of our arrival. They see our every move as a gesture of aggrandizement. Yet we see ourselves as liberators. But do the people we think we are freeing see us in the same light?

The troops from the south have fought hard. Operation Sunrise I. We have moved into the very heart of the peninsula. Now we are all battle-worn and bone-weary. We haven't changed our uniforms or boots for days. We look like strange insects created out of this landscape of red earth, white sands and green-black leaves; our camouflage uniforms are the colour of the vegetation. The trucks and armoured tanks are also painted in camouflage patterns, like leaf-covered branches of trees. They look incongruous to me.

The landscape itself has been transformed by war. Sometimes it seems that only the camouflage patterns of our uniforms and vehicles provide the green. There are desolate spots which are populated solely by helmeted troops running through desecrated groves, with guns, in heavy boots, taking cover, lying down flat. There is the periodic splatter of machine gun fire. What do the bullets strike? The enemy is never seen.

It is only on the army maps that the battles take place. The map of the peninsula shows thick black arrows, indicating the progress of the military campaign. Decisions are made in the boardrooms. Ground troops not enough, we need air power, naval power, gun boats, heavy artillery.

Guerilla warfare is never easy. I remember my history lessons. The Peninsular War, Spain, France, Ethiopia.

Guerrillas make the rulebooks of conventional warfare seem ridiculous. In the mountains, they use the natural formations of rock as cover. Here, in the thick jungles, they are impossible to find. But everywhere innocent people, uninvolved in the conflict, get caught up in the 'crossfire', that all-embracing euphemism used so often. Of course, in theory, one knows that civilian deaths are inevitable in any war. But I feel deeply uneasy. After all, now it's our own country that's being destroyed.

We all met after it was over, all of us who were part of Operation Sunrise I. The expressions on the faces of the men after they have reached the capital of the peninsula were like those of schoolboys after a victorious cricket match. A lethal match, but there is the same spirit of childish triumph though some of us have not made it.

Is it this boyish sense of triumph that impels men to go forward into unknown terrain? Our commanders try to inspire us before we set out on our forays. 'You are heroes, fighting for the motherland. Your patriotism will be rewarded. We are all together in this.'

I don't know why I am in this. Patriotism alone does not spur me on. I wonder why I am doing this when I fly over the peninsula, piloting the Sia Marchetti, the Avro or the Antonov. I ferry troops to the battlefield and support them in battle with air power, carry stocks of food and arms, and undertake reconnaisance flights. I also have to search out the military installations and training camps of the Tigers. When I see a military vehicle that might belong to them, I target it. It's not easy to find the exact position of their underground concrete bunkers, which are in the depths of the forest, concealed by palmyrah leaves. I know that a whole underground network of mazes lies hidden in the thick jungle; tunnels leading from village to village, to hospitals and ammunition dumps. Another life exists, buried deep. People live and breathe in the innermost depths of the earth. When I am flying, there is the excitement of knowing the seething life, the ingenious feats of engineering, exist unseen. What I can see is a mapped-out landscape: checkered patterns of red, brown, white, green and blue; cultivated fields, villages, townships, houses, *kovils* and churches, all toy-like and miniature.

War has its own distinctive language. A 'terrorist' is 'killed'. A 'soldier' 'sacrifices' his life. It's the eternal terminology, brought to fresh life in this current conflict. Who's to decide who is what, what is the difference between them? We're all groping blindly in the jungle, while day by day the war is carried deeper and deeper within, into our innermost beings. We too construct mazes within ourselves, tunnels through which our thoughts and feelings travel. Concealment and duplicity are now natural to us. We create our secret routes and travel through them, never emerging into the light of day.

In the beginning, for them, there was the Leader, who first took them in deep into those recesses. None of them could have gone in on their own. When they look upon the face of the Leader, it is not like seeing an ordinary man. The face that may seem colourless or even anonymous in times of peace takes on a heroic, epic aspect, like the deity whom you worship. So many thousands have been willing to die for the Leader, for the Cause. When that deified person dies, there is always another to take up his place, to inspire the people to queue up again, ready to be blasted to extinction, mutilated and maimed.

Sometimes I wonder what my own destiny is. I'm a pilot. Flying on missions gives a shape, a purpose, to my life. I like being up in the sky, far above terrestrial bonds. I have a friend, a monk who visits our home sometimes. He speaks of the *dewas,* the gods who dwell in clouds—be they warm clouds, thunder clouds, wind clouds, or rain clouds. I feel like a god myself when I am among the clouds, part of an exalted order. I have all kinds of fancies when I'm up there. I'm so much in control, much more than I am when I am down here. My mind takes on an agility that is unfamiliar to me. I feel I am a part of history. I want to possess a meaningful mission in a world filled with anonymous faces and unrecorded deeds. Perhaps that is what I want—to perform deeds which will sound like epics or the tales of war heroes I've idolized.

I know I am a hero and a patriot to some. But I'm not foolish, I also know what I am to others. I look down from the air at the peninsula. It looks so ordered, so patterned. But it's a pattern it is my mission to disrupt. War ceases to be black and white, heroic and epic because of the ordinary people who prevent the pattern from becoming neat. I remember a painting I saw in a book when I was in college. 'Guernica', that's what the art master called it. It showed the bombing of a village in the north of Spain, in Basque country. Province—what province was it? Viscaya. Yes. I remember the village in ruins, bombed buildings, the eyes of terror, the once-human truncated torsoes, snorting horses and bulls. The image of the bullfight is central to the painting. The bomber is the matador. It is so similar to what I see around me: a civil war, the civilian population under attack; General Franco, the inspiring leader; distortions of death, fleeing figures, men, women and children; the savagery and carnage in remote villages. It was painted over half a century ago, around 1937. Guernica was bombed out with the help of an external power, the Germans. After death and burial, no boundaries exist. Memory, like quicklime, destroys the thought of that agony. None of us are whole human beings any more. Our eyes reflect the images of Guernica.

How does one tell a civilian from a guerilla from the height at which I fly? Ordinary people too construct bunkers in their gardens, and take shelter when they hear the bombers fly overhead. We have all suffered and grown wary in this war. Both sides.

Sometimes I wonder, will the war ever be over? When? Will we live to be old men? Will the record of our battles be documented in military histories? Is the history of a small island like ours important to the rest of the world? I like reading books about history, especially about the two World Wars: the Blitz, the fire-bombing of Dresden, Hiroshima. And the names in today's newspapers: Sarajevo, Grozny, Rwanda. The clouds everywhere are tinged with the colour of blood, the wind rings with the wails of the dying. Death is an everyday fact I live with. All of us are caught up in this vast obsession with death. We have all lost so many friends in this ceaseless fighting. I sometimes wonder what my last moments will be like. A plane crash? A landmine? A stray bullet intended for someone else?

We had come into the peninsula as victors. It should have been a triumphant entry. But there were no banners proclaiming our victory, no guards of honour, no red carpets, no grateful people to welcome our generals with garlands. The roads were quiet, the surface churned up by the movement of armoured tanks, jeeps, motorcycles and the straggling columns of soldiers. The people seemed to have all gone away, fled in the aftermath of the victory.

And so we walk through the silence and emptiness of the countryside and make our own discoveries. Strange ones sometimes: a Pleasure Park for the citizens, a palace which some say was the palace of their Leader, where the last supper was held before the suicide missions were undertaken, where they all posed for photographs with the Leader. It isn't really a palace, but a mansion that had once belonged to a wealthy citizen, with elaborate and ornate trappings and beautiful paintings. It is difficult to explain these things to the people of the south. After all, none of us have seen the almost-mythical figure of the Leader, no one knows very much about him.

After our victory, we had hoisted the lion flag of the south. The de facto state of the north has its own flag too, bearing the image of the tiger. The two beasts are in perpetual combat, forcing us deeper and deeper into the jungle, where the endangered species is man.

The silence here has a palpable quality, I can almost feel it shiver on my skin. I hold my T-56 more firmly in my hands. What an exodus must have taken place before we arrived! Terrible things must have been told about us, the invading armies from the south, the shelling heralding our arrival. We think we are here to liberate the people here, though it is never specified who from. If they thought the same, why would they have fled?

And meanwhile there is the blue house. I step into it. This is not what I would have done in the south. If I were to visit a friend at home, I'd call out at the entrance, in anticipation of being greeted and welcomed. I would be asked news of common friends from the Air Force, from college, news about the fighting in the north and east. But for them, the war is very distant. Many of my friends in the south are still studying at the university or are young executives or bureaucrats. For them, my being in the Air Force has a kind of glamour attached to it. It makes them want to include me in the family. The parents of my friends, call me *putha* or son; to the sisters and younger brothers, I am *aiya* or elder brother.

Here in this empty house, I feel very alone. The peeling walls staring at me with animosity. The only sound I can hear is the echo of my footsteps on the cracked cement floor. There is no one to greet me, to offer me even a glass of water. Water has a different flavour here, tasting of this soil, this terrain. My friend Captain Pali says that the water in the well at the Fort Basilica at Pt. Pedro is clear and sweet. He is from a Kandyan village, and he says that the water from the springs and wells in his village is cool and fresh, and tastes of ferns and reeds. He's been in the army for ten years and has spent a lot of time in the peninsula. He believes that the other side fights with such single-minded intensity because they fight for a cause, their dream of a separate state in the north and east of the island. Eelam.

My home is at the southernmost tip of the island, close to the lighthouse at Dondra Head. I have often watched the strong beams light up the sea, there is a constant awareness that there may be danger to a boat at sea. There's no light here. Outside, it is growing darker and darker. I have a torch in my pocket, that will help me see my way through the empty rooms.

I feel a great sense of pity for the family who had lived here, whose home this was. I think of my home where my mother keeps everything in meticulous order. Every time I go back, my room is unchanged: the silver trophies on the shelves, the photographs of the college cricket and rugby teams, and old textbooks carefully preserved. There is order, a sense of life carrying on. I wonder where the people who lived here are now. Who were they, who lived in these rooms, walked in this garden and tended the plants and flowers? Did they willingly join the exodus out of the peninsula? Or were they forced to leave?

I push open a door. The wood is splintered, the door hanging on its hinges. Within the shadowy inner room, there is a strange luminous glow which emanates from a niche in the lime-washed brick wall, whose reflection flickers on the cracked glass windowpanes. It seems like a dim light bulb, but I know it cannot be that. There has been no electricity in the peninsula for some years now. I walk toward the niche, and am suddenly confronted by a statue of Jesus Christ. The people who had once lived here were Christians? We have that in common then: we worship the same god, pray to the same saints, chant the same litanies, though the language of the votaries would be different. But our prayers would still be the same: 'Give us this day our daily bread ... Forgive us our trespasses, as we forgive them that trespass against us ... Deliver us from evil ... Thine is the Kingdom ...

The statue glows, it seems, from both within and without, like the phosphorous lights that shimmer at the slightest ripple in the inky waters of Arugam Bay. The face, limbs and flowing robes of Christ shine, shedding light in the darkening corners of this empty shell. One arm of the statue is broken. I cannot see the expression on Christ's face, but does that matter? I am caught, transfixed between the incandescent glow of the statue and its fragmented reflection in the shattered glass.

This moment of intense calm does not belong to this place or time. All sounds of battle have receded from my consciousness. I feel an enormous sense of pity for the poor people who had to abandon their home and their shrine. The statue must have been a source of light and comfort to them, especially when darkness fell. Someone must have brought it for them from Europe, perhaps from Italy. And they had set it in this niche so that Christ could both physically and spiritually help them to see the light, in the darkness which was life on the peninusla these days. They must have looked upon the statue as a guardian in these uncertain and troubled times. Why did they choose to leave it behind? Couldn't they have carried it with them to wherever they were going, other parts of the peninsula or even beyond? I try to imagine the family who lived here—maybe there were young sons and daughters who are today asylum seekers in different parts of the world. Or are they involved in the struggle for Eelam?

I think of my brothers and sisters; think of them at this moment, as they surely must often think of me. What would I have felt if I had returned home to find it in ruins, walked into its emptiness with the hollow sound of my boots echoing in my ears? I am lucky, I have a home to go back to, a welcome to look forward to. In the south, we are now looked upon as heroes, patriots who are willing to sacrifice our lives for the motherland. And yet, it was not so long ago that we were regarded in a different light. When the revolution, the *bhishanaya,* was raging in our country, then the same army who had to put down the movement through violent means was looked upon with terror and hatred.

There are so many roles we have to play, and each involves duality and ambivalence. There are so many acts I commit, such as exhumations of the graves of dead subversives, that I have to justify. That the times were such, that we had to act as we did, that many saw us as their protectors. As example, we mention the border villages where they adore us, where parents are happy when their daughters marry a soldier.

Here, at this moment, alone in this shelled house, I wonder what the difference is between those who lived here and me. They have gone into exile. But in reality, we are in exile too. We have all been forced to leave the homes familiar to us, the lives that our families have lived for generations.

It must take so much courage to forge ahead, not knowing what lies before you, not bothering to lock the door behind you, for what is the point of locking up possessions that you will never see again? The bed you sleep on every night, the table you sit at, the mat you spread, things which are so integral to your everyday life, suddenly become unimportant. Nothing matters any more but life itself. To live. You can take only what you can carry or load onto a cart which you have to draw yourself.

And when you leave, you do not know whether there will be a return. And even return can be bitter, if you come back to see your house in ruins, denuded of all you had lovingly filled it with, of all that made it your home, by invisible takers. That's when you realize most chillingly that return is not possible, that you have to start all over again.

How shall we sing the Lord's song, in a strange land?

We wept when we remembered Zion …

I am an intruder here, in an unknown person's house, yet it's difficult for me to walk out. I can't run away. I have to obey orders or I will be considered a deserter, court-martialled. I have to constantly obey, obey, obey. This is my only moment of solitude, of freedom from the all-pervasive rules and regulations which bind me.

There's something happening within me, it's not a sudden revelation, it's just that I feel … a sense of being human again … of having the luxury of having feelings, emotions—simple emotions—without the need to bring in the complexities of thinking. I feel for the owners of this house as I would feel for my own kith and kin, if they were placed in a similar situation. I want to help them to come back to their home, to get over that feeling of displacement, of being banished from the consciousness of the rest of the world. It's not just this luminous icon that makes me think, it's the abandoned village with its empty dwellings. I wonder what they all felt when they heard of our approach—we who see ourselves as liberators on the most important mission of our lives. I remember a book I had read a long time ago where it said that at first Napoleon's armies were seen as liberators from reactionary autocratic governments. Yet things changed. Things always change … not always for the better …

I lean against a cracked wall. The light emanating from the icon seems to be almost from within, like stained glass windows in churches. Would I have knelt and prayed in the ruins of a church? Made the sign of the Cross? Our lives become meaningful now only if we think of them in terms of parables. There's the parable of the Good Samaritan, why isn't there a parable of an ordinary soldier? There's the story of the centurion's daughter, who was saved by faith. Many of my friends carry the ninety-first psalm in tiny leather pouches around their necks. I too possess a copy that my mother gave me, I finger the sacred words in their leather casing, and utter the words and phrases under my breath. There's one battalion commander who kneels down and prays with his men before they go out to battle. Their hallelujahs at the end of the prayer resound through the countryside. Casualties are supposed to be minimal in this battalion.

He is my refuge my fortress, with His wings He will cover me, shelter me. All the images we associate with Christ are protective, but what we pray for is at odds with what we do. Our missions often involve death. We seek to destroy, not forgive, our enemies.

Here, facing the statue of Christ, caught up in this silence, I interrogate myself. I look at the statue and try to think of the different names I know for him. The Saviour of Mankind, Salvator Mundi, the Light of the World, the Good Shepherd, the Lamb of God ...

The light emanating from the statue seems to be a symbol of the light of the world, it seems to be what I have been waiting for all these dark years.

The broken arm of Christ reminds me of Pali on the day that he was shot in his right arm and in his foot. He crawled in his own blood to reach safety, that strong instinct for survival impelling him. He would not have lived at all had not a boat drifted to a part of the coast where it was not supposed to be. No one should have survived. As it was, Pali survived, with thirty-six stitches in his arm. As he was convalescing in the army hospital in Colombo, watching the BMWs and the Pageros flashing by, the dancing on Galle Face Green, he told me he wondered if people knew at all that there was a war on in the north and the east? Would they need some cataclysmic event to make them realize? Pali's body had been awash with his own blood, his uniform and the dry earth along which he had crawled soaked. The militants were so close that he could see the expressions on their faces, intent on only one purpose, his destruction. He realized how intense that battle would be, outnumbered as the militants were. The women too engaged in battle, young girls … They are all completely convinced that they are fighting for the only cause that matters, he told me. Nothing else existed in their minds. Don't they remember Christ who shed His blood for us? How can they forget the communion service? Eat this in remembrance of me, drink this in remembrance of me. Go in peace … So much blood has already been shed, and there seems to be no sign of an end to the conflict.

What shall I do with this icon of Christ? I cannot bear to leave it in this ruined house. I know suffering was nothing new to Him: they scourged Him with whips, ridiculed Him. In His time, He was looked upon as a subversive element who dared to raise his voice against the mighty power of Rome. Yet today the names we remember Him by say nothing of His stand against temporal power, do they?

Shall I take the icon back with me to the camp and from thence to the south? I have no right to take it, but seeing Christ with the shattered arm, thinking of my wounded comrades and of the people who have gone away, I am overcome by feelings that I am not supposed to have. Don't take anything from peoples' houses, say the orders. I do not know whether I want to involuntarily transfer the pity I feel for the people to the broken icon of Christ, as a means of dealing with my emotions. And if it had been another image, another icon, another deity? I would have left it behind. I take hold of my T-56 in one hand. With the other, I carefully lower the statue from its niche, hold it close to my chest for a moment and then put it into my kitbag. I walk out of the house, looking around me carefully, both hands now free to hold the gun.

YOUR FATE TOO

Jesurasa

You stroll back home
from the beach
or maybe from the cinema.
Suddenly a rifle cracks
boots scamper away.
You'll lie dead
on the road.
In your hand
a dagger sprouts
a pistol too may blossom.
'A terrorist,'
you'll be dubbed.
No one
dare ask questions.
Silence freezes.
But
deep in the people's minds
indignation bubbles up.

Translated by A.J. Canagaratna

AMMA, DO NOT WEEP

Cheran

Amma, do not weep.
There are no mountains
to shoulder your sorrow
no rivers
to dissolve your tears.

The instant he handed you
the baby from his shoulder,
the gun fired.

On your *tali,* lying there in the dust,
blood spread.

In the heat of the splintering bomb
all your bright dreams withered.

What splattered from your anklet
were neither pearls
nor rubies:
there is no longer a Pandyan king
to recognize blood guilt.

On sleepless nights
when your little boy stirs restlessly
screaming out, 'Appa'.
what will you say?

When you pace the night, showing him the moon
and soothing him against your breast,
do not say,
'Appa is with God.'

Tell him this sorrow continues
tell him the story of the spreading blood
tell him to wage battle
to end all terrors.

Translated by Lakshmi Holmström

WHEN MEMORY DIES

A. Sivanandan

'Must you go tomorrow?' Uncle Para inquired of Vijay when they had sat down to the tea and *murukku* that Devi had set before them.

'Yes, grandfather. I've got to get back to work on Monday. I am sorry, but the next time I come—'

'Hmm, yes, next time. In that case, you had better bring me up to date on what's happening in your part of the world before you go to bed. And you, Yogi, had better tell me about what you young fellows are up to in town.'

'There's not much to say, really,' Vijay began, but at the end of two hours he had barely assuaged his grandfather's curiosity, and Yogi was yet to be questioned.

It was getting dark by now and the air was heavy with pent-up thunder.

'It's going to rain,' observed Uncle Para, 'this time for real. I wonder where that boy has got to.'

'What boy?' asked Vijay.

'Ravi, my grandson, Devi's boy. That's his plot up there.'

'Oh yes, I remember him. He was a baby—'

'No longer, I'm afraid. He is his own man now, does what he wants, goes where he likes, tells no one where he goes.'

'And the plot? I mean—'

'Does it when he pleases,' Uncle Para continued his catalogue of woe.

Devi, who had remained silent up to then because she had not spoken in English for a long time, now remonstrated with her father, in Tamil. Yogi nodded vehemently at what she said and Vijay got the drift of it, but the old man insisted that she spelt it out for Vijay.

'Tell him, go on, tell him. You've got a tongue in your head. You tell him.'

And she did. In halting English and Tamil, she told Vijay slowly, but feelingly, how the green of the chillies and the onions he saw over there was only the green of hope, not of expectation: 'his' government had flooded the South with cheap imports of foodstuffs from India and they had no market to sell their produce in. What good was a market garden without a market?

The government was doing this to them, she went on more passionately, just because they were Tamils, and now she spoke in Tamil only, but nothing was going to change that. That, 'they' could not take from them. 'They' had taken their land, their markets, their jobs, their children's education, but they were still Tamils and would die Tamils, and that, 'they' could not take from them—and with that she picked up the cups and plates and walked out of the room.

Uncle Para smiled bleakly. It was not like Devi to be so voluble in public. Something was up, something to do with her son, some suspicion perhaps of what he was getting up to, and she was preparing herself for it.

'You must have seen lots of little plots like this,' observed the old man, waving in the direction of Ravi's 'land', 'on your way here.'

Vijay nodded.

'Yes, Yogi pointed them out to me. I don't remember seeing that much green before.'

'You didn't, because there weren't any, not like this. And it is not just a matter of water, and the electric pump making it easier, cheaper.' The old man paused to light his cigar. Yogi pricked up his ears.

'It is also that a whole new generation has been pushed back on the land because there's no other outlet for them. Your government has closed down all the options. No jobs, no higher education' (Yogi nodded vigorously) 'no nothing.'

'The Colombo Tamils can go abroad, the town Tamils can go to the Middle East, but the village boys can only go back to their little bits of land and see what they can get out of it.'

His cigar had gone out as he spoke. He chewed out the wet end and spat it out and tried lighting it up again while speaking, and gave up.

'Have you seen so many young people in the villages, eh Yogi? How about Sudumalai? Isn't it the same there?'.

'Yes, you are right grandfather,' Yogi said sheepishly. 'I had never seen it like that before.'

'Not since your father was a boy, Vijay, have there been so many youngsters around. And they are trying very hard to make a living, some have tried to grow things never heard of in Jaffna before. In Sudumalai I'm told they've managed to grow apples. Apples! Isn't that right Yogi?

'But what's the use? As Devi says, there's no market. Your government has taken that too. And the will has gone out of the youngsters.

'See,' and he pointed towards Ravi's plot again, 'his friends come for him and he chucks up his work and pushes off. What's the point of working? The village is full of youngsters like Ravi, waiting for something to happen.' He removed his glasses and said more gravely, 'the British took away their past, the Sinhalese took away their future. All they have is the present. And that makes them dangerous.'

There was a clap of thunder and the rain began to pour down.

. . .

Vijay was arrested on his way home that evening. He had just returned the battered old van in which he had been ferrying voters to the polling booths in the neighbouring village, and was walking home when he was stopped by two men. It did not surprise him. The election had gone off too quietly for that, there were no government goondas about and he himself had gone around unmolested and unwatched. But what he had not anticipated was being stopped on a lonely road, at dusk, by plain-clothes policemen, and bundled into a car and carried off to Colombo. It was like something out of a gangster movie. Even the two men who had arrested him, apparently officers from the CID, looked like Edward G and Peter Lorre—and of course they were tight-lipped. They would answer none of Vijay's questions except to say that he was being taken to Colombo for questioning. Vijay was not even sure that they were lawmen; since outright violence was the style of the government, not this subtle gangsterism. It was only when he was ascending the steps to the notorious fourth floor of the Central CID that Vijay began to realize that he was in serious trouble.

The interrogation room was long and bleak and empty of furniture except for a stout mahogany table with a large mahogany chair at its head and a stool at the further end. The two men who had brought him sat him on the stool and left him, still without a word. He called out after them for a glass of water, but they chose not to hear.

Vijay slumped forward on the stool waiting for someone to come through the door, but no one came. He got up and walked to the one window in the room, but it was barred and covered with gunny sack and he could not see out. He took the papers he had in his pocket and tried to read them, but the light from the yellowed bulb set high on the ceiling of that vast room was too dim to read by. He walked around the room for a while, trying to keep his spirits up, but he was sick with hunger and tiredness. He lay down on the floor and slept, only to be woken every time he dozed off by the ringing of a bell just outside his door. He went up to the door and listened, but heard nothing. He came back and lay on the floor under the table, plugging his ears with pieces of paper moistened with spit, and fell asleep between bells.

In the morning, the two men came back and jerked him up, all bleary eyed and groggy with broken sleep, from off the floor and on to the stool, and stood on either side of him without a word. Five minutes later another man walked in and stood menacingly over Vijay. He was huge, enormous, well over six foot tall and almost as broad, or so it seemed to Vijay from where he was sitting, built like a tank. Only his face, set beneath a completely shaven head and lit up by small piercing eyes, was flabby and bejowled and sinful. He was fair-skinned, almost white, and wore a white suit, a Burgher perhaps thought Vijay inconsequentially. Hadn't he seen him somewhere before? In the papers? The man moved away and fitted himself into the big mahogany chair—yes, of course it was his chair, meant for him, meant to fit his stature not his station ... maybe he was a station-master ... Vijay could play trains ... he was getting light-headed, he must eat something ... soon ... he'll ask the man.

'Shall we interrogate him now, sir?' he heard someone ask. 'No, no, that won't be necessary.' The man's voice rasped and grated as though with a cough that couldn't quite come out. 'I've seen the papers.'

Vijay began to nod off. He was sure he had seen the man somewhere. We know all about you, the man was saying, and your conspiracy against the government. Your vice-principal has been very cooperative ... your connection with the Boys ... and your PLF ...

'Look at me when I speak to you,' the man grated out and his hench-men jerked Vijay's head up with considerable force.

'No, no, don't harm him. We must do this legally. He has connec-tions.' He chuckled and paused and chuckled again, his chins jollying each other along with each chuckle. Vijay knew that chuckle, he had heard it before, he was sure he had, the man chuckled again, of course he had, it was Sidney Greenstreet, that's who it was, Sidney Greenstreet from *The Maltese Falcon*. Vijay should have known it, known that laugh anywhere, the man had been a tea-planter in Ceylon once and had picked it up from beating the coolies.

'Take him away and put him in Welikade. Let them deal with him.'

Vijay tried to protest that he wanted to see a solicitor, phone his wife, a friend then, they had no right to put him in jail, anyway, not without a trial ... The man chuckled.

'Give him some bread and water before you take him,' he instructed the men and left.

Later that evening the men came back to take Vijay to Welikade jail and hand him over to the warden there. By now, Vijay had begun to realize that he was being treated as a terrorist and would have no recourse to friends or lawyers. The warden looked a kindly man, with a round moon-like face and a round moon-like body, and Vijay tried to start up a conversation with him. But moon-face merely beamed at him and handed him over to a guard who took him down past the noise and clatter of crowded prison cells, down a maze of empty corridors to a solitary cell in an uninhabited part of the prison. And suddenly Vijay began to be afraid. They were not just going to shut him up, they were going to shut out the world from him, shut him away from other prisoners. He would have access to no one, no one would have access to him, no one would know where he was, he was being made anonymous. Terror mounted in him and broke into a scream. But the scream clove drily to the roof of his mouth. He slid hopelessly to the floor.

In the unending days that followed, Vijay saw no one but his silent jailer, at meal times and slopping out. The food was inedible—rice, mostly uncooked, and a dry *mallung* or a coconut *sambol* that had gone off, and occasionally a piece of fish, iced and tasteless. The room, small and narrow and windowless but for a grille, smelt eternally of his shit. What once he had considered his staple diet was now a staple punishment, what was once a joyful evacuation was a burden he would rather carry. Once a day, his guard took him to an enclosed yard and walked him for half an hour like a dog. He asked for reading material, but got none, he wanted to know what they were going to do to him, but got no answer.

The old sensation of being written out returned more strongly, only now, the fear was gone, only recognition of the fear remained. He tried to think, just for the sake of thinking, tell himself stories, recall the world, but slowly he found his mind turning blank, his memory would not work for him, he was losing his touch with familiarity, the familiar things were not there for him to touch, they had been removed from him: people, time, books, laughter. He could not even feel his isolation any more, just a blankness where he used to be … this was how you went mad, he thought with a last thought … this was how they disappeared you … from yourself and the world. He was not being punished, he was being made absent.

…

Then, one day, Ravi disappeared for good. Or so it had seemed to Para then, so close had he been to Devi's sense of loss. But looking back now, he realized that Ravi had indeed come back, just once more, some six months later. Yes, of course, he had, how could he have forgotten. The laughter had gone from the boy, and he came dressed in army fatigues, a pistol at his side and a machine-gun in his hands. He had joined the freedom fighters, he said, and neither his grandfather nor his mother should expect to see him again. He was sorry he had left without telling them, but that was the day, that was the day … Ravi was crying … strange, an army man … with a pistol and machine-gun … crying … that was the day they had killed Gnani, his great friend Gnani, tortured and killed him, the Sinhalese army, because he would not tell who had robbed the bank with him, because he would not tell on his friends.

Devi had looked on her son, in a state of shock, unrecognizing. Para had buried his head in his hands and accepted. But Ravi had cried out, as though unable to bear his grandfather's acceptance, wanting his approval instead.

'You have never had to fight for anything, grandfather, have you?' Ravi had asked, and Para had been taken aback. Never fought for anything? he had bristled inwardly, chewing on his cigar. No, not like that, I suppose, not with guns and bullets and … not with my life. And not for my future. For my past perhaps, to keep something of myself, my language, my history against the encroaching British. Only, they were more subtle than the Sinhalese, they took away my past by stealth, the Sinhalese are taking away your future by force. And they are no foreigners, they are your countrymen, and that is hard. 'No, son,' he had said aloud. 'I haven't had to fight like you.'

His reverie broke as he heard Devi call from the other side of consciousness. 'Can't you hear me, father?' She seemed to be shouting, from some far-off place. 'Your food is getting cold.'

What had she managed to put together today, he wondered ... rice and *dhal* again ... full of stones, the rice ... he had broken his last tooth ... ah, well ... others in the village had less to eat ... they made sure that Commander Ravi's mother did not starve . . . out of love once ... out of fear now ... but Devi sent it all back ... to the children ... with their toy machine guns and empty, swollen bellies.

Once he had been proud of them ... the Boys ... the guerrillas ... the Liberation Fighters for Eelam, LIFE ... the Life-Boys. He chuckled mirthlessly ... what a silly joke ... senile ... no one to laugh with any more ... no one laughed any more ... when the Commander stopped laughing, they all stopped laughing ... LIFE was a serious business ... another silly joke. Oh hell, what did it matter ... it was time to die, anyway...

That day at Nallur temple, what a celebration that had been. The Boys had sealed up the army in the old Dutch fort and come out into the open at last. Everybody ran to the temple to see who it was who had come out of the bunkers. And they were stunned and proud to find not just their sons, but their daughters, in the guerrilla parade. Who'd ever have thought that Premi would have joined? She was the shy one in Kannamma's family, hid behind the curtains when visitors came. And Gowri, she was lame from birth, and here she was carrying a Kalashnikov. So that was where Mani had disappeared to? One by one, their relatives and friends counted them out, standing tip-toe in the crowd, shouting and yelling at each other. 'It's her, it's her, my baby...' 'Oh look, there is so-and-so ... Who could have thought...' 'Oh no, not him, he's too young.' Everyone vying with each other for the merit of the unknown contribution they had each made to the struggle for their own freedom.

Bliss was it in that dawn to be alive—how the memory of his alien schooling had come back to Para, then, turning it native. Bliss was in that dawn ... crashed by the crowd, but bliss ... barely able to keep his feet, but exalted ... couldn't see his grandson though ... or Yogi ... Devi had gone looking for her son, but did not find him. Ravi had kept out of it all ... through modesty or stratagem? ... the war was not yet over ... and he was not Commander, then, but *thambi,* everybody's younger brother ... and to be young was very heaven.

That evening Para had sat among his cronies in the toddy tavern of his youth and regaled them with stories of his grandson. His friends, not to be outdone, matched him, tale for tale, with stories of their own progeny—till, tired and proud, they rose unsteadily from their seats, proclaiming that it was the Boys who had raised them to their feet again.

Yes, Para had been proud of them, then, proud of the way they had brought back legend to a people starved of heroes and fed on fear, and prouder still of the practical way they had gone about relieving people's hardships with food redistribution centres and medical supplies and nurseries.

And then, they had begun to fight each other over who could serve the people better, which faction, which dogma, till the people mattered no more ... and the army came back ... and the war had to be fought all over again ... only this time there were no people in it, only armies and warlords and fiefs and kingdoms ... and the redistribution centres became places of ransom, medicines ceased to arrive and the nurseries grew into nurseries of war.

'Can't you see what you are doing?' Para had asked Yogi, who was in charge of their district but visited it less frequently since he was made Second-in-Command. When he did, though, he made it a point to look up his adopted grandfather and guru, if only to listen to 'the old man's lectures' as he put it.

'What are we doing, grandfather?' Yogi had challenged him affectionately.

'The Africans have a saying: when elephants fight, it is the grass that gets trampled.'

'Where on earth do you pick up these things?'

'I just read. Well?'

Yogi would not reply and Para had pressed him. 'Well?' 'Well, yes, all right,' Yogi had answered reluctantly, 'but you should speak to your grandson. I don't have his ear.'

'Nor have I. He never comes.'

'But you can't go on like this,' Para had continued. 'You are destroying everything you built. You must unite.'

'Unite with those who betrayed us? You can forget that one, grandfather. You know how he hates disloyalty, and informers. He has never forgotten Gnani's death you know: someone told on him and he died, refusing to tell on anyone.

'That's why we carry these damn things around our necks,' he added, fingering the cyanide capsule that hung from a string. 'We'd rather die than inform.'

Para had remembered the circumstances only too well, but he could not let Yogi go on that note. 'What happened to your socialism, son?' he had asked Yogi as he was leaving.

'Once we take power—'

'You'll keep it,' Para had laughed cynically, but knew that he had planted a seed of doubt in Yogi, so close had the lad grown to him since that day he had first come to see him with Vijay.

. . .

At ease with himself at last, Vijay put himself about, helping around the house, putting up with Nadesan's unfailing cheerfulness, assisting Sanji in the garden. The one thing he dared not do was to tidy up his room. Yogi's things were still there as he had left them all those years ago, the books on the floor, a cricket bat in the corner, the things so suddenly abandoned, and the legend 'Happy Birthday Son' chalked across the door. Chitra had probably left it like that to remind her of Yogi. What Vijay thought he could do was to buy some joss sticks from the shop round the corner and get the mustiness out of the room.

Halfway down the road he was summarily stopped by Kugan. 'You can't do that, *thambi*,' Kugan admonished him. 'The streets look innocent enough, but you are a stranger here. Anything can happen to you and no one will ever know. Not like Colombo.'

'Oh no, it happens there too, my friend, believe me, it happens there too,' and Vijay, sitting himself down on the verandah floor beside Kugan, told him the story of his arrest and detention and the scenes he had witnessed in prison.

'Yes, that was terrible, we couldn't believe that the government could do that, kill its own prisoners, it was terrible. It changed everything here, you know, it brought the various factions together for a time, and we mounted that attack on the barracks at Elephant Pass.'

'That's where you lost your leg, right?'

'And my arm.' He removed his blanket and showed Vijay an empty socket.

He didn't mind it though; it was all in a good cause. He himself had been a lowly toddy-tapper, but the Boys had accepted him as one of them. One day they would all be equals and the caste system would only be a memory. Wasn't that worth losing an arm and a leg for?

Vijay was moved by the man's dream. There was so much killing around that Vijay had forgotten why the war was being fought. The Boys themselves had forgotten. The gun, as Nadesan said, had taken over; the means had become the end.

Kugan was fatalistic about it. These things happen in a war, he said. What made him miserable was the Boys fighting each other, and that led to informers. And informers, for Kugan, were poison. He laughed, fingering the cyanide capsule that hung around his neck. No, there was no question about it, informers should be hanged.

Vijay had never understood the suicide pill. It was such a symbol of waste, of no-hope, of death as a way of life. It had such a finality about it. Maybe it was all right at the beginning when it symbolized a heroic refusal to inform, at least it implied choice; but now that it had been raised to dogma, belief, ideology, it symbolized the end of choice. And the end of choice was the beginning of terror.

'Loyalty and sacrifice are the things that hold us together,' said Kugan, reading Vijay's thoughts. 'Look at those other groups, just a bunch of self-seeking individuals. Yes, loyalty and a hatred of the army. Without that we'll come apart.

'Without that and Yogi. They all love him, the Boys. They fear Ravi, but they love Yogi.'

Vijay now began to keep notes of his conversations. He saw himself as a serious writer, a reporter from the front line at the least. He found an old exercise book in Yogi's room and every night, before going to bed, wrote down the things he had learnt that day, and the thoughts and reflections that arose from them, till writing itself became a discovery. And soon he had a feel for Eelam as he had never had before. He had understood it in his head, but he had not felt it in his imagination; and the imagination, he knew now, had to be felt to become material.

He was just putting his notebook away one night, some three weeks later, when he saw his bedroom window open stealthily and a man creep in. Startled, Vijay reached for the chair.

'Hey, hey, it's only me,' said the man removing his hood.

'Yogi,' yelled Vijay, leaping to embrace his friend. 'Yogi, you bastard. How are you?'

'Ssh, not so loud. This is a private visit.'

'Stand here in the light. I want to see how you look. Hmm, grown a bit, almost as tall as me. And I like that dashing moustache. You've put on some weight, haven't you?' Vijay asked, feeling Yogi's arms.

'Muscle, my lad, muscle.'

'But why this sarong and shirt—and hood?'

'As I said, this is a private visit. And I thought you'd like me to come in through the window again.' He chuckled. 'Besides, the army has been nosing around these parts the last few days.'

'You didn't come in through the window last time,' recalled Vijay, 'or did you? I know you left through it hurriedly.' He sat down on the bed and offered Yogi the chair.

'Nowadays I've got to come in through the window too,' laughed Yogi.

'Isn't this a liberated zone?'

'Yes, but it's never very stable.'

They chatted for a while about the situation in Jaffna, but Yogi, Vijay noticed, was giving nothing away. His demeanour was still very boyish and open, but beneath it had developed a more serious man, a thinking man, a man who listened above all, as Vijay discovered from the questions Yogi fired at him in the course of their conversation. What were Vijay's impressions, what had he heard, did he think the movement was winning? What was the feeling among ordinary Sinhalese people in the south? How could they be weaned away from government propaganda?

Vijay answered Yogi as best he could, coming up, finally, with his idea of reporting the war on radio. Yogi was enthusiastic about 'dispatches from the North', but not so sure that they could come from the front line.

That would not be possible as yet, and he would have to get permission from higher up even for the other thing.

'Funny, isn't it?' reflected Yogi. 'But for you I wouldn't have met the Commander.'

'Commander?'

'Ravi, your cousin, man.'

'When we went to Sandilipay, you mean? But we never met him that time.'

'No, but I knew who he was when I did, a couple of days later, in town.' Yogi smiled knowingly. 'With Veeran and the others. He came to see us, and we all knew that the talking was over.'

'What do you mean?'

'He wanted action, he wanted to do things, he wanted to get on with the business of liberating our people, not talk about it endlessly. He had an overall idea of what needed to be done to get rid of the Sinhalese occupation and he had detailed plans on how to do it. And he had worked out how we were going to get arms, and money to buy the arms, and when the arms stopped, he had anticipated that too, he would be ready by then to make them, landmines and explosives and ... You know that he is an explosives expert don't you? That he is the one who blew up Manipay and those other banks?'

Vijay saw the awe and reverence on Yogi's face and wondered how such a level-headed chap could be so wrapped up in one man.

'I know what you are thinking,' said Yogi, 'but there is something about him.' He went on hesitantly, looking for the words. 'A presence, you could say. Yes, a presence, quiet, aloof. But commanding of attention, of devotion even, there is that glow of certainty about him, you know what I mean. I don't know how to say it, but you could see straightaway that he is never going to lose. You can follow a man like that.'

'Where to?' muttered Vijay under his breath.

'Pardon?'

'Where to? To what end?'

'I don't follow.'

'What are you fighting for? Yes, yes, for Eelam, I know. But what sort of Eelam?'

'A socialist Eelam, of course.'

'But where's the socialism now?'

'How do you mean?'

'In the way you run things, your civil administration, law and order, that sort of thing.'

'What about them?'

'I know it's none of my business, but isn't it all very high-handed and top-down? You don't seem to take the people along with you. Or do you think you can take power on behalf of the people and then hand it over to them?'

Yogi did not say anything and, encouraged by his silence, Vijay went on. 'It never happens like that, you know, Yogi. That way socialism never comes. Those who take power don't give it.'

'But then, we'll never take power.' Yogi's voice rose in irritation.

'There's that chance, of course, but this way you are bound to end up replacing one tyranny with another. Where's your socialism then?'

'It will bloody well have to wait,' shouted Yogi, pushing back his chair angrily, 'till after the liberation.'

'Oh, Yogi,' rejoined Vijay, his heart filling with affection as he realized that these were not his friend's convictions, but those of the High Command. 'That way liberation never comes, and you know it. Socialism is the path to liberation, not just its end.'

But Yogi refused to be shaken of his anger, holding on to it tenaciously.

PUNJAB

BEGGING FOR ALMS OF FAITH

Pash

I have only one son, O Lord of faith!
The poor husband is not there to provide us.
After you roared men disappeared afar
Leaving women and vegetating creatures behind
To labour in fields and grow food in them.

You are all powerful, O Lord of faith!
Just a frown on your forehead
Turns flourishing families into herds,
Trampling others to dust
And to drive thin necks into each other.
I have only one neck, O Lord of faith!
Of my only son …
The poor husband is not there to provide us.

I shall worship totems you prescribe,
And recite psalms you have approved,
I shall hold all other faiths futile;
I have only one demand, O Lord of faith,
For my only son . . .
The poor husband is not there to provide us.

So far I have been an idiot:
The faith that my family professed
Never claimed my attention.

It was a sin to regard my family as my faith,
As an idiot I took my husband as the Lord;
Thinking that heaven and hell went
With the smile and frown of my family members.
I was a dropping of hell, O Lord of faith.

Your roar for faith's triumph
Has dissolved the mist of disbelief.
My feeble self will believe in nothing else
Only you will be the eternal truth for me.

What am I before your dogged disciples!
Less beautiful than thy sword at every stage,
Dim as compared to your light in every mood,
I am non-existent, only you exist O Lord of faith!

I have only one son, O Lord of faith!
Had they been seven in number
They could not have achieved anything else,
Your firy words give out fragrance
That drives astray sinners to your path.
I shall worship the bullet you adore,
I have only one son, O Lord of faith!
The poor husband is not there to provide us.

ENCIRCLEMENT

Anita Agnihotri

Her hands under the flowing tap, Kusumjit lets out a slight giggle. Why the giggle? Mahua's nerves instantly tighten as though at a deep-seated signal of danger. Before Kusum's arrival, she had carefully cleaned the glass-top table, the bookshelf, the pretty glass showcase on the wall. Old Dhananjay, his sight failing, misses patches of the layer of dust.

That's why once he'd sat down to cut the vegetables, Mahua turned her attention here. The hand basin is in the verandah. On a concrete shelf inside the net-covered verandah the indoor plants climb every which way—as they please. A leaf or two crinkled from a lack of light—these she's pinched off, and filled in with the healthier vines. The glass shelf under the mirror on the wall has been wiped spotless and, removing the assorted pins and clips usually left scattered there, she has placed a single red rose in a slim white bone-china vase.

Has Kusumjit spotted something out of tune? Mahua and Sushen have been to her flat in Barabani and seen its uncluttered, blemishless decor, combining good taste and aesthetics. They saw the red floor, which the young santhal girl wiped twice a day with cloth wrung out in disinfectant-mixed water. Kusum didn't like having carpets, she said they collected dust underneath and left marks on the floor. The beautiful sofas made of Assam cane, fitted with made-to-order cushions. The hand-embroidered covers, each one unique and lovely. On the centre table the flower vase with her own arrangement of full stems of *rajanigandha*. No TV in her home, no video. What she had was a collection of about two thousand books arranged on wall shelves in her bedroom. On the verandah floor, an *alpana* design drawn in white, a Tanjore brass peacock lamp placed at its centre. Who could imagine that this young woman was a district magistrate, that she spent ten hours a day in the office, and half the days in a month away on tour—on uneven roads in dusty villages!

'What made you laugh?' Mahua isn't able to keep the question from popping out.

Wiping her fair, slim bud-like fingers on the spotless white towel, Kusumjit giggles again.

'Look at that horse, and that red car. They'll never have a place in my life, in my home.' The wooden horse has its paint worn out. Bought by Mahua's Didi's mother-in-law for Mahua's Didi's son. The seat on its back is torn, the sponge inside visible. Still, Papan won't let go of it. He brought it home with him after almost a combat with Tatai. Didi said, 'Do let him take it. Tatai has played with it long enough, he's no longer of the age to ride a wooden horse.' This morning, Papan is off to visit his grandma, Mahua's mother. The horse stands in a corner of the verandah, chin pressed to chest as though it were upset. The red motor car has its horn broken, its steering wheel stuck. The boy managed to break even the fibre-glass seat. Toys don't last even a month in their hands. Still, those two have to be kept here—the boy insists on it. If Mahua puts them in the storeroom, he'd come here straight as soon as he wakes up, even before changing out of his night clothes, asking, 'Where's my horse? My car?'

Mahua catches herself just in time. She's terribly curious to know if Kusumjit is married or not. A rumour that she had married did reach Sushen's ears in the South Block after doing its rounds in the corridors of Shastri Bhavan and Krishi Bhavan—even that was some two years ago. But Kusum had not sent anyone an invitation. She hadn't even asked any of her friends on the telephone. So however strong the desire to ask, Mahua decides it'd be indelicate of her to ask any question of that sort, and keeps her peace.

'Have some of the chicken cutlet. And this is kofta, your favourite.'

'Wait, let me first have some rice with ghee.' With her fingertips Kusumjit lightly breaks the little white mound of rice waiting on her plate.

With puris on a glass plate, Dhananjay stands hesitating at the door. Mahua signals to him to take them back to the kitchen.

'Father died last month.' Kusumjit picks up a piece of fragrant lime from the glass bowl.

'Luckily I got some leave at the time. My brother also took leave. The two of us stayed up in the anteroom next to Father's bed, for the last fifteen nights he lived. Three days before his death; I had just walked into his room. Father had become very thin, because his kidney was slowly failing, he couldn't sit up unless propped with pillows. I walked in and he seemed not to have seen me, he kept looking straight at the white wall. I tiptoed to a chair by his bed and sat down, when he suddenly said, 'Guddi, do you remember, when you were little you used to jump on my back, cover my eyes, and ask, 'Father, where's your Guddu?'? And I used to pretend to be groping in the air for a long, long time before saying 'Here!' Today when you came into the room, I was suddenly reminded of that. I was thinking, you were small at the time, there were hardships in our life. A lot of things had to be kept from the two of you; now at this young age you've your own car, your own flat, yet you're so poor. You've no Guddu of your own, no little one to jump on your back.'

Annoyed, I said to him, 'Father, why are you saying these things? You know of all that has happened. If I feel that lonely, I can adopt a baby. Don't feel sorry about it any more.'

Father smiled sadly and said, 'No. I want you to know that I've no personal sorrow. You've grown up, you're accomplished, capable, you'll do what you feel is right. Spend some time with Dalbir. His mind is still much too soft. Dalbir's my younger brother, I don't think you've seen him, am I right, Mahua?'

'No I haven't. Your parents were there—in that I.B. in Daltongunj. I remember, your father brought hot chapatis to my place.' Mahua quite remembered the ever-smiling, simple gentleman, his affectionate personality.

Sushen is still not back. Amazing! Yet, Mahua called his office as soon as she got Kusumjit's call. Sushen was not in his office at that time either. After waiting, the two of them had sat down to eat. Without the man of the house. Mahua thought Kusumjit would be reluctant to eat. But she seems not even to notice. The girl, rather a woman now, hasn't changed a bit in the last twelve years. Five feet six inches of a slim, healthy body, hair pulled straight back in a short plait hanging below the shoulder, a wide forehead, bare like a desert, black-framed glasses, the face without decoration except for the black mole on the chin. Dressed in yellow-and-black flowered silk kurta-pyjama, a yellow-black striped silk scarf wound like a snake around the slim neck.

'Sushen has no idea when you went to Delhi! We had read about your transfer from Sultangunj. But where you went from there—we lost track. Well, won't you have a cutlet?'

'I've given up non-vegetarian food. Did I not tell you? Oh, sorry!'

Mahua feels a bit upset. The cutlets were so much work, and the fish curry. What else will she eat? Just that kofta, and dal. Such a whimsical girl! 'How long is it since you gave up?'

'Not quite like that. Only about six months ago I had to eat some, under duress, in order not to offend some people. As I'm not under duress here, why should I, don't you agree? You can give me some *dahi* instead, home-made.'

Mahua's own mind isn't on food any longer. Waiting with pricked-up ears for the doorbell. Sushen isn't showing up. Still she has had two cutlets, a couple of puris too, somehow, while they were still hot.

Mixing a spoon of sugar from the sugar pot in her bowl of curd, Kusumjit says, 'You just said you read in the newspaper about my transfer, do you remember what was written?'

Feeling a bit awkward, Mahua says, 'I don't know, I can't remember.'

'I know, even if you remembered you won't admit it. It was written that I was transferred for being unable to tackle the deteriorating law-and-order situation. Ramabatar Singh himself used this language at the news conference. The journalists noted his exact words down. Ramabatar was opposed to my being posted in Sultangunj right from the beginning. If one looks through the file, a confidential note from the D.G. (Intelligence) at the time can still be found, a note that said I was in secret sympathy with the terrorists, that Sultangunj was like a lake atop a volcano and bringing me there would mean that the situation would get out of control. The Chief Minister, of course, had not paid much attention to that note. The trouble with me is that I haven't learned the technique of kicking with velvet-covered shoes. My mother forgot, as you know, to put honey on my tongue when I was born.'

It was Sushen who had made that remark to Kusumjit, about honey on the tongue at birth. That's why Mahua hasn't forgotten it. About a year after he'd said that, it reached her ear after travelling via many others' ears. At the dak bungalow of Netarhat just before sunrise, when a freshly bathed Kusumjit stepped outside to join the rest of the group to watch dawn turn into day, Sushen took the camera out of his pocket. 'I'll capture that drop of water on your cheek,' he said.

'And once you've captured it, where will you keep it, in your bedroom or what?'

Insulted in front of his friends, Sushen went red in the face and, putting the camera back in its case, he said 'Did your mother put honey on your tongue-at birth? Doesn't seem so.'

'She did, too, it was neem-flower honey.'

Mahua continues to sit at the table, a little stiffly, her face lowered. The loose end of her multi-colour organdy sari flutters like a giant butterfly in the breeze from the electric fan.

Finishing the bowl of yogurt, with a practised hand Kusumjit takes a tissue out of her bag and wipes her lips. But the agitation inside her shows on her face. She continues:

'Do you know where Amitabh Menon first spotted me? At a reception for the vice-chancellor's daughter. I was talking with the V.C.'s wife, he came up on his own and said 'Hi!' with a light tap on my shoulder, which pleased the host endlessly. I was aware of his being one of those who could smell Oxford in the air. Without acquiring an intellectual or two like me to show off like stuffed deer heads on the walls of banquet halls, he couldn't have a good night's sleep. After barely a month, I was transferred from the education ministry and I joined his office.

'Mahua, you probably haven't seen their lawn, the flowers, flowers everywhere in winter. Impeccable decor, silver cutlery, China silk table covers, fragrant Darjeeling tea. Frequent parties, going on tours. On special airplane trips to places with him, really, I won't lie, Mahua, I was taken in. And the A.D.C. gentleman, so handsome, over six feet tall. Recited *shayeri* to me in my chamber every day after lunch. Got my nickname from somewhere, and mooned, 'Oh , Guddi, I'm so lonely, no compatibility with my wife.' It was like getting drunk on sherry. I still didn't know it, Amitabh was unable either to swallow me or to spit me out. I didn't know the young man had been briefed and sent to keep an eye on me. Later when I came to know this I felt nauseous with disgust. By then I had received a telegram in the postal files. From a mother whose son had been missing. Her young, college-attending son, couldn't be found. At the highway crossing he'd been picked up one evening by a gray-coloured jeep with a red roof light. Would he help her? I sent it on, he just sent it back to me like a dry yellow saal leaf, with the two letters A.M. added on and no instruction whatsoever.

'One letter, then two. Gradually over a month and a half, when I had a pile of seventy five letters and telegrams about missing husbands, sons, daughters and wives, all of them returned like that, then one day I picked up the whole bunch and went to Amitabh Menon's room.

'Who's going to bring them back?'

'Arre, Kusumjit, don't be so agitated. Sit down, will you have tea, or orange juice?'

'Sir, I feel terribly disturbed. These letters are supposed to be answered by you. Every day I read them helplessly. Please tell me, who is supposed to find them?'

'Not a line of Amitabh's fair opaque face stirred. He said, 'Kusumjit, you're young, inexperienced, you can't see the future. We're in a terrible crisis. You're losing sleep over these people; so many of *our* boys have needlessly given their lives, why can't you hear their wives' cries? We're crawling each day through this terrible conspiracy. Terrorist encounters each day. In all this disturbance, maybe a few came in our custody, is it possible to find them now?'

'The news bulletins were coming in on the terminal. Menon pressed a button—and the districtwise count started coming in. The numbers of officers and constables killed—during this month—twenty in one, ten in another, thirty in yet another. In a mild but solemn voice he said to me, 'Take a look also at these.'

'Swarup Singh in full uniform came into the room, saluted him, and took a seat. The smell of alcohol, sweat and blood seeping out of his whole body. Laughing, Amitabh said, 'Listen to what this crazy poet girl is talking about. Haven't you told her about Sanju's wife yet ?'

'Poets are a case apart, Your Excellency, what was the subject of your research in Oxford?'

'The influence of Eastern cultures on the West? Hah hah.'

'The two men's hearty laughter filled the whole room.

'I knew Sanju's wife. A young woman of twenty-five, wife of the police super of Garbatalao, recently widowed. With two small children. Out jogging one morning, Sanju was shot dead by assassins—at very close range. The story of Mili's untimely widowhood was written with a flourish in the newspapers. What wasn't written was that for some three months prior to that she had made her separate bed. Mili is a cousin of Tridib, my friend from college days. When he first joined this new post, Sanju used to seethe with excitement. The arrests, the encounters, liberating village after village. It was the joy of winning war that he wore on his forehead. The longer it went on though, the more tense and weary he became. There was no turning back. Towards the end, he began to spend increasing amounts of time in the torture chamber.' At home, he would get dead drunk. Mili's husband had proudly told her how a confession was extracted from the notorious terrorist Dipak—'His nails were torn off one by one—that's what it took!'

'You stood and watched this?'

'Watched? I had to get it done.'

Dipak's body was never found. He was a student, a third-year engineering student, who had disappeared from his hostel one day. Dipak's elder brother's wife sent someone from her village to hand-deliver a letter she wrote to Mili some time ago after being informed about Dipak by another student's father. 'Your husband is an SP, please try and see if the boy can be found.'

'Why do you act like this? As if you'd lose your job if you didn't do these things?'

'You don't know, Mili. We have to motivate each and every *sipahi*, sub-inspector, and inspector who's out there. Our battle is against darkness. Know what Swarup Singh says? Who's to stand by them if we back down in the name of principles? It's a personal commitment.'

'Sanju didn't even think of his two children's future! Two months later he was killed. So, it's not that I didn't know about Sanju!'

'At a party after a few days, the same topic again. I was sitting alone sipping a lime juice, when Swarup Singh materialized before me with four or five officers.

'Have you heard how Kusumjit the poet describes our campaign?'

Young Shamsher, his face red from agitation and the glow of beer, said to me, 'If in spite of being one of us, you say bad things about us, then what justice can we hope for from the outsiders?'

'There was a lot of talk then, jokes being flung back and forth. But, at the time, I just couldn't figure out who was spreading this poison against me.

'At one point I found myself alone again.

'After some time, Amitabh turned me away. Swarup was going around saying, 'If our boys get demotivated, then who's going to fight this battle?' There was discussion in the cabinet—some intemperate remarks also reached my ears. 'Export the Oxford stuff back. No need for it in this country.'

'Alone at the Barabani flat after a long time, I dusted the rooms. Then back to Sultangunj.'

It's now eleven at night, Sushen still isn't home. At this time, naturally, there's no one in his office, to pick up the phone. Mahua and Kusumjit are now sitting in the drawing room. On the centre table lies a little silver plate with cardamom seeds and paan arranged in it.

Maybe Sushen has gone to his club! He gets so carried away playing bridge that sometimes entire nights are spent there. Mahua's beautiful brows are gathered together in a frown. Absently, she has stepped out and is pacing under the portico. 'Why don't you stay the night here, Kusumjit?' She's shown no sign of getting ready to leave, though it's very late. Politeness requires that Mahua ask her to stay. She's really strange! She has stayed on for so long, yet hasn't asked Mahua a thing about her. Nothing at all about her son, her home life, Sushen's posting here. Has Dhananjay fed the terrier ? It's asleep cuddled under a thin cover, in its box, whimpering on and off in its sleep.

From the mosaic bathroom, Kusumjit emerges dressed in Mahua's kurta-pyjama. Since she is about four inches taller than Mahua, the kurta looks a bit short on her. Still, because of her slender figure, she actually looks quite nice in it.

Putting her fair feet up on the soft cushion of the cane stool, Kusumjit continues:

'The atmosphere in Sultangunj then could truly be described as having a picnic on top of a volcano. The Janabadi Morcha's secret bands had fanned out across the villages, throughout the countryside. Of the landlords, quite a few handpicked heads had rolled in the meantime. Rumours could be heard about some five men sighted below the hills in the evening darkness, carrying two AK-47s between them. Already, in many of the villages in those areas, specially in Haripura, Gadania and Gadalpur, there were factories that churned out country pistols. But until then, there had been no morchas of the landless. Nor of the marginal farmers. According to the intelligence report, it was after the preceding year's freedom congregation of bonded labourers that membership of the Janabadi Morcha suddenly soared. The closer it got to harvest time, the more widespread the tension about cutting the crops landlords had planted on lands that were State-owned or over the ceiling. A two-battalion force was dispatched from Barabani. Throughout the district in fact, the rumble of trucks kept spreading like caterpillars in night's darkness.

'I had come to Barabani for a meeting. There I got the news that in a press conference he called on short notice, Amar Mahato had announced that an interstate ring of extremists had been uncovered; that a youth arrested very recently had confessed under interrogation about the roots and branches of this ring. I was surprised. I had left Sultangunj only two days ago. How come I knew nothing of it? From where did this ring materialise? Worried, I called the office.

'The P.A. hurriedly said, "Madam, the criminal is held in the circuit house, not at the police station. Amar Mahato Saheb has given instruction that Madam should not visit the circuit house for two days. Some weapons, explosives, and so on have been found on him. The bomb squad was sent for yesterday."

'I was even more suspicious after hearing this. I asked the driver to head straight for the circuit house. Evening had set in when I got there. Outside the circuit house there was just the one iodine vapour light. There were four police jeeps waiting, the IG's car with the red light on top, and uniforms everywhere I looked. Seeing me approach, the crowd parted in two. Armed guards stood posted outside room no. 2. Pushing open the door, what I saw—'

'What did you see?' Mahua's sleeping nerves were suddenly jarred awake.

'You were asking me, Mau, why I've stopped eating meat and fish. Touching meat or fish reminds me of that night. A young boy was lying in front of the bathroom's Closed door. A slender, fair-complexioned boy with a thin beard and loose long brown hair dirty from dust. He had on a pair of jeans and a red-and-green check shirt, his hands were tied behind, his feet also tied up. The face was turned on its side to the floor, where two pools of fresh blood had collected, the nose still bleeding. On the point of pushing the door I heard a sharp moan, Amar Mahato had just moved back after dealing a booted kick to the boy's abdomen. A bottle and a glass stood on the table. Two police supers were inside, one from Barabani, one local. For an instant I felt dizzy, about to throw up … But next moment I recovered and shouted— "Stop! What are you doing?"

'The super Keshabnath rushed up to me, 'Madam, why are you here? Please, come outside.'

'I was furious. "In my circuit house, without my permission, how dare you, this boy—"

'Almost drunk, Amar Mahato came forward swaying, "Boy! Whom are you calling a boy ? Notorious criminal, an extremist with the Janabadi Morcha wing here—"

'The officer from Barabani said, "Assault weapons have been found in his bag."

'Where are they, I want to see.' Before they could get in my way, I ran to the corner and picked up the 'Adidas' bag. No, it had no bomb; you know what it had, Mau, a tube of toothpaste, men's underwear, a towel and a book, it was a play. Dropping the bag I shouted at them, 'Get out, get out of here.'

'Amar Mahato said, "Madam, we're forced to report your conduct. You've interfered with urgent government work. We're taking him to the police station. Sipahi, pick him up!"

'I said, "No, he isn't going anywhere. Until the time he's produced in court in the morning, I'm going to sit right here. The armed guard can stay inside the room."

'Keshab, who was my colleague and friend, in whose cool verandah I have so many times had tea and pakodas to the accompaniment of the tinkle of his wife's gold bangles, now said, "Madam, you're reacting terribly emotionally. This is a matter of keeping public order. If something happens tomorrow as a result of this, we'll lose our jobs."

'I said, "To hell with your bloody jobs." After I said this, they stood in a knot away from me but inside the room, and conferred with each other. After a while, that officer from Barabani politely approached me and said, "I hesitate to say this, but we've to take the criminal to the urinal for a bit, as it's a matter concerning whether he belongs to a particular community—".

'The boy, I still didn't know his name, Uttam, he was crying from pain, his face still down. I shook my head. "Whatever it is you want to check, do it here, in front of me."

'Then they left the room, leaving the boy there.

'Amar Mahato was swaying, he was fuming, and undeterred by any Janabadi Morcha ambush coming that very night, he went back to Barabani.

'With the sipahi's help, I got the boy's hands and feet untied and took him to the bathroom. Must have been badly injured inside his abdomen, he was spitting blood in the basin. A third-year student, he belonged to an amateur theatre group and wrote poetry.

'Why did you come here?' I asked him. Amar Mahato had earlier parodied my asking the same of him and sneered, 'Why don't you ask him what he's doing *here*?' To which I had said, 'Maybe next you'll ask what I'm doing here. I thought the Constitution guarantees a fundamental right of movement.'

'The boy was visiting, staying for a few days with a relative in Barabani, wanted to learn about the farm labourers' organizing in this area. That's why he was found wandering in villages. I took down the address of his sister and brother-in-law back home, their telephone number. Both of them were established doctors, running a large nursing home in Bakhtiarpur. Uttam was duly produced in court. They had no choice, because that very morning my press conference was held at the circuit house. The journalists were all there and most of what I said concerned human rights—which in their language was support for the terrorists. In three days, telex messages were received from the police branches of different states. No case pending against Uttam. Before I could organise Uttam's bail, Ramabatar Singh then took up the reins. He summoned me and said, "He'll be tried under the national security law."

'I said, "Impossible. Someone without a single police case against him in any state—"

'Then are you asking that I lose face? The interstate ring was mentioned in my press conference statement—'

'Why should I worry about that, I wasn't consulted beforehand, was I?'

'Kusumjit Kaur, your conduct is truly regrettable. This kind of narrow communal attitude—we didn't expect this from you. Because the criminal comes from your own community, you're today—'

'Sir, I see nothing regrettable in it. I can't accept an argument that because he's from my community I should let him be thrown in the fire. If he were a Bhumihar, would you have let him—'

'Shut up. You're overstepping the limits. You realise, don't you, that you can be transferred this very instant? Don't forget you're a district magistrate at the government's wish—'

'You're the one who is overstepping the limits. Do not implicate me in any plan to call a dog mad before shooting it. And I want you to know this. Kusumjit is a district magistrate at the wish of the government, but no power of government can break Kusumjit as a human being.'

'I marched out of the historical building ringed with huge lawns that now served as Ramabatar Singh's bungalow. The next morning I got the transfer order, inside an envelope, which lay very still on the tray cloth. Raju said someone came and delivered it in the night. I also read the newspaper headlines: the worsening law-and-order problem, my inability to deal with it and hence my transfer. Uttam was admitted to the hospital with abdominal wounds. There was a danger that gangrene might set in, so part of his intestine had to be surgically removed. After the surgery he lay unconscious with high fever on the dirty sheet in one of the hospital beds. I went there to see him. While I sat watching the ribcage of his thin chest rise and fall with his laboured breathing, some words from his drama book that I had glanced at in the circuit house that night floated back before my eyes

Today it's time to play with fire, Heer and Ranjha,
Sweetheart's face may be like the moon, still it's ice cold.
Today all around the barbed wires guarding our lives
The ground is on fire, in red-yellow flames of fire
And the tears have dried up into bits of hot cinders ...

'For several months after this I suffered terrible depression. I carried on with the work in a routine manner, yet the whole time my head was ready to burst with the tension. In the corridors, friends asked with barely suppressed smirks, "What went wrong?" All that I had believed the entire time seemed to be dissipating like smoke. Dalbir came up and made me go home with him. I had three sessions with a psychiatrist. But the problem did not get solved. On top of it, Mother was unwell; her old ischemia acting up. My parents were slowly getting worn down from worrying about my future. They began to put pressure on me, "Get married, you must get married. We want to see you married so that we can die in peace." One day there was a big fight. Father became furious and said, "You just have to get married, you aren't going anywhere until you do it. After that, whether you get divorced or do whatever you like, we aren't going to check on that."

'Then, did you get married?' Mahua asks, as if from the bottom of her fatigue. Her nerves are all drowsy, but curiosity does not allow her to give up.

'I did. I'm not going to mention his name. You people don't know him. He was a good prospect, actually. Plenty of money. Smart young man. Read poetry and stuff. Wanted to find out from me who was the nominee for my insurance policy. The day I took the decision to marry him, I knew the marriage was going to last just three months. In a manner as though I were walking on glass, I wore the bangles, put the glitter-spangled veil over my head, walked out of the beauty parlour in full bridal regalia. While putting the ring on my husband's finger, I thought, just three months to get through, that's all I've to do! Basically, I didn't have any need for a lifemate. All I needed was to find myself again. But my parents, my brother, my would-be husband, none of them let it be so. In four months I had managed to get a legal separation.'

It's now three in the morning. Mahua becomes listless with worry. Where's she going to search for Sushen? The night world sleeps with folded wings. Hospital emergency, police station, Mahua has none of the telephone numbers on hand. Yet, she must begin the search.

Kusumjit is distracted, her eyes on the wan moonlight outside the window. 'You know, Mahua, in the last ten years, I've grown really tired searching for answers to these two questions.'

'Ten years ago, I hated the fundamentalists. Now I'm afraid that perhaps I don't hate them any more. Perhaps they're the ones who have got it right, not I. Decay must have started somewhere at the very core of my identity. Otherwise, why would so many people question my integrity on the grounds of my religion, the community I come from, why do they push me away casting doubts on my objectivity? The effort I made in coming this far and to stick to human rights issues has been met with my getting labelled all kinds of things to do with religion and communalism in response. The other thing I've seen is: how endlessly eager people are to probe into what could be a single woman's talisman of protection. If she's not sheltered by a man, then everyone from the woman who gave birth to her to her flesh-greedy male friends, starts thinking she must have something wrong in the head, why should she want to live alone, she must have some sort of mental disease—'

In a voice now tearful, Mahua shouts at her. 'You're neurotic, totally insane. From eight in the evening you've been talking continuously, all of it one-sided talk. Sushen is still not home, and you don't have the slightest concern, no consideration, no empathy—'

With profound sadness in her voice, Kusumjit replies—'Don't worry about Sushen, Mau. He's all right, in suite no. 302 of the Sabera Hotel. I'm sure he'll be back home in the morning. He called me in Delhi even before I came here. He was happy to hear that I've a conference here. He said, "Mahua will be away for two days, we can spend a night together." When he heard that my divorce was final, Sushen said he was sorry. Still he said, "So, you're a free bird now." In other words, I'm there of course, easily available, and when Sushen has the time, when he's in the mood—he will be asking for my company. Twelve years ago, this girl had proposed to him, in a train compartment in the middle of the night—do you know of that, Mau? Pushing my eager, upturned face off his lap, Sushen turned me down, saying, "We've different religions, we come from different communities." He said that his carefully built cosy family of parents and brother and sister would be threatened. However, if occasionally I wished to have his company, he would have no objection to that.'

'And today, the cosy family of his is of no consideration at all. Especially when it comes to a night of union with a female body from a different religion. Mahua, didn't you go to your mother's?'

Bewildered, Mahua says, 'Believe me, he hasn't told me anything. Nothing about your posting, about your coming here. It was my son who wanted to go to my mother's place, so I sent him. I thought, it'd be a nice surprise for Sushen. To come home from office and find me here alone.'

With deliberate care, Kusumjit folds the clothes Mahua lent her for the night and sets them down. Putting around her head her own black-yellow striped snake of a scarf, she reaches out to touch Mahua's shoulder in farewell, 'So long!' Mahua stares at the darkness outside, listening to the night birds call faintly as if in a dream.

COMB YOUR HAIR, MY DEAR!

Mohan Bhandari

For me, it was nothing short of a miracle. You could even say, a bizarre incident. It happened on Wednesday. On 3rd of May 1989. My *chacha's* son Gulzar came from Calcutta. Accompanied by a Bengali old man. Name was Nikilesh Basu. Face wizened. Yellow teeth. On the nose rested thin, gold-framed, clear-glassed specks. Though he had only a few hair on his head, they were well combed. Dark brown. With streaks of white. He was wearing a *khaddar kurta pajama*. A *khadi* shoulder bag hung around his neck. It had two or three books, a newspaper, a towel and a comb.

Bapu's last wish was that on his death, neither tears be shed nor religious rituals observed. For *bhog* ceremony, no cards be printed or advertisements inserted in the newspapers. No one should be allowed to make speeches either. 'No one will have anything worthwhile to say. They'll just tie themselves up into knots ...' is what *bapu* had said.

Gulzar had told the Bengali old man that his *tayya* was a poet. A people's poet. He used to write in conventional meter. *Korha, Dorha, Baint.* All in all, he had left six manuscripts behind, '*Jan,* The quarrel between Tea and *Lassi,* The fight between the daughter-in-law and the mother-in-law, Morcha of *Jaito,* The *Malwai* Warriors, and The Well-dressed Women of Malwa.' Only one of these, *Jan,* had been published. The rest were lying unpublished. There were another three or four copies, which contained a couple of poems in an odd meter, and a few *hakimi* recipes.

In course of conversation, Gulzar had also mentioned it to him that I had been drawn into militancy. And on account of my militant activities, I had stayed underground for nearly three to three and a half months. Then having managed to wriggle out of this *chakravayuh,* I had returned to the compelling demands of domesticity. So impressed was he with whatever Gulzar had told him that he decided, on the spur of the moment, to accompany him, that too, in those very three clothes he was wearing on his body, then. The solemn air of the simple *bhog* ceremony, work-a-day gossip, simple, artless jokes of the villagers and their inoffensive ways of teasing or pulling each other's leg did impress him a great deal. Though my father was known to have led a rather sedate life, it was the revolutionary nature of his last wish that had left him totally perplexed.

People would come surging in, eager to meet this stranger from another State. Especially among the children, he had become a real cynosure. Though not quite fluent in Punjabi, he could still manage to speak it fairly well.

After some time I felt that he was taking a little more than ordinary interest in me. Listening to me, he would be all ears and occasionally narrow his eyes rather meaningfully, too. He was observing my speech, my gait, my interaction with other people and other such little things about my personal behaviour so minutely that I became somewhat restless. I was beginning to get a little suspicious about him. Deep inside, I was almost frightened. 'By thus keeping me under a constant vigil, was he trying to ferret some secret out of me?' I wondered.

'Come, let's get aside and talk,' I finally suggested.

'No, first let me talk to the village people about this, that and the other. Besides, your relatives are all here ... You *attend to* them. Serious stuff we'll talk at night ...' He narrowed his eyes, again.

'I hope this man isn't from some secret government agency?' Pulling him towards one side, very hesitantly, I asked Gulzar in all innocence.

Hearing my suggestion, he burst into laughter. Loud, raucous and uninhibited laughter. Then he said, '*Oye,* he's my neighbour ... an idler. Gets a very handsome pension. His wife died long ago. He has three sons. All of them are officers. Married and settled. And his income is simply unlimited. He's somewhat eccentric. All his time goes into reading and writing. He likes to rush into every such place in our country where militancy has reared its head; his shoulder bag conveniently slung across.

He meets up people, and visits their houses, too. I tried my best to explain to him, old man, just forget it, don't go to Punjab. If you land up in their net, they won't let you off the hook so easily. They'd just make mince meat out of you. But he simply refused to listen. In response, all he did was just bare his yellow teeth. For the past two months, he has been touring towns like Taran Taran, Patti and Batala. What he tells me is—'I'm doing a survey. Later, I'll write a book, *The Impact of Terrorism upon People.*"

I felt palpably relieved.

For a long time, both of us, the brothers, had chatted about him. And laughed, too.

That night, I had an interminably long conversation with Nikhilesh *babu.* The first thing that impressed me was the range of his knowledge. He was talking about the history of the Punjab, the character of the Punjabis, their habits and tastes with such ease as though he were a Punjabi himself. Though he talked with rare insight about the several wars of the Sikhs against the Mughals or the British, the smugness of the local overlords and their eccentricities, he appeared to have a special interest in the revolutionaries of Punjab. And now in the terrorists.

'Will Khalistan ever become a reality?' I posed a straight question.

'Is that your opinion?' It appeared as though he wasn't really prepared for this kind of a question. Narrowing his eyes, he meditated a little and said, 'Not like this ... though this is not something beyond the realm of the possible. But it's not going to make much difference to the people ... I mean, the common people.' He paused awhile, took a little breather and then spoke, 'Pakistan was also created. But come to think of it, what difference has that made ...?'

'Anandpur Sahib Resolution ...' I was about to initiate the discussion when he started nodding his head.

'It's all right. I've read all those documents ... now what's objectionable in them? Tell me.' Then he spoke on his own, 'No, nothing whatsoever.' He was talking with an air of self-confidence.

'May it always be a victory for the *Khalsa* ...? I picked up the main thread of his argument.

'That sentence?' He laughed.

'*Hanh!*' I was serious now.

'Who was responsible for drafting it? ... Anyway ... let's just concentrate on the main issue. And the main issue is that this doesn't appear to be a very sensible thing to say.... These victories are not to be proclaimed in this manner. This either happens or it doesn't. Wherever Khalsaji is ... that's where the victory always is.... Just look at any foreign country ... Why go far.... In Calcutta, they really dominate. Isn't it, Gulzar?'

Showing *off* his yellow teeth, he cast an eager look towards my *chacha's* son. Gulzar started laughing.

'*The Impact of Terrorism upon the People?*' Once again, I steered the conversation towards the subject of his research. *The Roots of Terrorism, Amritsar* ... my purpose in referring to these two, three titles was to create an impression that I had an academic interest in the subject as well.

He looked at me, searchingly ... narrowing his eyes, somewhat. Then his lips trembled ... as though the yellow teeth wanted to know, 'What have you read, really? It's all stuff and nonsense.' Then he spoke softly, as though Pooran was speaking from within the well. All I heard was:

'This is nothing but journalism; all so superficial. Pure romanticism or, at best, it could be classified as pure fiction. This is hardly research ... As far as I go ... well, I'm still trying to study the problem ... examining the issues!' He shot a sudden questioning look at me.

'Examination!' I laughed. 'Yes, examination is still on ...' He offered. 'Still, you must have come to some conclusion?' I was curious.

'Results?' he sought a clarification. 'Oh, yes ... the results.' With his hands, Gulzar made a gesture as though he were squeezing a lemon.

Either seeing him do this or listening to his words, he just broke into a smile. Then he came out with something, the gist of which is as follows:

It's always so very difficult to draw the final conclusions. Perhaps, even impossible. It is quite clear that the population of youth in all the terrorist-hit states is going to witness a precipitous decline. The ratio of women would increase proportionately. On an average, people of the future generations would lose, not gain height. And the stomachs of most of the people would puff-out like those of the pregnant women. Their eyes would shrivel up and shrink. Like the Chinese. Or they would slit open so much as to nearly pop out of the sockets. Deaf and dumb would become a common enough sight. The light of the sun would be so strong as to start scorching the eyes or the bodies of the people. People would slow down considerably, walk at a pace much slower than before. Their bodies would become much heavier, and more difficult to drag around.

People would be forced to walk, with their legs wide apart. Men and women would enjoy sex just like rats. Though darkness would appear rather alluring, the nights would be terrifying—everywhere the animal instinct would rule the roost. Cowardice would be on the rise among the people—and to cover it up they would resort to all kinds of mean and petty deeds. And often such acts of cowardice would be proclaimed as the heroic deeds. Trust would simply disappear. Suspicion would spread like a contagion. The only time people would display their courage is while coping with their cowardice.

And only on the *bhog* ceremonies would the fairs be held.

. . .

The next day, they tucked in *bapu's* manuscripts under their armpits. And set off. 'We'll publish them,' is what Gulzar had announced before leaving.

. . .

'My autobiography?' I had started thinking.

. . .

This was just one of the snippets. Now let me tell you how I was greeted when I returned home:

'. . . You son of a whore! You've really crossed all the limits . . . pushed me into the fires of hell! For which past birth are you wreaking such a vengeance on me? *Oye,* my flesh! You have disgraced us so thoroughly that now we can't even show our face to anyone . . . It's worse than life-in-death for us . . . You, seed of a whore! Bastard, he thinks no end of himself as a bloody *kharkoo* . . . '

Coughing and breathless, *bapu* had been reduced to tears all over again.

These abuses were hurled by my *bapu.* So I kept listening. Quietly. There was so much I could have also said or talked about. But who would have listened, anyway? Neither earlier. Nor now. Nobody would have paid attention to me, anyway. Nobody would have heard me out or nodded his head in agreement. Suddenly tears welled up in my eyes. Mother's memory came back with a vengeance. Had she been alive, she would have driven herself crazy, crying her heart out. She would have kissed my forehead repeatedly. She would have held me close to her chest, over and over again. She wouldn't have uttered a word. Even if she had, it wouldn't have been anything more than just this: 'O cursed one! What made you choose such a path? Why did you make me feel the heat of your separation?' And if somewhat irritated, she would have probably said, 'There are only three things in life that keep a man on the straight path—love, respect or fear ... just these three.' Perhaps, she would have wound up with some such parting shot as 'A *beri* close to a banana tree, bad company ruins many lives, my dear.'

Why did my *bapu* beat such a humble, gentle and affectionate mother of mine to death? Somewhere inside me, a deep sigh rose.

...

It was as though all hell broke loose.

Hellish days. Equally hellish nights.

The fifth night was on its way out. It was barely half way through. Perhaps, more than half of it was over already. That's when *bapu* was able to settle down a little. Hardly settle down? He was still tossing and turning. Sometimes, towards his right. Sometimes, towards his left. Then his loud, muttering sound rose: *'Oye,* Buddheya! Have you come? ... Get away ... stay back ... You bloody mother fucker ... khh ... khh ... khh ... *hai'*

Crazy *bapu!* Which age is he living in? Would he put up a fight against 'them' solely on the basis of such hollow assertions? After all, they're not the same boys who used to pluck muskmelons off the fields on the sly. Such pitiless, blind power! What mercy could one expect?

When finally she came, a mild tremor ran through my body. Then I collected myself. 'O you intelligent one, if she is the same person, we'll see what's to be done?'

A smile flickered on my plaintive lips. So much lay hidden behind this smile. Annoyance, anger, hatred, bitterness, sarcasm, complaint, ridicule and pride. As though someone were to first put one's own past on the palm and then start mocking it. And were to say: 'Take all this back! Whatever you gave me.'

Regardless of whatever the people say, it's not at all easy to shake off burden of the past. The past was now walking right behind me. Almost like a ghost. Sometimes it would appear to me in the guise of my *baba,* sometimes as a dust-smeared *sadhu,* or the usurious *bania,* and sometimes my mother or my elder sister. Occasionally, it would even appear to me in the guise of that agent who had, on the promise of sending me to Dubai, duped me of fifteen thousand rupees. All these faces that hovered before my mind's eye appeared to me to be 'the agents of God.' All of them arrayed at their respective positions. Doing their respective duties. What a bizarre *tamasha* is this? Here it's in the God's name that everything is usually done. Including coercion. Even the tolerance and patience to bear it. Grace, contentment and acceptance. Everything is in His name. But contentment is something I'm yet to see anywhere. This, too, must be His grace.

While I was still contemplating all this, smile flickered on my lips, yet again. Why feel annoyed at *bapu's* abuses. These were still straight and uncomplicated. But every time he muttered 'this new *kharkoo*,' and dusted his *chaddar off,* his words would get stuck in my throat. They were still stuck there. For the first time I realised how even a good word could sometimes turn into an abuse and pierce through someone's heart, almost like a bullet. That, too, a word your own *bapu* shoots off.

As I shook these thoughts off, my attention was suddenly drawn towards the room. Through the window, the moonlight was filtering in. In the alcove on the wall right opposite, the mirror neither lay sprawling on its back nor straight up. Reclining at an awkward angle, it could have easily slipped off and be reduced to smithereens. I felt enraged at my wife, Jeeoni. How lazy and indifferent she has become! Shards of the mirror could have easily pierced the hands and feet of the children, leaving them blood-spattered. Very likely that Pappu might end up stuffing one of these shards into his mouth. He was barely a year and a half old. Though innocent-looking Rimpi was much wiser. She was well into her sixth year. Holding Pappu's hand, she would have immediately chided him, 'O you fool, once you swallow a piece of glass, it's so difficult to take it out. Want to kill yourself? I'll tell your *bapu,* I …'

Jeeoni tuned over to the other side. In the moonlight, even her worn-out face appeared rather innocent to me. The hair on her head were all tangled up. Hardly a head! It was more of a wild overgrowth. The faces of Pappu and Rimpi appeared rather dirty and grimy to me. As though, these had not been washed ever. Every night, they must be crying themselves to sleep. What to talk of lullabies, they must not have been mollified ever. Such an indulgence is possible only in the good times. Who sings lullabies to the dark, inky nights? On such nights, lullabies simply die a quiet death. And my attention drifted again towards the alcove. The vial of collyrium was lying upside down. And pray where was the thin, collyrium glass rod? It appeared as though the comb had fungus on it. And the overhanging cobwebs were swinging freely in the air. I got up. And poured myself a glass of water out of a pitcher perched upon a platform. After drinking water, as I came to, I was suddenly reminded of something. Taking long strides, I walked up to the door. Standing on the threshold, I cast one longing look towards the moon. Then I immediately slammed the door shut. And returned to the bed. Lying there, I had kept turning my thoughts over for a very long time. Sleep was eluding me. I felt like waking Jeeoni up. But didn't have the heart to do it. For the past several days, she hadn't so much as spoken a word to me. All she did most of the time was sob her heart out. The children would stare at me as if I were a rank stranger. Fear lurking in their *eyes*. As though I was some devil. I understand all this. After all, I'm their father. It's a different eye that is often cast towards the fathers. Pure. Untainted. Soaked in affection. One that you would want to wink back at and say, 'O there you go!'

'What's this you've done?' Something inside reprimanded me.

'The new *kharkoo!* 'Again, something seemed to get stuck in my throat. I was peeved.

It did occur to me, once, that I should tell *bapu,* 'Why, you, too, had taken 'Amrat' against the wishes of your father. Had grown your hair. And taken active part in the movement for Punjabi Suba. Had faced the police atrocities and been beaten up as well. Had been to the jail also. You, too, were a 'new *kharkoo,*' then.' But I held my counsel.

It was because of me that *bapu* was tortured. For days on end, he was detained at the police station. Was beaten up. His turban came off. And the beard was pulled. All because of me. I don't know why but now whenever I'm in his presence, a sudden sense of inferiority overtakes me.

In his own times, he had been a poet, too. He enjoyed a good deal of respect as well. He would visit fairs and festivals. Or even hold special courts. In those days, *bapu's* face would be aglow, all the time. Among thousands of persons, the only one I had eyes for was my own *bapu.* Wearing a turban with a long, flowing tail. His hands covering his ears.

People would stand tiptoe just to be able to catch his glimpse. They would watch him, wide-eyed and listen to him with respect. But once the fair dispersed, *bapu* would become an ordinary person all over again. He wouldn't do much work. Nor would he get money from any source. Irritated, *baba* would often tease, calling him 'a shirker.' I could never reconcile to such a divide in my own thoughts. Was it really simple poverty or the lack of literacy or that of compassion and concern?

Sometimes I would think to myself.

Once he got his manuscript published. *Jan.* In those days, he just went ahead and spent as much as five hundred on it. He carried the book to the fairs. He sang the poems. People gathered. They listened and applauded. Tiptoeing. That time, *bapu* was hoping that the he would be able to sell all the copies. But he could barely manage to sell five or seven copies. Crestfallen, he came back to the village. On reaching home, he deposited the bundle on top of the grindstone. 'It didn't sell:' This was about all he could manage to utter, sheepish as he was.

Dragging in at his *chillum* and releasing a cloud of smoke in the air, Baba Burra Ram had mimicked him, grinding his teeth, 'Nothing sold!' Then in an exasperated tone, he had said, 'How would it sell? It's not something precious. Five hundred rupees down the drain. This son of a whore! ... Bloody good-for-nothing progeny!'

Hearing this, his *bapu* had sunk into the ground where he stood. He was the same person who never allowed anyone to outwit him. One who would hold the court right through the night and have the audience eating out of his palms.

. . .

And today, he was in such a situation. Who was responsible for it? It was as if I was reeking of inferiority.

'What have I ended up doing?' Somewhere inside, a deep sigh escaped me.

. . .

I presented myself. The village *panchayat* accompanied us. The respectable people of the village: Sadda Singh, sarpanch, Bhag Singh, the saw-mill owner, *Jathedarni* Daler Kaur, Pandit Brij Lal, Nagahi *bhagat* ... all of them forwarded an application after signing it, 'We stand guarantee for the good character and behaviour of Buddh Singh, son of Sadhu Singh 'Zakhmi,' grandson of Burra Ram, resident of Bahmani Nihangan ... and farther testify that he would put in an appearance in the police station as and when he's required to do so.' Then Pandit Brij Lal winked at *bapu.* *Bapu* followed him into the adjacent room. After a minute or so, the in-charge of the police station also walked into the same room, pretending to adjust his belt. All of them returned after about ten minutes. *Bapu's* face was looking somewhat like a flax spindle.

On their return to the village, *Jathedarni* said laughingly, 'Mal, what if you'd run into the police alone?'

Bhagat Nagahi was the one who responded on my behalf, 'It's as true as the broad daylight. Seeing his suspicious movements, the raiding police party would have challenged him. On being challenged, he would have fired a few shots at the police party in self-defence. In the return fire, he would have been killed on the spot. Under the cover of darkness, two of his accomplices would have managed to escape. From the encounter site, they would have recovered two or three Chinese AK 47 assault rifles, 249 rounds, one H.E. 36 hand grenade, one country-made pistol, and perhaps 51 or so empties ... and then a cash prize of twenty or twenty-five thousand announced on his head would have been given away ... and that would have been the end of the matter, my *bhai!* And my lion-hearted son would have lost his precious life for a price less than that of opium.' With these words, he gave me a warm hug and burst out crying like a child. As though he had managed to retrieve his own son from the jaws of death.

The poet's heart inside my *bapu* melted, too, as he suddenly became emotional. He rested his hand on Bhagat Nagahi's shoulder, as two tears rolling off his eyes silently got lost in his bushy, white beard.

'This is no matter, really. Encounters do take place.' I don't know from where I had been able to summon up so much of courage. Hearing these words, ten or twelve pairs of eyes had stared at me, all of a sudden.

He was the same Bhagat Nagahi who, several years ago, would not think twice before taking his pot shots at me. Once in all innocence, he had said, 'Which caste do you belong to?' I just happened to say, 'Carpenters ... the progeny of Vishwakarma.' Hearing this, he had first clapped loudly and then burst out laughing. Then he said, 'Ask Sadhu. The one who sits on the platform, stringing words together. Tell him to write poems on his family history.' After a while, he had shot another question, 'You've seen your grandfather, haven't you? Luckily, you had become quite a vagabond while he was still alive.'

'Yes, I do remember having seen him. He used to just sit around in the courtyard, smoking his *chillum.* And its *gurh—gurh* sound would be heard from afar. In his ears, he always wore earrings.' I said.

'In a way, well, what do I say, you must have seen it yourself that he always went around without too many clothes on his body. All that he often carried with him was a simple *khadi* towel, just the way Gandhi used to. He was somewhat allergic to clothes. Plenty of money he had to keep himself warm. Money is what he gave on interest to people. And often he charged interest rate, three or four times that of the market rate. He'd keep people's jewellery. Mortgage their property. In your house, gold was often weighed in the scales meant for weighing grains. We've heard that you have as many as four bricks of gold in your possession ...' Seeing his furtive glances, I first felt a little nervous, then frightened and finally started trembling. A lump had come into my throat. And just as I was about to break down, he had started patting me affectionately. He had caressed my face and back. A little later, after I had composed myself, I had pulled myself away, jerking off him as if stung by a bee.

'*Oye,* why don't you speak up, now? You're really very clever!' Running his tongue over his chapped lips, he had broken into a simpering smile.

I felt much lighter, as if suddenly several tons of weight had dropped away from me. That moment, it just occurred to me that I, too, should play some trick on him. If nothing else, I should, at least, set a scorpion inside his *dhoti.*

I had already resolved that under no circumstances would I disclose it to him that after *baba's* death, *bapu* had dug up every inch of the house in course of a single night. But all he had found from one of the corners of the house was a small wide-mouthed vessel. And it barely had two thousand rupees, stamped with the Queen's impression.

'It was Telu *bania* who actually used to lend money on interest, one who had been killed by the robbers.' I had tried to evade the feeling of inferiority. '*Bacchu,* robbers had attacked your house, too ... that's what claimed your *baba's* life, in fact. That's when he decided to drown himself in the river,' he insinuated rather meaningfully.

'But what do all these things have to do with 'which caste do you belong to'?' With a view to get rid of him, I had tried to distract him.

'Yes, that's right! We just started rambling. If you're scared of that 'poet,' then I'll tell you something. Your grandfather wasn't getting married. Once, he was caught red-handed with the daughter of one of those ... what do you call them ... those who go from street to street, riding the carts ... selling the kitchenware. It had really created a lot of ruckus. Finally, he had to marry the same girl. For a long time, they had continued to have dealings with each other as well. Do you know these cart-owners are supposed to be Rajputs? You are one of them.'

I was quite perplexed. I don't know when Nagahi Bhagat just slipped away from there.

That very evening, Bisheshar, son of the *brahmins,* and I were busy enjoying the swings on the banyan tree. It was late in the evening. Though the sun had still not set. While playing, we had started clambering up and jumping off the trees. Finally, we came and stood on the bank of the pond, not very far from the tree. We saw another banyan tree in the pond, as large as the other one. Sprawled as much as the other.

Bisheshar started saying in the manner of an adult, 'There are several banyan trees beneath this one. Underneath. Deep down, right up to hell. Their roots have spread all over, right from one end of the earth to another.'

Talking in this manner, we came and stood under the banyan tree. He looked up, 'Wow, that's great! Just look up through the leaves!' He said, his mouth wide-open. I did exactly what I was told. 'Can you spot the top boughs anywhere?' He spoke in the same tone. I made 'tch' sound with my mouth. As much to say, no. 'Now it's touching the sky. Almost like the tip on a storm's head … endless. Come on, let's play 'tree, tree.'… Just imagine that both of us are trees. Do you know where our roots are? In our ancestors. And as spirits, they keep roaming the heavens.' Then I don't know what occurred to him that he suddenly opened his mouth wide and screamed, 'Have you ever seen a woman naked?' Completely thrown off-balance, I said, 'No, why?' 'I've seen it, in that hutment over there. Where that ebony dark *sadhu* lives … your mother also visits that place at night.' I saw that somewhere between the mound and the cemetery, peering from behind a thick grove of trees stood that hutment playing hide and seek with the trees.

'She goes to deliver the *roti,*' said I, feeling somewhat exasperated. 'O yes, she must be going to deliver the *roti* … but why does your *bapu* always keep thrashing her? Like the grams, every day without fail? *Henh?*'

I was on the verge of tears. I had no reply to his query. That moment, I felt that I should go and drown myself in the pond.

'What are you thinking about? O you low-caste one! Fly off to your house. Night is about to descend. That ebony dark *sadhu* is going to release the witches soon … Tying their beards with the branches of this banyan tree, they'd dance here.' With these words, he simply vanished. I, too, took to my heels. And ran after him.

...

Almost a month after this incident, one day, Daler Kaur accosted me in the street itself. That time, she looked different from what she does now. Now she is as fat as a mattress. That time, she was young and nubile. Almost like the branch of a mulberry bush. Slim. She had been married for almost a year. Shouting *'deora, deora'* she would often come rushing in, wrapping me up into a warm, bear hug. Making me sit on her lap she would give such a tight hug that I would start screaming. Then she would pinch these cheeks of mine ... Oblivious of everything, she would start showering me with kisses. So much so that I would almost be blinded.

She was very friendly with my elder sister. What she regretted was why this sister of mine have to marry Duhajoc? She had remained married for barely a year. Then she died. Holding me close to her chest, she started crying bitterly.

'My parents, the cursed ones, have thrown me also on a moth-eaten *Jand*. Sitting in the hutment, he keeps churning his opium. That crazy fellow, who just needs about two bowls to lose his head - and then a handful of opium. Trust him to earn even a single penny! Let him go to hell, that stupid fellow ... thin as reed. No intelligence. Doesn't even die. My life would go by, just like that.'

She dragged in a deep sigh.

Then she struck the chord of memories again, 'One day, all of us had gone to town. Well, what did we buy, not even so much as a trashcan? All of us bought a *khaddar-crepe* suit each ... then *bhai,* we got ourselves glass bangles. Had some water from the pump. Started winding our way back, walking down the middle of the street. That's when your sister asked for *gol-gappas* worth one *anna.* And there she was pitted against your mother. Known to be extremely stingy. She kept saying, 'I'll treat you a little further down the road ...' Finally your sister lost her cool and said, 'O mother of mine, we're almost out of the bounds of the town, now.' So *bhai,* we had to reach the outer limit of the town and that we did. That was it. Jingling our bangles, we returned to our village ... now your mother often thinks back on those times and cries her heart out ... but time once lost can never be regained ... Your mother became a regular patient ... burdened by so many sorrows ... To top it all, there was this temperamental father of yours ... Could easily redeem hundreds like him ... liquor is, of course, something he had been having for a long time ... but now he began to hit the bottle rather hard. Besides, he started chasing other women, too. After all, grazing in someone else's manger doesn't always give one contentment ... the very same Santi, of the butchers ... Come on, the one who was married to one of the Mann's. Woman is a woman, after all!' As she said this, Daler Kaur, who had been crying all along suddenly started laughing, and seizing this opportunity, she pinched one of my cheeks as well.

...

'There we are, *hai, panchayato,* we've reached the village. March forward now!' Kehru, the *tonga* driver, caressed the back of the horse.

'On some days, you must roam the streets as well,
For the *baghi* is always parked in the courtyard.'

Brij Lal 'Dhidal' touched a common chord as soon as he disembarked from the *tonga*. We had reached the outskirts of the village. Nearing the main gate, where we were to go our separate ways, Brij Lal sidled up to my father and whispered into his ear, 'Sadhu Singha, the brick has already fallen into the well. Now nothing can prevent it from getting wet. Once you get arrested, you learn to take mere chiding in your stride ... Just marry him off now ... Sooner than later.' Once again, Sadhu's face turned ashen pale.

The very next morning, I overheard a few voices: 'You see for yourself, Sadhu ... and then come to a decision ... *Bhaiyaji,* this is the way things change with time ... He was to die, anyway ... But by joining hands with that *sadhu,* he's certainly ruined your life ... We've fallen on such bad times! Age is not respected any more. It just happened the day before ... early hours of the morning ... it was still quite dark ... dawn had barely cracked, *bhai* ... What would a stupid person like me know ... My embarrassment is so acute, I can't really get myself to tell you ... I had stayed awake the whole night long ... So in the wee hours, I thought, why don't I go and give fodder to the cattle... As I was walking towards the manger, a basket on my head, what do I see, but ... Now how should I tell you ... My younger daughter-in-law ... that lamb of a girl ... was lying, her legs entwined with that of the boy ... lost to the world. During the day time, when I tried to explain it to her, she tells me most unabashedly, *'Bebeji,* now times have changed ... You should have turned your face away and gone your way.' Peeping at my *bapu* through a veil half drawn over her face, Santi started again, 'Now, what should I tell you?' If you lift your shirt, you only end up exposing your own stomach … This daughter-in-law of mine is a real calamity … she's like a leaping flame … this daughter of a whore!'

On hearing this, the string of beads leapt out of *bapu's* hands. All he managed to say was: '*Waheguru! Waheguru!*'

Santi turned red, like an unripe gooseberry. Cool as winter. She said, '*Bhaaiya,* I had come to tell you … *bai,* you should thank God. That the boy has come back home, safe and sound. Thousands of dangers lurk all around. God forbid … if something unfortunate happened, you would condemn yourself all your life … By the grace of God, he's now as tall as you … has a family, too … And you are known to have a bad temper. Don't have a confrontation with him. Hold him close to your chest and hug him.' With these words she took her leave. Barely had she crossed the threshold when *bapu* first hollered loudly and then broke into punctuated sobs.

First I just kept lying in a somewhat determined manner. 'In a way, this man is a murderer of my mother and sister. I'm not going to speak to him at all.' It was as though resentment had arisen from deep inside me. But when he didn't stop crying, my heart started to melt. After all, he is my *bapu*. He had brought me up and had me educated. His support had made it possible for me to get a diploma in mechanical engineering from a polytechnic. It's another matter that I failed to get a job. It was around this time that I got obsessed with the idea of going to Dubai. Somehow found an agent. *Bapu* invested all the money. It turned out to be a fraud. And it took us quite some time to recover from it. Operating from a small factory inside our house, both of us would try and do whatever little work we could get. Together.

Technology was slowly making its way into our lives. We, too, were impacted by it. The *jats* went ahead and bought themselves tractors. Threshers began to be installed. Tubewells replaced the ordinary wells. All the traditional implements such as sickles, ploughshares, ringlets of the bullocks et al were rendered useless. The factory had to be shut down. I had some experience of the latest techniques. Despite the fact that I knew my job, I was at a loose end. Still, I refused to sit back, twiddling my thumbs. I started repairing the faulty machines. After all, I was a mechanic.

But *bapu* was not quite satisfied. All he wanted was hard work so that he could live it up. Worried on my account, he started to hit the bottle rather hard.

That's the time, acts of terrorism became a daily occurrence in Punjab. The railway stations were gutted. Every other day, eight to ten persons would be slaughtered. Then pulling people down from the buses, they started shooting them senselessly. The number of such persons began to rise ever so imperceptibly. Now, much before the sunset, people would shut themselves up inside their houses. What was really happening? And why? I just couldn't comprehend all this. Newspapers would be agog with the stories of how the divide among the Hindus and the Sikhs was becoming sharper, and how the terror prevailed everywhere. All this had us surprised. For in the villages, such things were nowhere in evidence. How could it, when it didn't exist at all? After downing a quarter or so, *bapu* would start letting off his steam. 'This calamity is actually the creation of the urbanites. They just can't digest their food. Swollen with self-conceit, bloody-hell! They're hungry for power. What else is it? Their internal squabbles have ruined the Punjab. They are into brokering power. And the ordinary, hard working people or labourers are the ones who are paying a price for it!' He would often talk in this manner for hours on end.

I was never a staunch supporter of religious orthodoxy. Though my *bapu* had been persecuted, even sent to jail twice, first during the Punjabi Suba agitation and then during the Emergency. But all this had not made a separatist out of him. In this respect, I really admired him for his convictions. In his own days, he was known to be quite a progressive person. And his white flowing beard bore testimony to this fact.

Then a major incident happened. Operation Bluestar. For a long time, the world attention had been focussed upon Harmandar Sahib. The army laid a siege to it. Pitched battle was fought. The *Akal Takht* was razed to the ground.

The village boys, who had already started wearing their beards loose just to be able to keep up with the Joneses, now wore saffron-coloured turbans as well. They would often call on me. With tears welling up in their eyes, they would ask, 'We've absolutely nothing to live for. These butchers have ruined us completely.'

I would listen to them attentively. Then assuage their feelings, saying, 'Doesn't matter, it'll be constructed again.' Hearing such words, they would be struck dumb.

'What kind of a Sikh are you?' Some of them would complain. 'He's a traitor.' Others would announce their verdict. Most of the people in the village had started condemning me openly. Young boys would sneak away to organise clandestine meetings. They had even started contemplating the possibility of eliminating me. All kinds of rumours had started floating around. Some would say, 'Sant ji is in Pakistan. He would show up at the right time.' Some would even say, 'Sant ji comes riding a white horse. At night. *Bai,* yours truly has been a witness to it, of course, in flesh and blood. *Morcha* must continue …' Several households would play his cassettes rather unabashedly.

I found all this rather strange and bizarre. Occasionally, I would think all to myself that soon enough the circumstances would become normal. It had to happen, anyway.

On the 31st of October 1984, all we got to hear on the radio was that our adorable Prime Minister Mrs Indira Gandhi had been shot dead by her Sikh bodyguards. I don't know why it felt as though the announcer was stressing the word 'Sikh' rather unnecessarily. This had me rather worried. All through the day, I had confined myself to the bed. I don't know where my thirst and hunger had suddenly vanished.

The very next day, I went to the house of Pundit Birj Lal. He did have a television in his house. I found that the main hall room in Pandit ji's house was jam-packed. With men and women. The women were busy watching the TV. And crying, sniffling through their veils. In the entire hall, I couldn't spot even a single Sikh from our village.

TV showed how the Prime Minister's dead body had been kept on a raised platform. And how people were queuing up for her last *darshana.* 'TV is really a blessing. The entire nation can pay its homage to its dear, darling Prime Minister, Priyadarshani Indira Gandhi,' I thought to myself as I peered somewhat harder. I couldn't spot a single Sikh on the TV as well. Though I did hear some slogans in the background, 'We demand blood for blood.'

It was as if something convulsed inside me.

'Where have they gone?' I asked Pandit ji

'Who, they?' Pandit ji stared at me somewhat differently.

Then almost everyone sitting there started giving me strange looks. In much the same manner. What kind of a look was this? I just couldn't get myself to utter a word. Looking into my eyes, they had probably sensed my fear. Until today, I haven't been able to figure out to why my tongue had stiffened that day. Why couldn't I get myself to utter the word 'Sikh.' I decided to beat a retreat. In sadness and dejection.

The newspapers came. All censored. The empty boxes almost appeared to be mocking right in the face of the people. Seeing these empty boxes, emptiness began to penetrate deeper into the souls of the people. It was as though each person was trying to fill up this emptiness with his own rumours. The rumours shrieked. Delhi, Kanpur, Jamshedpur ... and in several other Purs, too, the riots broke out. Clashes between the Hindus and the Sikhs. Thousands of people were killed, burnt alive and their houses set on fire ... Finally the people started staring rather hard at those boxes in an effort to recognise the faces. To find out as to what kind of people had died? Sikhs would say, Sikhs. And the Hindus, Hindus.

When I got to know that thousands of Sikhs had been killed, something snapped inside me, with a 'cracking sound.' It was 'terror.' The first danger-alarm.

My thoughts were diverted. And started moving off in a particular direction. And finally landed in a dark, narrow street. All other doors were shut on me.

Now I had started socialising with 'Kharkoo' Sikh youth. Outside the village. Someone, who had come from outside, was busy lecturing. Hearing his words, my hair almost stood on the edge. Then there was no looking back. An endless round of lectures followed.

I was beginning to get convinced that if we continued to be treated in the manner we were, soon we'd become an extinct race. We'd lose our identity altogether.

Meetings had become a daily affair. Every day, the same things were discussed. Coloured in the same thoughts. Apart from that, we just couldn't think of anything else. And finally, I, too, was soaked in the same colours.

After some time, all of us were taken to an undisclosed destination. And the schemes were made on how to 'eliminate' people.

I found myself in the middle of a seemingly insignificant confusion. All the members of our group were a determined lot. They were the kinds who could easily be trusted to act on the orders of the commander. And they refused to forgive anyone who either showed hesitation or mercy. Anyone who tried to beat a retreat from the chosen path was simply eliminated. I found one of them to be somewhat more gregarious than others. After I had won his confidence, once I asked him rather hesitantly:

'I've never killed a man in my life. What should I do?'

'This is hardly anything. I swear in the name of the Guru, it doesn't cause any qualms whatsoever. Just fire the shot. And that's the end of the story.' He was speaking with a disarming ease and spontaneity.

I remembered. Once after the riots, I had had to run an errand. To Ambala. The train journey. All the passengers seated inside the compartment were quiet. Even if someone did speak, it was in whispers. Terror-ridden whispers almost like deathly silence. Corpse-like faces. Tears suddenly welled up in the eyes of a lady who was sitting right next to me. Streaming down.

'What happened, *bibi* I asked out of a fellow feeling.'

'*Bharaji*, is that a way to kill really? Slow torture. First put a tyre around someone's neck and then set him on fire. Or to make someone drink petrol, and then light the match ...' I just couldn't bear to listen to her words, soaked as these were in sobs and tears. Pretending to be indifferent, I had started looking out of the window.

Deep inside somewhere, I almost felt throttled.

'Just fire the shot. And that's the end of the story.' How uncomplicated my companion was. He was doing his best to help me prepare psychologically. 'Go for at least two of these 'actions.' Don't shoot if you don't want to. Well, that's a concession for you ... this would help you overcome initial hesitation.' He laughed. Though I had never seen anyone of them laughing ever.

They took me along on one of their 'actions.' We were to eliminate the family of one of the informers.

We left at night. Knocked at the door. It opened. Four people shrank away, screaming their lungs out ... three women pleading with their hands folded... In less than a minute, all of them had been reduced to a heap.

'Kill this little one of the snake as well.' Though I was stunned, my attention was drawn towards a year old child. He was staring at us and smiling. His arms akimbo. As if he was saying, 'Lift me in your lap.'

...

We got our orders from above. That we have to strike in Delhi.

Our commander chalked out the programme, 'Look, all of you must proceed from here, one by one ... Even in Delhi you should stay at different places ... Don't even disclose to one another where you're staying ... The next morning at quarter to six, all of you should assemble... at such and such place ... Five of you ... That's where you'll get the 'ration' ... right on the spot ... After the 'action,' you've to deposit the 'ration' at such and such place ...' All the code-words were obvious enough. 'Ration' meant arms.

I made up my mind. I'll spend the night at my elder brother's house. At Pitampura. I reached there a day ahead of the appointed day. In the evening. I made assessment of the people around as soon as I got there. On reaching home, I was somewhat surprised. My brother was lying on the bed. All bandaged up. 'What kind of a driver are you? Why so many bandages? Are you all right?' I asked him, laughing.

'It was one of those accidents ... ! Was in the hospital. Only last week, I returned home ... now I'm much better.' He was spontaneous.

For the past few years, we had not even been corresponding with each other. Meeting was, of course, out of the question. But still with a great deal of warmth, he said, 'So, tell me, how is *bapuji* ...? And your children ... Is everyone all right?'

'Everything is fine.' I just summed it up in three words.

'You?'

'You can see for yourself ... as strong as a *tahli.*'

'And how's your work?'

'It's fine.'

He didn't have the faintest of notions about my activities.

'But ... how did this accident happen?' I expressed concern.

'Just like that ... Coming from the ring road as I neared the big *chowk,* my brakes failed. There was a large crowd—teeming right ahead. I just couldn't think of anything. Lo and behold! Steering the vehicle towards the left, I just rammed it into the pavement. Of course, some of the passengers did get hurt ... others had minor bruises.' He paused awhile. And stroked the wounds on his knees gently. Then he started off, again, 'It was *Waheguru's* intervention that saved the people.' Words were simply flowing out of him. Spontaneously.

'But just look at this ... how badly injured you're?' My
emotions spilled over.

'*Oye,* Singhs hardly ever bother about such things ... we take no
notice of such injuries.' He replied.

'Bloody hell, you should have ploughed through the crowd.' The
kharkoo within me thundered.

'*Oye,* how could I kill them ... so many people? Is this what the
dharma of a Singh is?' He became somewhat emotional as he spoke.

After the dinner, we went off to sleep. Before retiring, I told him
that I would be leaving in the wee-hours of the morning. As I have
some work.

The next morning I left the house. I was to catch an auto rickshaw
or a taxi from some place away from the house. In order to reach that
spot, I had to walk through a small garden. I was striding forth. The
words of my brother were trailing behind me, 'How could I kill them
... so many people? Is this what the *dharma* of a Singh is?'

I raised my arms overhead, piercing the air. Then I suddenly jerked
my hands backwards. And started walking on ahead.

I reached the garden. And started following the pathway running
through it. All around, the trees were steeped in silence. Loaded with
fruits. Multi-coloured flowers blossoming on them. The leaves were
... squarish, triangular, round, long ... pointing towards the sky. The
bright rays of the sun broke through them. like the smile on the face
of that child—who had hurled his arms towards us. 'Lift me in your
lap ...'

Slowly the rays embraced the entire garden into their fold. The
divine glow emanated from the leaves. A swing-like rainbow. I saw.
I stood rooted to the ground. 'Wow!' I don't know when this word
escaped my lips.

'What are you looking at? Son, these sights are for the living, not
the dead!'

I turned towards the voice. A seventy or seventy-five year old man
sat on a bench, smiling towards me, his head bent over the round head
of his umbrella.

I came to myself. And started retracing my steps.

'What happened, son? You're going back?' The old man called out
from behind.

'Yes, *baba,* I had strayed off the path.' It was as though the words had simply tumbled out.

In the evening, I returned home.

...

I got up with a start. Walked across to *bapu's* bed. And almost threw myself over him, squeezing him into a warm embrace. He, too, threw his arms around my neck. Our embrace was a long one. As long as several miles. This time, *bapu* neither sobbed nor sighed. All he said was:

'Budhe, we've really been caught in the cross-fire.' 'Don't worry, *bapu! We're* not alone. We'll see ...' I reassured him.

'All right, then, go and attend to your family.' He said. The dawn was about to break.

Wriggling out of *bapu's* embrace, I walked towards *Jeeoni's* bed. I looked at her face as she lay there, sleeping. Then sitting in front of her, I shook her a little.

'*Bhagwane,* it's time to be up, now! Just look at it, the day has already dawned. Sunlight is already filtering in.' I ran my hand over her head.

She got with a start. We looked at each other. Straight. Into the eyes.

'What have you done to your hair, Jeeoniye?' I don't know what was the sentiment behind my words. Love, longing, magic or command. Stretching out, she raised herself from the bed ever so slowly. On getting up, she walked across to the alcove. After cleaning up the mirror, she put it straight up. Then she lifted the fungus-infested comb. Cleared off the cobwebs. Set the *pihri* down. Then after sitting down on it, she started running the comb through her hair. Each time the comb got stuck in her dry hair or pulled at the skin of her head, tears would rise to her eyes.

Mesmerised, I kept staring at her for a long time. Then I said: 'What thick hair you've got?' Her eyes started brimming over with tears. Heaving a deep sigh, she said, 'There are all tangled up. And these knots would take their own time to untangle.'

MY BLEEDING PUNJAB

Khushwant Singh

In the last few years, I have got into the habit of keeping a diary on events in the Punjab. Some of the pages are reprinted here. They record ups and downs in the scenario, and my own corresponding swings in mood—often hopeful, more often despondent.

...

JUNE 1989

From the Punjab comes both good and bad news. First, the bad. Khalistani terrorists have picked up yet another target in their nefarious designs to divide Hindu from Sikh by concentrating their fire on the *Hind Samachar* group of papers published from Jalandhar and Delhi. That is not new because they have already killed the founder Lala Jagat Narain and his son Ramesh Chandra as well as some reporters. Now they have trained their guns on poor hawkers who distribute their papers. They are soft targets because they are unprotected: they do not have political bias; most of them can't even read the papers they hawk. Selling papers provides them and their families their *dal-roti.* Killing them is not going to kill the *Hind Samachar.* On the contrary, in all likelihood, more people would want to know what is it in the publications that the terrorists want to prevent their reading them. Their circulation, already much the highest in the region, is likely to thus go up higher.

The *Hind Samachar* group is accused of having an anti-Sikh bias. This is not true. They have an anti-Akali bias—which is altogether a different matter. I have had many differences with them. I think they were wrong in asking Punjabi Hindus to declare Hindi as their mother tongue, opposing the Punjabi Suba and supporting Operation Bluestar. However, since they felt they were right, they had every right to say so. That is what freedom of the Press is all about. At the same time, they carried everything I wrote on the language problem, the Suba movement and Bluestar without changing a single comma. Pressure was brought on them to drop my column, but they refused to give in. They regularly carry long, eulogistic articles on the Sikh Gurus and Sikhism. Next to *Ajit, The Hind Samachar* papers are the most widely read by the Sikhs. I hope they will not give in to this murderous blackmail.

Now the good news. In two different villages in the Punjab, gangs of terrorists were taken on by the villagers themselves without the police being anywhere in sight. And in both, the villagers beat their would-be killers to death. That's the kind of guts villagers have to show to rid themselves of this menace to civilised living.

And the best news of all was of the two young Sikhs who laid down their lives and prevented a massacre of Hindu fellow passengers travelling in the same bus. This was true heroism and the kind of martyrdom the Gurus would have blessed. Their names will be honoured for years to come. Meer Anees's lines are apt:

> *Sab hain Waheed-i-asr yeh ghul*
> *chaar soo utthey*
> *Duniya mein jo Shaheed utthey*
> *surkhroo utthey*

> All of them are unique in all times,
> Let this be bruited in all lands
> Wherever in the world men rise to
> lay down their lives for a cause,
> They rise again covered with glory.
> ...

DECEMBER 1990

It grieves me to note that our protest against the code of conduct for the media dictated by the so called Panthic Committee (no one knows how many there are) has claimed its first victim in the cold-blooded murder of

Rajender Kumar Talib, Station Director of All India Radio in Chandigarh. He was only doing his duty and had nothing whatsoever to do with the discussion that had been recorded earlier by the Delhi Radio Station between S. Sahay, ex-Delhi Editor of *The Statesman,* the retired Director General of AIR and Doordarshan and myself with C.S. Pandit acting as the moderator. All we said was that no one had the moral right to tell the media what it should or should not say—neither the government, nor proprietors of papers nor the public. Media people worth their salt have their own personal codes of conduct of which the most important is that they must never give in to pressure of money or power, nor knuckle under threats of violence. This so-called Panthic Committee had issued a diktat which required us, amongst other things, to use the honorofic Sant before the name of Bhindranwale and describe terrorists as freedom fighters for Khalistan. I remember when I was Editor of *The Hindustan Times*, I had issued instructions that the title Sant was never to be used with the name of Bhindranwale.

Bhindranwale was then alive. I have never used the title nor have any intention of using it in the future. As for the Panthic Committee's freedom fighters, I described them as *looteyrey* (robbers) because that is exactly what I think they are: killers of innocent men, women and children, abductors and rapists, living on extortion and smuggling of narcotics. It can be held against me that I am bold enough to say all this because I live in comparative security provided to me in the Capital. What about media persons in Punjab who are exposed to these gunmen all the time and have already lost over 150 of their colleagues to killers? There is little people like me can do for them except express our sympathy and solidarity. It is for the government to provide them better security so that they can discharge their duties without fear. The battle for the freedom of expression has to be fought to the bitter end no matter how many of us fall to the assassins' bullets. In the end it is we, wielders of the pen, who will win and not thugs armed with AK-47 rifles.

. . .

According to *The Statesman* of 22nd May, 1989, criminals who murdered Dr. Ravinder Ravi, writer and professor, in Patiala had four other names on their hit list: Playwright Gurcharan Singh Arshi, Editor of *Nawan Zamana,* CPI leader Jagjit Singh Anand, novelist Kulbir Kang, and myself. Although I have put my name last, I am apparently on the top of this mini hit list. According to leaders of the All India Sikh Students

Federation, the Khalistan Commando Force and Khalistan Liberation Force, our heads are to roll because of our 'anti-Sikh writings.'

I think it is time these killers were told in plain language what is and what is not anti-Sikh. At the risk of being accused of indulging in self-praise, I will start with myself. What the English-speaking world knows of the Sikhs, their religion, history and their achievements is largely through my books published in America and England. All the entries on Sikhism in the *Encyclopaedia Britannica* are mine. I, more than any other person, am called upon by foreign radio and television networks for comments on events in the Punjab, particularly regarding the Sikhs. I have never made myself out to be a man of religion but zealously retain my Sikh identity and am emotionally involved in the Sikhs fortunes. I condemned Bhindranwale because I regarded him as anti-Sikh; I condemned Operation Bluestar because I regarded it as anti-Sikh and anti-nation. I condemn terrorism because killing innocent people is condemned by our gurus as a sin. I make no distinction between Hindu and Sikh victims of violence: my heart goes out to the widows and children who have been deprived of their bread-earners and I do the little I can for them. I know our gurus would approve of that. I oppose Khalistan because I know it will spell disaster for the Sikh community as well as the country. There is nothing anti-Sikh about any of this.

The three other writers on the assassins' hit list are doing more than me in spreading the message of goodwill between the two sister communities. They do so at enormous risks to their lives because they too feel that this is what the gurus would have liked them to do and because they feel it is the best thing to do for the community and country.

And now let me tell our would-be assassins what is anti-Sikh. Killing an old *Jathedar* of the Akal Takht was anti-Sikh. Killing Sant Longowal was anti-Sikh. Killing Master Tara Singh's daughter, Bibi Rajinder Kaur was anti-Sikh. Hanging innocent Hindus was anti-Sikh. I could extend the list of their anti-Sikh activities to several pages. Those who committed these crimes disgraced their gurus and the religion they profess.

In spite of the massive security that surrounds me wherever I go, they came very close to getting me. The story unfolded itself when I happened to be holidaying in Goa two years ago. Armed police were posted in front and at the rear of my hotel room. Four men accompanied me when I went for a stroll on the beach. I protested to the D.I.G. Police of Goa against this unwarranted intrusion into my privacy. Very gently he explained why I needed so much guarding. The police officer happened to be the one who had interrogated Jinda who had murdered General Vaidya in Pune and then absconded. A year later, he was captured in Delhi. On his person they found a plan of my apartment showing the chair by the window where I normally sit to read and write. Jinda confessed that he had visited my apartment, gone to the kitchen to ask for a glass of water and taken a good look around to mark escape routes. He also admitted that he had followed me up to Kasauli but at village Garkhal, two miles short of Kasauli, felt he was being shadowed and returned to Delhi where he was captured. He is now under sentence of death for the murder of General A. S. Vaidya. He was asked why he wanted to kill me. He admitted that he knew very little about me and had not read anything I had written. But his bosses, who directed him, felt that I had to be eliminated because I was an enemy of Khalistan. Jinda was told that I would be an easy target and would evoke a lot of publicity.

I am not a brave man but being slain by a terrorist does not disturb my night's sleep. Manini Chatterjee of *The Telegraph* and *Sunday* came to get answers to a questionnaire drafted by her editor. The last question was, 'How would you like to die?' I answered quite candidly and without bravado, 'I would like to be shot by a Khalistani terrorist. At my age (77), a quick end would be preferable to wasting away with some old-age disease in a hospital. It would also give me the halo of martyrdom and the feeling that I had given my life to preserve the integrity of my motherland. Terrorist threats do not deter me, and many others like me, from writing what we are writing and doing what we are doing. If they succeed in getting us, I am sure many others will rise to continue this *Dharma Yudh* against these evil men.

HER DUE OF A DAUGHTER

K.S. Duggal

The crowd in the market was bursting at the seams—Hindus and Sikhs, both men and women, rich and poor, young and old, some buying and some bargaining. Somewhat amused, Malkiat watched it for a while. And then, perhaps as a reflex action, he took out his carbine and pulled the trigger. Tuck, tuck, tuck, an unending hail of bullets. Crimson-red blood gushing out of the dead and the dying splattered the market all over. After he had finished the magazine in the weapon, Malkiat took his finger off the trigger, and with total nonchalance looked around and then walked with a steady step towards his jeep which he had parked across the road under a *neem* tree. After occupying the seat, he put his hand in the right hand pocket to fish out his bunch of keys, switched on the ignition and drove away.

What to speak of anyone challenging him, none even dared to look at Malkiat. And it is not as though there were no policemen either in uniform or in plain clothes around. There were at least half a dozen of them, fully equipped, but the moment, Malkiat started shooting, they vanished into thin air, as it were.

He had not gone far on the main road when Malkiat took his jeep onto a *kachcha* road with a view to misleading those trying to chase him. Covered by the dust raised by his own vehicle, Malkiat continued to drive like mad. Before long, he had driven more kilometres than he cared to count. He was in Mand, the territory where the writ of the police had never run—the hide-out of the dreaded outlaws. Anyone from the establishment who dared to intrude into this territory never came back unharmed. Many of them were never heard of again.

After driving for an hour or so, Malkiat abandoned his jeep and, with his weapon slung around his shoulder, he entered a thick jungle covered by old trees and ever grown thickets.

Here Malkiat was safe and out of danger. He had left his vehicle on the *kachcha* track. In the event of his being chased, the security people were welcome to take possession of it. He couldn't care less. It hardly mattered. He, too, had filched it from the roadside in the town. If the owner was lucky, he would have his vehicle restored to him, otherwise the sub-inspector's family would have the pleasure of joy rides.

Sitting under the cool shade of a Gulmohar tree to rest for a while, Malkiat dozed off. He hadn't had enough sleep the previous night, or maybe he was too tired. He snoozed for quite some time. Suddenly he got up. He was perspiring all over. What a queer dream he had:

Malkiat's Khalistan had come into being. There was no Hindu, no Muslim, no Christian, no Buddhist, no Jain, no Parsi, nor any Jew left. There were Sikhs all around—long beards and unshorn hair tied in buns, orange-coloured turbans and *dupattas.* The *Khalsai* banners, the Panthic slogans, and shouts of the Sikh salutation—*Bole So Nihal, Sat Sri Akal.* A network of canals, but all canals overflowing their banks and turning the soil marshy with saltpetre all over, diminishing the prospect of a rich crop. Physical verification exercises in schools and colleges to ensure that students wore their shorts as prescribed by the *Panth* and that they carried a kirpan on their person. Smithies working day and night to make swords and steel bangles. Some saying their prayers, others singing holy hymns while some others engaged in drills and military manoeuvres. Some called themselves *Nanakpanthis,* some others belonged to the *Khalsapanthic* faction; and yet others who subscribed to the cult of 'Degh,' while others swore by 'Tegh.' Then they began to find fault with one another and started abusing each other. Slogans were raised all over. They started issuing statements against one another. Public meetings were being held to run down the rival group. Processions were being taken out to slander one and all. At one such meeting they came to blows. There were cases of assault on a procession. Then the sniping started. Their relations deteriorated to a point of no return. They were perpetually arraigned against one another. This gave their neighbours the opportunity they were looking for. One side helped one faction, the other started camps to train the youth of the rival party. And then all of a sudden, the bullets started raining. Blood was flowing from the wounds of the dead and the dying, the whole place was covered with corpses. But who was it playing this bloody Holi, as it were? It was Malkiat. How could it be Malkiat? And yet Malkiat it was. His height. His looks. It was Malkiat. And Malkiat suddenly got up. He was perspiring all over.

What a weird dream! Malkiat wiped his perspiration from his face. He also tried to wipe out the eerie images hanging before his eyes. How everyone was being slaughtered around him!

As he was trying to forget his dream, Malkiat noticed a leopard sneaking in a bush a little further away from him. It looked as though the leopard was about to pounce upon him. Malkiat picked up his gun and taking a quick aim fired a shot at the leopard. The shot missed the beast and it made good its escape.

Evidently, there would be more of shikar around. Holding his gun in his hand, Malkiat started to look for it. He had the rest of the day to himself; it was risky for him to be seen either on the road or in a habitation until it was dark. The police must be on the look-out for him.

Malkiat couldn't understand how the leopard had escaped his shot. It was hardly a few steps away from him.

What had become of his aim? Shame on him! And also shame on the weapon he was holding!

Again and again Malkiat wondered how he could have missed his aim. He went around looking for *shikar,* but nothing came his way. Up the hillocks, down the ravines, luck did not favour him. Malkiat was thankful for his silly dream; but for it, he would have continued to sleep and the leopard would have devoured him.

Malkiat wandered in the jungle the whole day. By now he was tired of roaming about aimlessly. He was also hungry. The evening shadows had already begun to lengthen. It was time he looked for a habitation where he could spend the night. Soon, he noticed smoke rising from a cluster of trees in the distance. As he moved in that direction, he heard the soothing noise of the chime of bells of the village cattle returning home at dusk. He quickened his step, and when it was about to get dark, after hiding his weapon in the bag slung over his shoulder, he entered the village.

It was not a village; it was a biggish town, linked with a *pucca* road. As he crossed the road he noticed a *Nishan Saheb* aloft a pole in a Gurudwara. He, however, decided he would not go to the Gurudwara if he could help it. Ever since the Operation Blue Star, Gurudwaras were under the constant surveillance of the police.

He must have some rest in a *dhaba* on the roadside. He was hungry. He must first eat and then decide where to spend the night. He walked to the first *dhaba* he came across and went and sat on a *charpoy* under a tree.

He drank some water and then ordered a meal. As he was waiting for the *dhaba* boy to bring him his tray of food, he was suddenly taken aback, someone came and put his hand on his shoulder from behind. It was Tarsem, one of his close friends. He took him along to a rented room inside the *dhaba*. 'One who has killed twenty-five people in the morning must not be seen sitting on the roadside,' he whispered. There were five other militants sheltered in that room.

The Government had announced an award of one lakh of rupees to anyone who would help the police in apprehending Malkiat. The announcement had been made on the radio several times during the day. They had also been announcing Malkiat's description time and again. The first thing his friends asked him to do was to change his clothes and put on the dress of a local peasant.

Jodianwala was the name of the town. His fellow-militants had planned to loot the local bank first thing the next morning. Malkiat might as well join them.

Jodianwala! Malkiat heard the name of the town and it rang a familiar bell in his mind. He remembered that Banto, a girl from their village, was married to a youngman in this town. She used to be their neighbour. Malkiat was in a queer predicament. How could he loot a bank in a town where a girl from his village was living? What would she think when she comes to know of it? He would not be able to show his face to his own village folk. No, he was not going to join them in this adventure. Malkiat was having one drink after another but it seemed to have no effect. He was in a great dilemma. How could he harm anyone in a town where a girl from his village lived?

When Malkiat told his companions what was bothering him, they agreed to let him be. He need not join them. They appreciated his

predicament. A young girl from one's village is like one's own daughter
and a daughter deserves every consideration.

In the meanwhile, they saw the regional news bulletin on TV. The
killings in the morning were the lead story. They showed Malkiat's picture
also. The announcement of the award was made when the grim visuals
of the slaughter were being shown. His companions filled their glasses
again and drank to his health. It was something only a man with Malkiat's
nerve could have done. They kept drinking till late in the night.

The next morning his companions, after having their bath and reciting
Nitnem (prescribed daily prayers), set out on their mission. Malkiat did
not go with them. He sat on the rear verandah all by himself.

Malkiat couldn't forget the fact that he was in a town where a young
married girl belonging to his village lived. He could not possibly leave
the town without giving her something. He must meet her and give her
a present, no matter how small. It was a must.

Malkiat remembered Banto's wedding. What a large marriage party
the bridegroom's people had brought. Some of them had stayed at their
house. The members of the marriage party had to be put up with relatives,
friends and neighbours. And what a charming doll of a bride Banto had
turned out to be! She was only a stripling at the time. Hardly thirteen.
She must have grown up by now. She perhaps even has some children.

She used to call Malkiat *Veera* (brother). He had once climbed a
Beri tree and had shaken its branches for her to gather the *bers.* Coming
down the tree, Malkiat had his hands and arms full of bruises because
of thorns. But to see Banto giggling with joy made him forget all about
it and he had walked away happy and contented.

His companions should be back soon after completing their task.
In the meanwhile, Malkiat thought he would go over to see Banto and
fulfil his duty as a brother of the girl from his village. Malkiat found out
the address of Banto's husband and left for her house.

He did set out for Banto's house but Malkiat never came back.
Everyone in the town knew him. His picture had been flashed on the TV
the previous night. Every child in the street was talking about him.

A NEW POLITICS OF RACE
India and its North-east

Sanjib Baruah

I

There was a time when the peoples of North-east India were described as belonging to the Mongoloid race.[1] Today Mongoloid and other racial categories such as Negroid or Caucasoid—and indeed, the very idea of

---

[1] The term 'Mongoloid' is especially unfortunate because of the association of the term in medical science with mental retardation. When in 1866, John Langdon Down observed that a group of children with mental retardation (Down's syndrome) shared certain appearances and characteristics he described them as 'greatly resembling people of the "Mongoloid race".' Down described one child as follows: 'The boy's aspect is such, that is difficult to realize that he is the child of Europeans; but so frequently are these characters presented, that there can be no doubt that these ethnic features are the result of degeneration.' He could explain the so-called Mongoloid features of the retarded 'Caucasoid' child only by a process of degeneration. Medical practitioners continued to use the terms 'Mongolism' or 'Mongoloid' well after biologists had abandoned racial categories. But in 1965 when the World Health Organization awarded a prize to the British geneticist Dr. L.S. Penrose for his contributions to the understanding of 'mongolism,' the delegation from Mongolia, that was now a member of the World Health Organization, quietly protested the use of the term. WHO then stopped using these terms (Leshin, 2003).

race as a biological category—have no standing in scientific circles. For there is more diversity of gene types within what was once thought of as a single 'race' than between 'races'.

But while race may no longer be accepted as a scientific category, it does not mean that human beings would stop making distinctions based on stereotypical phenotypes or skin colour. Arunachalis, Assamese, Garos, Khasis, Manipuris, Mizos, Nagas and Tripuris may indeed have some phenotypical similarities related to genetics. Thus one may be able to say that someone is from North-east India based on looks, though he or she may not always get it right. For 'human populations ... possess a wide genetic potential which increases in variation through chance mutations or new generic combinations in each generation. ... Completely stabilised breeding isolates ... are exceedingly rare' (Bowles, 1977, cited in Keyes, 2002: 1166). And of course, most of us realise that what we think of as the 'North-eastern looks' are not unique to peoples from the region. For instance, peoples from the western Himalayas— those from Nepal or the Uttaranchal—might share features similar to those found among peoples in the eastern Himalayas.

Race as a social category is the product of practices. There are visual regimes of labelling, and individuals encountering those labels from childhood may internalise characteristics associated with those labels and learn to adapt to the socially constructed racial order.

African-American intellectuals have long recognised the role of visuality in the politics of race. The writer bell hooks—even her way of writing her name without capital letters is an intervention in the regime of visuality—describes her project as one of 'resisting representation' and of constructing an 'oppositional gaze'. 'We experience our collective crisis as African-American people', she writes, 'within the realm of the image' (hooks, 1992). The project of black liberation, for her, is thus a battle over images.

The Indian image of the troubled North-east is increasingly mediated by a visual regime constructed by popular films, television, pictures in magazines and newspapers, and limited contacts with people from the region. Thanks to improved communications, Indians today are quite mobile; and North-easterners travel to other parts of the country more than ever before. There are a large number of students from the region in Delhi, Bangalore, Mumbai, Pune, Kolkata and other cities. They are now a 'visible minority' in a number of university campuses. A disturbingly large number of them tell stories about their experiences of being racially labeled as 'Chapta' (flat-nosed), 'Oriental' or 'Chinky'.

A large number of North-east Indian young women are employed in upscale restaurants and shops in Delhi—their 'Oriental' looks and English language skills being considered desirable for these positions. Many of them live in ethnic ghettos, for instance, renting rooms and apartments in *'lal dora'* areas: the urban villages of Delhi. Apart from rents being affordable, they feel physically safer than in upscale neighbourhoods. Compared to landlords in elite neighbourhoods, these landlords of more modest means are tolerant of North-east Indian eating habits—for example, fermented dry fish, beef chutney and pork: and they are less inclined to impose restrictions on the lifestyles of their tenants. However, racially marked niches in the labour market or in settlement patterns have the danger of reinforcing racial thinking. Incidents of violence against North-east Indian women in the country's capital may partly reflect the racialisation of the divide between the mainland and the North-east.

While many North-easterners travel to the mainland, thousands of Indian soldiers and members of the various paramilitary organisations make the reverse journey to the region to fight external threats as well as on counter-insurgency duties. In the streets and paddy fields of the region security forces stop and interrogate North-easterners every day. The soldier himself faces an unenviable situation: the most peaceful of surroundings can quickly turn hostile and he has to be alert against possible offensives by militants. Some sort of racial profiling becomes inevitable under these conditions, especially since we have no laws prohibiting it. As Indian soldiers return home, their stories of 'treacherous' rebels hiding behind bamboo groves and jungles spread through friends and relatives. . . . The shared visuals of this regime provide ways of putting those stories and faces together.

North-east India's fractured relation with the mainland has been described as a cultural gap, an economic gap, a psychological gap and an emotional gap. The shared visual regime now carries the danger of this fault-line becoming racialised.

II

Mani Ratnam's film of 1998, *Dil Se,* is a love story between a woman militant from the North-east and an All India Radio journalist. The male protagonist, Amar, played by Shah Rukh Khan, travels to the North-east to speak to fellow citizens for a radio programme to celebrate the fiftieth anniversary of India's independence. He develops a relationship with a local woman Meghna, played by the Nepalese-born Manisha Koirala.

If Bollywood gossip is to be believed, Manisha Koirala was chosen for the role partly because of her 'small eyes'. Director Mani Ratnam, according to Aishwarya Rai, 'definitely wanted a small-eyed girl in *Dil Se*. She had to have that kind of physical features as she was supposed to be from Assam' (Rai, 2000). The cast of *Dil Se* also included a number of Assamese actors, among them film-maker Gautam Bora, who played the role of the chief of a militant group.

The film's story[2] unfolds between Indian independence or August 15, the fiftieth anniversary in 1997 and the Republic Day on January 26. While the All India Radio reporter, Amar, embodies the Indian nation, Meghna represents the horrors of life in the North-east torn apart by insurgencies and counter-insurgency operations. Amar defends the nation against rebels bent on tearing it apart.

The North-east of *Dil Se* is a dangerous place where women are raped and families are destroyed. Life in Delhi could not be more different: the file portrays it as a middle-class city where tranquil family life and traditional family values prevail. Meghna in the nation's capital is a danger to both nation and family. She is on a suicide mission to blow herself up at the Republic Day parade. As a guest at Amar's home she is an awkward presence at a time when the family prepares for his arranged marriage. 'Had it not been for the army, the nation would have been turn to shreds,' says Amar to Meghna. It is 'your nation, not mine,' says Meghna in defiance.

Am I making too much out of a film? Perhaps. But what if we are beginning to look at people from the North-east through the prism of a visual regime exemplified by films like *Dil Se*? What if after nearly half a century of counter-insurgency, the counter-insurgent gaze is framing our way of seeing people from the North-east?

[2] This and the following paragraph borrows a few ideas from the discussion of the film by Priya Joshi in the course material she provides for her course on 'Nationalism & Popular Hindi Cinema' at the University of California, Berkeley.

Films like *Dil Se* and pictures in newspapers and magazines enable people to put together a mental picture of the North-east and its people. The gaze of the Indian army patrol, reinforced by films like *Dil Se*, gives meaning to what it is fast becoming a racial divide.

III

There are signs that we are slowly beginning to recognise this new politics of race though we seem to be as yet unsure whether to use the 'r' word. A Manipuri journalist wrote in a national daily that, 'physically the people of the North-east are closer to Southeast Asia and China. However, 'this *racial* divide,' he said, is not appreciated 'in a sensitive manner' (Singh, 2004). The journalist told me that the 'r' word was edited out at one place in the printed version. He had actually written, '*racially* the people of the North-east are closer to South-east Asia and China.' Apparently the editors substituted the term 'physical' for 'racial'. However, his second usage of the 'r' word—in racial divide—remained in the published text.

Let me turn to a small sample of writings by North-easterners who have been students in mainland India, recalling their experience of being seen as different and encountering racial labels. 'I did my schooling in a boarding school in India,' recalls a Manipuri living in Kuala Lumpur, Malaysia. He was the only student from the North-east in that school. He posted the following on an email discussion group: Being the only minority I was subjected to many racist comments. ... The one that I still remember clearly was my being called 'Chapta' (flat-nosed for the fortunate ones who never heard the term) The word 'chinki' ... is peddled around with not even a little thought of whether the term could offend someone, by even my closest friends. I came in contact with some Mayangs (the Manipuri term for other Indians) here and it shocked me that despite my being there amongst them they refer to the other Asians as chaptas still with no consideration that I now find it offensive. Even on my bringing up the issue they just laughed if off saying they saw nothing offensive in it. So I have now resorted to referring them as 'Pakis' and that really seems to anger them. For those who don't know about it, 'Pakis' is a racist term used in Britain to refer to people with the sub-continent features (Pakistani, Indian, Srilankan etc.) So the next time you hear any Mayang using the word chinki or chapta, call them a 'Paki'. I think once this word gets common usage as a term to refer to them by all people of the North-east they will finally realize what it is to be referred by a racist term (*Manipur Diaspora*, 2004; cited in Ray 2005).

In Kuala Lumpur, he wrote, because of his features he had a hard time convincing people that he was an Indian. He got tired of explaining that he was from India since he 'didn't look like the Indians they knew'. On the other hand, he said, he was 'able to melt into the crowd and it was easier making friends with the Chinese and Malays' (*Manipur Diaspora,* 2004; cited in Ray 2005).

At a seminar in Pune a Naga student joked that after coming to Pune he became 'half Naga, and half Indian', while he was 'a complete Indian' before. He elaborated that in Pune, shopkeepers, doctors, teachers, and government officials, everybody treated him as Japanese or Chinese because of his features. He was asked to show his passport when applying for admission to college (cited in Das, 2004). While doing fieldwork in Manipur, anthropologist Sohini Ray asked a young student about his first visit to Mumbai. He told her that 'the first thing he and his companions found difficult was that every other person asked them where they were from, and stared at them.' When they said Manipur, people asked where it was and if it was really in India. To avoid such uncomfortable encounters, after a few days they started saying that they were from Thailand, because 'it was more convenient' (cited in Ray, 2005).

An Assamese woman describes her first year as a student in Delhi University (1996–97), as follows: 'I didn't look "Oriental"—the politically correct term they'd devised in lieu of the derogatory sounding 'chinky'. So I didn't have to face some of the stupider questions. My friend from Mizoram was asked if she needed a passport to come to India. The "Oriental" looking among us,' did not have to go through hazing, she recalled since 'Indians are always nice to foreigners' (Goswami, 2004).

IV

The emergence of a racial label to include all 'indigenous' North-easterners fits nicely with the category 'the North-east' that since 1971, in the words of a retired senior civil servant who played a key role in designing this political order this has 'emerged as a significant administrative concept … replacing the hitherto more familiar unit of public imagination, Assam' (Singh, 1987a: 8). In 1971 a number of the new states were created (though not all of them were states at the beginning), and another piece of legislation gave birth to the North Eastern Council (NEC). These two laws were 'twins born out of a new vision for the North-east' (Singh, 1987a: 117).

Unlike the distinction between tribal and non-tribal that is an important part of our vocabulary in discussing the North-east, the racial label has the advantage of including all those who belong to the troubled region, and are perceived as being connected to the troubles. For instance, a majority of the plains people of Manipur and Assam are not 'tribal' which, after all, is an arbitrary governmental category. However, the Assamese and Manipuri insurgencies are among the most potent in the region. Thus the distinction between tribal and non-tribal is not very useful when it comes to discussing insurgent North-east India. Since tribal and non-tribal North-easterners share certain stereotypical phenotypes in common, the racial label has become more functional.

The racial label incorporates meanings that predate the era of insurgency and counter-insurgency. Willem van Schendel, writing mainly with Bangladesh and the Chittagong Hill Tracts in mind, comments on the 'remarkably stagnant view of the hill people' that has prevailed in South Asia. The classic nineteenth century Western assumptions about social evolution from a state of savagery to civilisation was superimposed on the ancient South Asian distinction between civilised society and nature. The later distinction, indicated in the categories *grama* (village) and *aranya* (forest), implies a relationship that is complementary but always unequal. These two traditions, writes van Schendel, combined to generate a dominant view that considers the tribal peoples as remnants of some

hoary past who have preserved their culture unchanged from time immemorial. Backward and childlike, they need to be protected, educated and disciplined by those who are more advanced socially (van Schendel, 1995:128).

The visual label of race that transcends the colonial categories of tribal and non-tribal and reaches out to pre-colonial categories such as the *Kirata* people—used to describe the people of the periphery—may now give a new lease of life to some old Indian prejudices.

Responsible Indian officials, have from time to time used the metaphor of children to describe the peoples of North-east India. In February 2004 the Mizoram Governor, A.R. Kohli, described the entire region as a spoilt child. Contrary to the charge that the North-east is 'the most neglected region,' he said it is 'in fact, the most spoilt child in the country'. The central government, he said, 'showers funds and other goodies' liberally on the region. But the funds are not properly utilised or they do not reach the intended beneficiaries. A news report paraphrased the governor as comparing the region 'to a petulant child who is showered with goodies but does not know what to do with them' (*Telegraph,* 2004).

Such sentiments are also found in the language used by B.P. Singh, the former civil servant who played a key role in the creating of the North-east as an administrative category. In an article published in 1987, he concluded:

There is no tangible threat to the national integration ethos in the region despite the operation of certain disgruntled elements within the region and outside the country. But in the context of a history of limited socialization and ethnic conflicts, and rapid modernization after 1947 the unruly class-room scenario is likely to continue in the region for years to come. (Singh, 1987b: 281–2).

'Unruly class-room' is a telling metaphor. In the North-east Singh seems to imply, what is needed is a paternalistic and disciplinarian teacher—someone who knows what is good for children and, occasionally uses the stick for their own good, the role that he probably sees the coercive apparatus of the Indian state playing in the region.

These passages smack of attitudes and habits of mind that long predate the politics of counter-insurgency. But while these prejudices are old, they have acquired new meaning in the context of India's failed policies in the North-east. While Singh's metaphor of an 'unruly class-room' rationalises the coercive response to insurgency, Kohli's description of the region as a 'spoilt child' expresses the frustration with the failures of a policy of nation-building through corruption, or what Jairam Ramesh calls 'using corruption as a mode of cohesion' (Ramesh, 2005:18).

V

What are some of the consequences of the racialisation of the divide between India and its North-east?

MOTIVATION FOR MILITANCY

According to Manipuri intellectual and politician, Gangmumei Kamei, a major motivation for joining insurgent groups in Manipur is the social discrimination that young Manipuris face in different parts of India because of their appearance (cited in Ray 2005). Race has been a factor in the Meitei religious revival movement of the 1940s as well. Some revivalists converted to the newly formed faith 'only after returning from pilgrimages to Mathura and Brindavan, where their South-east Asian features raised curiosity and animosity among the local population.' The racial divide, according to anthropologist Sohini Ray, is central to understanding the Meitei urge for constructing an alternative history. A constituency for an alternative geneology emerged when 'the whole idea of sharing a common ancestry with the people who are hostile to them for their looks' became unacceptable (Ray 2005).

PERPETUATING A DIVIDE

While official narratives about counter-insurgency view each North-eastern insurgency as distinct, the racial label disrupts this narrative. As a result the differences between political conditions in different parts of the North-east have no effect on popular perceptions about the 'disturbed' region, since racial thinking does not allow for such distinctions. For instance, the Mizo insurgency that ended with a peace accord in 1986 is usually portrayed as a success story. Yet that did not mean that Mizo relations with mainland India are any different from that with other parts of the North-east. Even today Mizos such as Laltluangliana Khiangte complain about mainstream India not understanding their culture and traditions, and about Mizos being mistaken as South-east Asian tourists in the national capital (cited in Singh, 2004). After nearly two decades of a peaceful Mizoram, as Manipuri journalist Khogen Singh puts it, Mizos 'still don't feel fully at home outside the North-east' (Singh, 2004).

HIJACKING OF COUNTER-INSURGENCY

There is evidence that the racial divide sometimes subverts counter-insurgency operations; and they get hijacked for other purposes. For instance, it was reported that in the Karbi Anglong district of Assam Indian security forces, ostensibly there to deal with the security threat posed by insurgencies, became partisans in local land conflicts between tribal Karbi and Hindi-speaking settlers. The settlers Karbis refer to as Biharis had over time acquired informal control over what is formally designated as public lands, and had consolidated a 'considerable amount of economic and political power'. They now seek formal change in the status of those lands and formal land titles (MASS 2002: 11–13). In Karbi Anglong's ethnic configuration and the growth of insurgency, the loss of land by Karbis to 'Biharis' is a factor. Many Karbi young people have come under the influence of the United People's Democratic Solidarity (UPDS). But in local armed land conflicts, because of racial solidarity, 'Bihari' settlers have occasionally secured the informal backing of Indian security personnel stationed in the area to fight the UPDS (MASS, 2002: 21).

FACILITATING MILITARISATION

The racial divide facilitates the relentless militarisation of the region. Consider for instance, the recommendation to strengthen Indian military presence in Manipur made by E.N. Rammohan, a senior Indian police official who was Advisor to the Governor of Manipur. In order to stop the penetration of the government departments by militants, Rammohan recommended that battalions of the Central Reserve Police Force (CRPF) should guard all government offices and the residential neighbourhoods housing central and state government officials in the state. Furthermore, he recommended that ten battalions of the Central Para-Military Force (CPMF) be deployed in the Manipur Valley in a 'counter-insurgency grid'; and six to eight battalions be deployed in each hills district, where roads are few, with 'helicopter support to effectively dominate them' (Rammohan, 2002:15). Were it not for the racial fault-line it is unlikely that such policy options would have been seriously considered.

LEGITIMISATION OF CORRUPTION

The leakage of funds allocated for North-east India's development can be best described as insurgency dividend. The figures are staggering. Jairam Ramesh estimates that the annual expenditure of the Government of India on the eight states of North-east India, including Sikkim, is about Rs.30,000 crores a year. With the region's population at about 32 million, he estimates that the government annually spends about Rs. 10,000 per person in the North-east. This money is not going into development. In Ramesh's words, it is going to ensure cohesiveness of this society with the rest of India through a series of interlocutors who happen to be politicians, expatriate contractors, extortionists, anybody but people working to deliver benefits to the people for whom these expenditures are intended.

A surer way of improving the economic conditions of the intended beneficiaries, he suggests, might be for the Indian government to open bank accounts and deposit an annual cheque of Rs.10,000 for every poor family in the North-east (Ramesh, 2005:18-19).

The racial divide facilitates the sharing of the insurgency dividend between local political and bureaucratic elites, and outside contractors and suppliers. Not unlike western businessmen who justify bribing politicians and bureaucrats in the Third World in terms of local norms, the image of the North-east and its people in this new visual regime is that of a modern frontier where corruption is just a part of the natural landscape. Even the 'chinky' students from the North-east in Delhi, after all, appear more 'modern,' 'westernised' and affluent than many of their mainland peers, apparently confirming the corruption-friendly image of the region. It is hardly surprising that when it comes to doing business in the region, 'make a fast buck and run' appears to have become accepted practice. Even today's much-lowered levels of inhibition and moral compunctions do not apply to India's modern but wild North-east Frontier.

VI

Things did not have to turn out this way. As an Arunachali minister once said at a meeting in Mumbai, 'Why can't you think that in a big country like ours a few people may even look Chinese? Come to Arunachal Pradesh, he said, people in areas bordering China will greet you by saying *Jai Hind*' (cited in Das, 2004).

In everyday conversations North-easterners resist mainland India's representation of the region. But intellectuals, artists and activists will have to develop what bell hooks calls an oppositional gaze. Khasi commentator Patricia Mukhim believes that because of its geographical location, policy makers in Delhi think of the North-east primarily in terms of its 'strategic importance'. The region, she suggests, is treated as 'enemy territory, which needs to be subdued by force'. But 'you cannot buy allegiance with force,' she warns and calls for 'an entirely new approach' to the region (Mukhim, 2004).

A new approach must start with the domain of representation. Our policies have an impact on the way the North-east and its people are represented. For instance, softening our international borders—opening up the region on the east and the north, and encouraging close cross-border interaction—can slowly change perceptions. The region seen as a gateway to a friendly transnational neighbourhood will evoke very different emotions than those of a frontier or an 'enemy territory'—a danger zone where foreign and domestic enemies conspire against the Indian nation. Policies that could transform the South-east Asia within India into a dynamic gateway to the South-east Asia of world political maps. This could be the foundation for a new social contract between India and its North-east. This could radically change what it means to look North-eastern in India. The battle for the future of North-east India is also a battle over images.

REFERENCES

Bowles, Gordon, *The People of Asia,* New York: Scribner, 1977.

Das, Arup Jyoti, 'The Half-Indians' (Unpublished essay), 2004.

Goswami, Uddipana, 'Misrecognition' (Unpublished essay), 2004.

hooks, bell, *Black Looks: Race and Representation.* Cambridge, MA: South End Press, 1992.

Keyes, Charles, 'Presidential Address: 'The Peoples of Asia'—Science and Politics in the Classification of Ethnic Groups in Thailand, China and Vietnam,' *Journal of Asian Studies* 61 (4) November, pp. 1163-1203, 2002.

Leshin, Len, 'What's in a name The 'Mongol' Debate,' *Down Syndrome: Health Issues,* 2003 (website) http://www.ds-health.com/name.htm (accessed 16 September 2005).

Manipur Diaspora, 2004, Manipur_Diaspora@yahoo-groups.com Archives, e-mail No. 367.

MASS (Manab Adhikar Sangram Samiti), *And Quiet Flows the Kopili* [*A* Fact-finding Report on Human Rights Violation in the Karbi Anglong District of Assam] Guwahati: Manab Adhikar Sangram Samiti, 2002.

Mukhim, Patricia, 'Life under Martial Law,' [Shillong Notes]; *The Telegraph* (Guwahati edition), 21 September 2004.

Rai, Aishwarya, ''I've not come here looking for fame,' Interview by Kanchana Suggu http://www.rediff.com/entertai/2000/mar/29ash.htm (accessed 16 September 2005), 2000.

Ramesh, Jairam, 'North-east India in a New Asia,' *Seminar* (550) June 2005, pp. 17–21.

Rammohan, E.N., 'Manipur: A Degenerated Insurgency,' in K.P.S. Gill and Ajai Sahni (eds), *Faultlines,* Vol. 11, New Delhi: Bulwark Books and the Institute of Conflict Management: 1–15, 2002.

Ray, Sohini, 'Boundary blurred? Folklore/Mythology, History and the Quest for an Alternative Geneology in North-east India' (Unpublished manuscript), 2005.

Singh, B.P., *The Problem of Change: A Study of North-east India,* New Delhi: Oxford University Press, (1987a).

——, 'North-East India: Demography, Culture and Identity Crisis,' *Modern Asian Studies* 21 (2): April: 257–82, (1987b).

Singh, M. Khogen, 'As Indian as You and I,' *Hindustan Times,* 10 September 2004.

The Telegraph 'Governor Slaps Spoilt-child Tag on North-east,' *The Telegraph* (Guwahati edition), 14 February 2004.

NATIVE LAND

Robin S. Ngangom

First came the scream of the dying
in a bad dream, then the radio report,
and a newspaper: six shot dead, twenty-five
houses razed, sixteen beheaded with hands tied
behind their backs inside a church . . .
As the days crumbled, and the victors
and their victims grew in number,
I hardened inside my thickening hide,
until I lost my tenuous humanity.

I ceased thinking
of abandoned children inside blazing huts
still waiting for their parents.
If they remembered their grandmother's tales
of many winter hearths at the hour
of sleeping death, I didn't want to know,
if they ever learnt the magic of letters.
And the women heavy with seed,
their soft bodies mown down
like grain stalk during their lyric harvests;
if they wore wildflowers in their hair.
while they waited for their men,
I didn't care anymore.

I burnt my truth with them,
and buried uneasy manhood with them.
I did mutter, on some far-off day:
'There are limits', but when the days
absolved the butchers, I continue to live
as if nothing happened.

WHEN DEBATE HAS NO ROOM

Niranjan Chakma

Grass leaves here
clad in pungency of gunpowder;
Lies the spiritless body of a gang raped
hill woman on the lobby of a *Jhum Tong*.

And of course,
The frantic movements of
some aberrant youths, up for autonomy
Completely changes the meaning of . . .

Hither and thither
Dirty tricks of gunpowder traders everywhere.
Terror grips you often,
Conscience takes the other way then.

Is that all?
Now terrorism is a cheap commodity
Perhaps cheaper than a child's toy.

So, no more anxiety—
No more questions.
It is high time—

POETRY IN A TIME OF TERROR

Robin S. Ngangom

There is no such thing as an innocent bystander. If you are a bystander, you are not innocent.

—Czeslaw Milosz

I wrote my first faltering line in the relative innocence of childhood. I was about eleven or twelve years old then, and caught as I was in the flush of youth, I wanted to explore the world by writing ornate and sentimental poetry. Since life was ignoring me, I thought I could engage the attention of kindred hearts through friendly and softhearted verse. Naturally, my poems were mostly inspired by romances and adventure stories, especially *The Thousand and One Nights,* but it was essentially dreamy-eyed adolescent stuff. I still haven't grown out of it.

One favourite poem of mine began with these lines: The boy stood on the burning deck. That well-meaning world is no longer recognisable now; the sacred landmarks have disappeared long since. Only dim memories of hoisting the country's flag on a holiday, or leading a blind man by the hand, or praying in temples on a feast day, remain as mute reminders of that sacred past. Manipur, my native place in Northeast India, is in a state of anarchy, and my poetry springs from the cruel contradictions of that land. Manipur boasts of its talents in theatre, cinema, dance and sports. But how could you trust your own people, when they entrust corruption, AIDS, terrorism and drugs to their children?

Naturally, the Manipur that I ritually go back to from the laid-back hill town of Shillong every year is not the sacred world of my childhood, because

> *Childhood took place*
> *free from manly fears*
> *when I had only my mother's love*
> *to protect me from knives,*
> *from fire, and death by water.*
> *I wore it like an amulet.*
> *Childhood took place*
> *among fairies and weretigers*
> *when hills were yours to tumble*
> *before they became soldiers barracks*
> *and dreaded chambers of torture.*
>
> *Childhood took place*
> *before your friend worshipped a gun*
> *to become a widowmaker.* [1]

Having acknowledged this growing restlessness within myself, poetry became an outlet for pent-up feelings and desires, where I can bare myself without actually being demonstrative. Poetry, therefore, has remained an underground exercise with me. It perhaps began as a dialogue with the self, and has become an illegitimate affair of the heart, because I believe in the poetry of feeling, which can be shared not cerebral, intellectual poetry which is inaccessible, and which leaves the reader outside the poet's insulated world. I suppose I've always tried in a naive way to invite the reader into my small world. Perhaps I've written poems because I've felt this desperate need to be understood, and to be accepted:

> *I want to describe myself again and again*
> *to people who do not know me.*
> *That is why I always look for paper and ink,*
> *even in the midst of a terrible loss,*

[1] Robin S. Ngangom. 'A Libran Horoscope'. Unpublished poem, 2000.

or, a dangerous illness.
Because someone said
the spoken word flies
but the written word stays.[2]

In many ways, my own Meitei culture, which is part of my childhood, has shaped my thinking. Perhaps we all mourn the fate of our homeland, as the Sicilian poet Quasimodo has said. And though I've never remotely imagined myself as any conscience-keeper, I've often tried to speak of my people, and of the terrible things happening in Manipur:

First came the scream of the dying
in a bad dream, then the radio report,
and a newspaper: six shot dead, twenty-five
houses razed, sixteen beheaded with hands tied
behind their backs inside a church
As the days crumbled, and the victors
and their victims grew in number,
I hardened inside my thickening hide,
until I lost my tenuous humanity.

I ceased thinking
of abandoned children inside blazing huts
still waiting for their parents.
If they remembered their grandmothers tales
of many winter hearths at the hour
of sleeping death, I didn t want to know,
if they ever learnt the magic of letters.
And the women heavy with seed,
their soft bodies mown down
like grain stalk during their lyric harvests;
if they wore wildflowers in their hair
while they waited for their men,
I didn t care anymore.
I burnt my truth with them,
And buried uneasy manhood with them.

[2] 'I Want to Describe Myself'. Unpublished poem, 1995.

I did mutter, on some far-off day:
There are limits, but when the day
absolved the butchers, I continued to live
as if nothing happened.[3]

But it may be mistaken to see only geographical, or cultural, or linguistic differences. I don t agree with the view that a writer requires a tradition to lean upon, to till the soil which others have made fertile, and harvest ideas for himself. A writer can be influenced by anything, and he would be able to write in any country other than his own. But he has to reclaim his individual voice. It is natural for someone from the Northeast of India to exploit the folk traditions he grew up with, to write of the hills when he is living in the hills. It is Shillong that has moved me into this kind of poetry, Shillong with its gentle hills, the Khasis with their rich oral literature:

I told you the stories of old
on soft Sundays, of Manik Raitong
and Ka Likai. Only the stones of unknown gorges
weep for them, I said.

We awakened sleeping melodies
and talked of native lands,
and my foolish youth.
Where the pines
read the lips of the wind
and silent rain drums the hills,
the cottages dry their eyes
and open them in the dusk.
The land of the seven huts,
they've named these hills.
You would belong here
if you would listen to your heart.[4]

[3] Native Land. In *New Statesman & Society,* London, 14 July 1995, p. 41.
[4] 'I Told You the Stories'. Unpublished poem, 1992.

If I had not made use of this hillworld, my poetry would have been false. You would notice this preponderance of images from the hills in many of my poems the vast pines, the mountains with their great rains. But this, I've realised, is mostly artless, inoffensive poetry.

For someone who has suffered from a fundamental poverty of experience, I ve been naturally inclined towards the personal lyric. I don't have faith in inspiration, but since poetry cannot originate in a vacuum, I've also left my influences open, and have allowed myself to be ambushed by political events, books, biased memory, a dogged sexuality, womankind, films, streets even. But my poetry seems to be drifting towards something more. It is no longer a mere diary of private incidents, or a confessional. I've been trying to come to terms with this change of heart, which is even more distressing than the shattered love of a woman. And I've perhaps opened my eyes to insistent realities and have stepped out of the proverbial ivory tower. If anyone should ask now why my poems do not speak of my land's breathtaking landscapes, its sinuous dances, its dark-maned women, I can only offer Neruda s answer: Come and see the blood in the streets![5]

The writer from Northeast India, consequently, differs from his counterpart in the mainland in a significant way. While it may not make him a better writer, living with the menace of the gun does not permit him to indulge in verbal wizardry or woolly aesthetics, but is a constant reminder that he must perforce master the art of witness.[6] Forces working under slogans that have been twisted, slogans such as self-determination, rive my society. We have witnessed growing ethnic aggressiveness, secessionist ventures, cultural and religious bigotry, the marginalisation of minorities and the poor, profit and power struggles in government, and as a natural aftermath to these, the banality of corruption and the banality of terror. Further, the uneasy coexistence of paradoxical worlds such as the folk and the Westernised, virgin forests and car-choked streets, ethnic cleansers and the parasites of democracy, ancestral values and flagrant materialism, resurgent nativism and the

[5] Pablo Neruda. 'I'm explaining a Few Things'. In *Selected Poems* (Penguin Books, 1985, Harmondsworth).

[6] Michael Ignatieff. 'The Art of Witness'. In *The New York Review of Books,* Vol. XLII, No. 5 (23 March 1995).

sensitive outsider's predicament, make the picturesque Northeast especially vulnerable to tragedy.

And what can a poet-aspirant do in such contrary circumstances, when he can no longer nurse a magical vision of the world? For the first time, I've begun to understand Camus's words: Whatever our personal weaknesses may be, the nobility of our craft will always be rooted in two commitments, difficult to maintain: the refusal to lie about what one knows and the resistance to oppression.[7] Today, when cruel suppositions are made about the conceit of the artist, innuendoes that the poet has become a world unto himself and should be brought to his knees; when there is a sharp divide between modish criticism and literature, when literary schools are merely reactionary and seem to be turning their eyes from what is known as the human condition, I would again like to reaffirm my indebtedness to my fellow men. Today, when heartrending events are happening all around a poet, when all he hears are chilling accounts of what man has done to man, how can he close his eyes to the brutalisation of life and remain solipsistic? Anyone with even an iota of conviction is in immediate danger if he speaks up; a gun points at you if you don't observe a prescribed code of behaviour! how then can I claim that I am living in a free society?

In contemporary Manipuri poetry, there is a predominance of images of bullets, blood, mother, the colour red and, paradoxically, flowers too. A poet from Imphal told me of how they've been honing the poetry of survival with guns pressed to both temples: the gun of revolution and the gun of the state. Hardly anyone writes romantic verse or talks about disturbing aspects of sexuality because they are absorbed in writing the poetry of survival. This has resulted in criticism that contemporary Manipuri poetry is hemmed in by extreme realism. There is, of course, a danger of the images listed above becoming hackneyed. And maybe poets should try to strike that fine balance between realism and reflection, as Israeli poet Yehuda Amichai skilfully does in The Diameter of the Bomb. The opening lines of this poem read like statistics and a news report that we often ignore as we go on with our daily lives: The diameter of the bomb was thirty centimetres and the diameter of its effective range about seven metres. And in it four dead and eleven wounded. But the lines that follow make us reflect on lives obliterated by violence; they reveal

[7] Albert Camus, Nobel Prize acceptance speech, 1957.

how violence transforms men and women, regardless of nationalities; and also how such mindless acts make one reflect on the indifference of a god who, if he exists at all, should never have allowed his creation to be erased or reduced to an absurd drama. But poets also have to write about the here and now. And writing about it lends a sense of immediacy and vividness to their poetry. I call this the poetry of witness. Reviewing the Chinese emigre writer and 2000 Nobel laureate Gao Xingjian's work, translator and critic Mabel Lee comments: Alternatively, the nonconformist could remain in conventional society and survive by feigning madness or could achieve freedom, transcendence and self-realisation in literary and artistic creation[8]. In Manipur, when the reality becomes oppressive, a few poets frequently seek refuge in absurdist irony often directed towards oneself, in parody, and in satire. It is a rejection by these poets of the extreme realism I've mentioned; they in turn, also reveal an inclination towards the surreal. In Manipuri poet Y. Ibomcha's Story of a Dream, murderous bullets turn into luscious fruits, and in Thangjam Ibopishak's I Want to be killed by an Indian Bullet, terrorists appear in the guise of the five elements. This kind of verse is a reaction to the absurdity of violence and death, when the Manipuri poet's existence is reduced to negotiating the subject matter of guiltless addicts, child soldiers, and young mothers with AIDS.

Literature that is not the breath of contemporary society, that dares not transmit the pains and fears of that society, that does not warn in time against threatening moral and social dangers such literature does not deserve the name of literature; it is only a facade, claims Alexander Solzhenitsyn. But here lies a paradox, because the writer is not beholden to anyone, let alone to society. He must be true only to his own world and to himself. A writer is not a self-assigned conscience-keeper. Living in society, he will talk about his milieu, the people with whom he is in touch with daily. But you cannot expect a writer to consciously promote, say, ethnic harmony, as a part of his writing programme. You cannot expect a writer to be a public relations official on behalf of any organisation, or a propagandist for any cause. On the other hand, there

---

[8] Gao Xingjian. *Soul Mountain* (Introduction), transl. Mabel Lee (Perennial/ Harper Collins, 2001).

is often a defiant and self-damaging streak in him that sometimes incites him to confront authority. When in 1964 Joseph Brodsky was asked by Soviet authorities what he did for a living, he replied that he wrote poetry; he was immediately arrested on the charge of social parasitism. Is the writer a social parasite or a conscience-keeper for his society? One thing is certain he values his freedom above everything else, and will protect it fiercely.

I think the task that literature of the Northeast must address is what Albert Camus called the double challenge of truth and liberty. Truth, because what can the writer hope to accomplish now except to tell the truth? When the unspeakable is out there, being enacted and quickly consigned to oblivion, when cruel things are done but never undone, and when media machines are busy feeding the world one-sided lies, the writer can only tell the truth about what he knows. Literature cannot bring harmony or a moral revolution by telling us what we must do. And forces are always at work to rob the writer of his freedom. Liberty, therefore, is a necessary precondition, which the writer must fight for in order to tell the truth he knows; freedom is the lifeblood of his art.

During these pessimistic times, the responsibility of the writer is much more modest than what well-meaning people would like him to shoulder, that is, to change the world into a better place through his efforts. But at most, poetry of the Northeast can only mirror the body and the mind of the times, as in Thangjam Ibopishak's Poem:

> Now, in this country
> One cannot speak aloud,
> One cannot think in the open.
> Hence poem,
> Like a flower I sport with you.
> Before my eyes, incident upon incident,
> Awesome, heaving events,
> Walking, yet sleeping,
> Eyes open, but dreaming,
> Standing, yet having nightmares;
> In dreams, and in reality
> Only fearsome, shivery instances.
> So around me, closing eyes,

Palms on ears,
Moulding the heart to a mere clay object,
I write poems about flowers.

Now, in this land
One should only think of flowers,
Dream about flowers,
For my little baby, my wife,
For my job,
To protect myself from harm.

Surrounded as we are by playthings we don't need, when a man's worth is determined by what he can buy, we are continuously taught to be grateful to the capitalist god. What we have inherited then are the tyrannical fetishes of market capitalism, murderous technologies, and grisly ideologies that would leave a cursed earth for our children. How can poetry sing the praises of this age, or compose hymns to Mammon? For me, poetry can never be an ally of this numbing materialism or a party to mindless violence. Materialism, wherever it abounds, begets a particular kind of terrifying alienation, for the simple reason that we forfeit our ability to love when we place commodities above our fellow men. And someone who cannot love is always alone.

These hostile forces have often compelled poetry to burrow deeper into itself; it has retreated into its shell of obscurity and isolation. In such precarious times, writing poetry is always a defiant gesture that poets make against power and money, insensitivity and terror. Poetry cannot help anyone to get on in life, or make a successful human being out of anyone. But poetry should move us; it should change us in such a manner that we remain no longer the same after we've read a meaningful poem. For all these reasons, a poet can never be a conformist. He may not be an anarchist, a nihilist, or an inquisitor, but by the token of his verse, he is a natural dissident. Czeslaw Milosz questions the efficacy of poetry in his Dedication: What is poetry which does not save/ Nations or people?/A connivance with official lies/ A song of drunkards whose throats will be cut in a moment. But he will also not espouse his native language or champion his people s cause unquestioningly. As he says in My Faithful Mother Tongue:

Now, I confess my doubt.
There are moments when it seems to me I have squandered my life.
For you are a tongue of the debased,
Of the unreasonable, hating themselves
Even more than they hate other nations,
A tongue of informers,
A tongue of the confused,
Ill with their own innocence.

Poetry is always an act of subversion. And paradoxically, the poet is perhaps the most ironic realist. No more for him the security of an ivory tower or the temptations of Utopia. In Who Is a Poet, the Polish writer and poet Tadeusz Różewicz offers with certitude an ambivalent definition:

a poet is one who writes verses
and one who does not write verses
a poet is one who throws off fetters
and one who puts fetters on himself
a poet is one who believes
and one who cannot bring himself to believe
a poet is one who has told lies
and one who has been told lies
one who has been inclined to fall
and one who raises himself
a poet is one who tries to leave
and one who cannot leave

Each word must be fashioned from a private hurt, and writing poetry is like trying to keep a deadline with death. Perhaps I am always dying/ Yet I listen willingly to the words of life/ that I have never understood wrote Quasimodo. That is why I've always felt that poetry should not merely amuse us or make us think: it should comfort us, and it must heal the heart of man.

GO, GIVE THEM THE NEWS

Sameer Tanti

Go, give them the news
tell them the water is waist deep now
they have to give the boats alone
the graveyards are to be dug up tomorrow
that should tell them all

Go, get the news across
take a lamp with you as you go
all lamps may have burnt out there
no oil may be, for the wicks which stand
all these belong to when the evening deepens

Go, get the news across
don't you tell them though
that the men are all lost
that with the roads
the courtyards too are lost
don't tell them of the firing at Kokrajhar
or of the homes and fields mortgaged

Go, tell them the news
know his walk well before you confide

hear his voice
measure his shadow if you can
with these ten, these ten fingers

Go, get the news across
inform the police before you leave
rehearse before the mirror
what all you would say
give your address before you leave
so that town-folk get to know of you
Is it true really?
Could be false
may not be
then it's a fact
Yes, yes, it is
Go, give them the news.
It's true
it could
that's right, it may not

THE SORROW OF WOMEN

Mamang Dai

They are talking about hunger.
They are saying there is an unquenchable fire
burning in our hearts.
My love, what shall I do?
I am thinking how I may lose you
to war, and big issues
more important than me.

Life is so hard, like this,
nobody knows why.
It is like fire.
It is like rainwater, sand, glass.
What shall I do, my love,
if my reflection disappears?

They are talking about a place
where rice flows on the streets
about a place where there is gold
in the leaves of trees,
they are talking about displacement
when the opium poppy was growing
dizzy in the sun,
happy, in a state of believing

And they are talking about escape,
about liberty, men and guns,
Ah, the urgency for survival!
But what will they do
not knowing the sorrow of women?

BASAN'S GRANDMOTHER

Bimal Singha

The old woman was milking the cow and the bucket was reverberating with the flow of foaming milk. Bansiram, whose name had been shortened to Bansi or Basan, stood motionless behind the cow, the strong sunlight striking his round, sweating face, the blue pupils of his eyes moving restlessly around. The fat woman all of a sudden turned the cow's nipple up and the milk hit Basan's face in a thin jet and entered his mouth below the flattened nose. He grinned. The old woman giggled merrily and the veins stood out on her thick neck. It was an everyday farce they enjoyed enormously.

Uprooted from the bank of the river Meghna, the old woman had been wandering about aimlessly with her small family till she found shelter on a hillock beside the river Howrah in the hilly state of Tripura. That was more than a decade ago. A small piece of land, reclaimed through hard labour, was all she possessed now to keep life going. In all, there were nine members in the family including the tribal boy, Basan, whose parents lived on the adjacent hillock. Basan's father used to be a Jhum cultivator previously and the family now worked on the Assam-Agartala border road as daily wage earners. Suren, the old woman's son, along with his wife and sons, joined the work force of road construction as did Basan's parents; so the old woman and Basan reigned supreme in the hillocks throughout the day.

The little plump child seemed to be the only link between the two neighbours from the hills and plains: Basan had forcibly occupied the big, safe, warm bosom of the old woman from the very beginning and would not allow her own grandchildren to touch her. Suren had once squeezed Basan's soft, round cheeks and said jokingly, 'Looks like he's established exclusive right to occupy my mother's lap, as if it were the district council for the hill people!' Seeing him suck happily at her dried breast, Basan's mother burst out laughing, 'Look, just look at the two of them. You must have been Basan's mother in your previous birth, dear old woman. Now, do one thing, just start eating boiled pumpkins, the small ones. And there will be plenty of milk in your dried breasts!'

Well, she knew that herself, didn't she? The old woman cooked delicious curries with pumpkin and tiny prawns, but her breasts remained as dry as before. How about small, boiled, green pumpkins? Oh, the shame! She let it go at that and in her sub-conscious mind despised the hill woman for trying to exercise control over *her* Basan. She chanted gloomily to herself: It's dog's urine, the other woman's child. As soon as the little cuckoo learns to fly it quits the crow's nest.

Never mind if the little cuckoo flies away someday, the old woman told herself resignedly, and like a poor insect got herself helplessly entangled in the magical spider's web of love. And it is not only love and friendliness that guides our life, there are periods of fear, hatred and jealousy too that overwhelm us. A petty incident sparked off a quarrel one day. A goat from Basan's house freed itself from the leash and chewed off the bean plants in Suren's luxuriant kitchen garden. Suren's wife asked the hill woman to tighten the leash but a little while later the animal tore off the weak jute cord, came over and made a horrible mess of Suren's vegetable garden. Suren's wife yelled, cursed and called loudly but the other woman did not hear her. Suren's wife flew into an uncontrollable rage and flung a sharp piece of bamboo at the greedy goat, which ran away with a profusely bleeding leg.

The hill woman's small almond-shaped eyes glowed with resentment. Her whole face flushed red with anger and hugging the bleeding goat, she stood fuming in Suren's courtyard and cried out. 'Shame on you, woman. You're not going to eat its raw meat, are you, shameless woman?'

'How dare you blame me?' Suren's wife rushed out of the kitchen, furiously tying her unkempt hair. 'Don't you try to say that I slaughtered your dirty animal.'

'Ah-ha, if it's not you, then some devil from across the hills came all the way to kill my goat, eh?'

'Shut up, I say.' Suren's wife turned crimson with rage and shrieked at the top of her lungs, gesticulating. 'Very well, then. Just try and send in your nasty beast again to eat off my plants and I'll cut it into pieces.'

'Come, come along, cut my pet if you dare!' The furious woman pushed Suren's wife with both her hands.

Suren's wife screamed out all on a sudden. 'Oh, save me! She's killing me!'

Everyone from both the houses rushed out with a look of shock and embarrassment on their faces. Suren's wife looked around with blazing eyes, gesticulating wildly, and burst out menacingly. 'Get out, you witch. Get out of my house, I say!' She caught hold of the other woman's neck and shook her violently.

Basan's mother ran away crying and, standing in her own courtyard, brandished a broomstick and hurled her choicest obscenities at the other woman, shouting and dancing madly up and down the courtyard.

It was at that stormy moment that the old woman made her appearance on the battleground and raised her big leg in a gesture of kicking. 'Shut up, you shameless whore.' She roared, throwing up her strong hands. 'Your goat has massacred my lovely plants and what do you do—curse us and abuse us in return! We'd just tried to drive away the beast, nothing more.'

'Where had you been when I was pushed around in your house?' Basan's mother shouted threateningly. 'Just try to enter my house and I'll smash you to a mould, you old bitch.'

'Your house! Thoo!' The old woman spat in her direction. 'What the hell do you have in that stinky hole of a house, tell me that. Don't forget you borrowed salt this very morning from me, my filthy wretch!'

'Don't be proud, you fat bitch!' Basan's mother shouted back. 'Did your grandson return my spade?'

Suren's wife picked up a spade and flung it across the courtyard in her direction. 'Now fry it and eat it.'

The storm subsided and the women in both houses went on giving vent to their venom, cursing and swearing. Quite unaware of the brawl, Basan awoke late in the afternoon and holding a piece of bamboo between his legs as his horse, went towards Suren's house, calling his Thakurma. His mother gripped his hands and dragged him away, cajoled him, lured him with banana and fried maize seeds and at night told him fairy tales in vain. His Thakurma's wide warm bosom kept beckoning him with a tremendous force till around midnight sleep finally came over him. On the other side, the old woman paced up and down the courtyard restlessly, thirsty for the warm embrace of a pair of chubby arms, the capricious looks in a pair of blue eyes, the heavenly laughter of an innocent child. A strange sensation of longing choked her and she repented the uncalled for brawl in the morning. She sighed and consoled herself with the thought that Basan was after all a child of tribal parents who spoke a different language and had a lifestyle quite different from the plains people. But ... but all humanity is fascinated by the mirage of love and admiration and it is only such a heavenly feeling that has placed man far above everything else.

In that village of daily wage earners, the only dheki for pounding rice was available in Basan's house. The day dragged on and the following day, Suren's wife and daughter after long hesitation stood on Basan's courtyard carrying a basketful of rice on their heads and eyed the dheki in a corner. Basan's mother stopped smoking the hookah and flashed them a resentful look. 'Go and make your own dheki. Don't you feel ashamed after what you did yesterday?' A queer feeling of delight and revenge made the hill woman's chin quiver as she concentrated on her smoking, 'I forbade you to enter my house, didn't I?'

The mother and daughter exchanged quick meaningful glances and slowly retraced their steps towards home, the sarcastic abuses of the hill woman ringing thunderously in their ears, 'Why are you so shameless?'

Towards evening, Suren's eldest son set out for the rice mill in the town with a sack of rice in a rickshaw and ran into Basan's father. He had been to his daughter's house and was quite unaware of the happenings in the house. He heard everything and forced the son to return home with the sack of rice. He faced Suren's wife and said in a voice charged with emotion, 'It's my bad luck that such an ugly thing happened in my absence. Why, isn't my dheki for your use? That goat is a god-damn beast, but we're human beings. What do we spoil our wonderful friendship for? Come, come, forget all this childish brawl, please, please!' He dragged the woman across the courtyard and standing in front of his hut called out to his wife. He beckoned Basan's mother to touch Suren's wife's feet and ask for forgiveness. The hill woman bit her underlip, mused for a moment or two and bent down. Immediately Suren's wife held her in a warm embrace and silent tears rolled down their cheeks and into their mouths. The sun was shining once again from behind the dark clouds and Basan instantly occupied his most comfortable place on earth, the old woman's large, warm bosom, unnoticed by others.

To mark the happy occasion of the re-union, they organised a kirtan, a noisy community singing at night with drums and cymbals and the next day the Bengali settlers and the hill folks set off together to crush stones on the Assam-Agartala road through deep jungles and across the hills. The road was trying to climb up the highest hill of Baramura. But then there was a certain fear writ large on the rugged sweating faces of the labourers, some of whom were drawing figures absentmindedly on the dust while others unwrapped their banana-leaf food packets and ate silently. The air seemed to be charged with a certain gloom and uneasiness. Debendra, a knowledgeable villager, crouched on a piece of brick under a tree, looked about the fields of green paddy and said in his high-pitched voice, 'I'd been to Champaknagar, you know. At least three thousand Bengali refugees were slaughtered by the hillmen in a single night at Ranirbazaar area. And at least fifty thousand houses were torched. Imagine! You can't live in this land, can you?'

Suren's wife was looking for lice in the hill woman's head. She laughed out aloud. Before you tell these cock and bull stories, 'tell us if you've seen these things for yourself. Is there a total of fifty thousand houses in the whole of Agartala? Ha!'

'What do you know of the world, old woman?' The wise fellow barked at her savagely. 'Is it any good to talk to one who's never read a newspaper or listened to the radio? Ask those who keep track of the happenings around us. Have you seen any lorry on this road for the past three days?'

Well, it was a fact. The woman kept silent.

'Hundreds of thousands of people have taken shelter in Agartala town leaving all their belongings behind.' Debendra glared at the increasing number of listeners around him and cleared his throat noisily. 'Hundreds of women were tied to trees and had their breasts cut off. And there was a bamboo basket full of children's heads!' He paused for breath. 'The hill folks will cross the Baramura hills and proceed towards Teliamura, butchering people and burning down houses, and on the way they will surely not spare us.'

'But what the hell are the Bengali men doing?' A voice from the crowd demanded angrily.

'What can they do against the hillmens guns and daos? Of course the locals of Agartala are taking full revenge.' Debendra sounded important. 'They've started slaughtering the hill folks with swords and bombs. They've cut up lots of the hill folks, put them in sacks and flung them into the river. Why, you won't find a single hillman in the whole of Agartala. Go and see for yourself, if you don't believe me. Well, truck loads of Bengalis are roaming around the valley looking for those flat-nosed hill people. Just wait, you'll see them over here pretty soon. Outwardly these folks of Tripura appear to be very innocent, don't they? But inwardly they're all very cunning.'

A dark shadow of panic and mistrust crossed their faces. Nobody could understand what they were going to kill each other for. A numbness gripped their thoughts. The tense silence was shaken by Suren's loud voice. 'Well, you've told us a lot about what you heard at a shop in Champaknagar. I had been at Champaknagar till ten yesterday and nobody uttered any such nonsense to me.'

'It's strange you didn't hear anything.' Debendra flared up. 'The big merchant himself told me so.'

'Tell us whatever you've seen yourself. Is it any use just repeating what some chatterbox narrated here and there and everywhere? You gain nothing, do you?'

Debendra rolled up his sleeves threateningly and gnashed his teeth. 'You want Bengalis blood being a Bengali yourself. Ha?' He pointed an accusing finger at Suren and glared from one numb face to another. 'He's a traitor and ought to be slain first. A stooge of the hillmen! There will be no peace with him around.' His face assumed the shape of a wolfs and cunning gleamed in his narrowed eyes. The uncomfortable silence was broken by the sharp whistle blown by the overseer from Punjab. The sullen-faced labourers trudged towards the hill with their tools.

Sometime ago the labourers had stopped work on the question of wages. Debendra was then an ordinary labourer like them and he had managed to create a rift between the hill and plains labourers that had culminated in a riot. He was rewarded with promotion to the prize-post of sardar for breaking the strike so easily. Now, as Suren filled the basket of a woman with soil, he hissed, 'Have you heard what that fellow said? Make a mountain out of a molehill, as they say. Is it any good terrorising the poor labourers?'

Debendra who was smoking, overheard him and shouted, 'What is the hillmen's stooge telling you?'

People were scared and did not go to work the next day. Basan's father went to Champaknagar to buy salt and was taken aback at the exorbitant price. Asked to explain, the shopkeeper howled ferociously, his eyes blazing, 'You're lucky, I've sold salt to a hillman. Go away. It's bad time now.'

Stunned with disbelief, the hillman could not understand the reason for such insult. He gulped and dared to ask, 'I'm taking things on payment, am I not?'

Debendra was sitting in a corner of the shop. He looked at the shopkeeper and dropped a hint with his eye. Immediately the shopkeeper jumped down from his cot and snatched away the packet of salt. He roared. 'Now, get out of here. Both your money and salt are gone. See what you can do. Get out.'

'We're good at heart and that's why we take care of you.' Debendra smiled slyly. 'You don't know when we're going to cut you into pieces though.'

Dumbfounded, the poor hillman turned purple with impotent rage. His tongue went dry, he gulped repeatedly not knowing what to say and stepped out of the shop, trembling with insult and injury. Outside he was aware of several pairs of eyes turning towards him in suspicion. There were very few hillmen in the market. He looked around seeking a familiar Bengali face who would dare protest against the injustice on his behalf. He returned home empty handed, the feeling of insult and injustice gnawing at his heart.

It had been three days now since they went for work and hunger and fear stared them hard in the face. The two families shared a big jackfruit brought by Suren. People started migrating to safer places or deeper into the jungle. A breath of mistrust and fear had suddenly rent the air. At nightfall the whole locality shivered with the feeling of an impending disaster. When the pangs of hunger became too painful to bear, the men and women of the two houses came out and went hurriedly in the direction of the work site.

The old woman was alone at home looking after Basan. She could not pacify the hungry, nagging child till she found a few seeds of the jackfruit, burned these and gave them to him to eat with salt. A gentle breeze was blowing across the hillocks like all other days; but the old woman felt it to be the harbinger of a coming storm. An unknown fear took possession of her senses and she almost hated the overwhelming silence all around her. Would they come back home safely—the folks of the two houses? She wondered and licked her dry lips in anguish. She heard a bird calling in panic and gave a violent start. She held her breath in endless anxiety, straining her ears to hear her people returning home.

Night had fallen and the old woman did not feel like lighting up the lamp. The hill child kept whimpering with hunger. All of a sudden she heard a fearful scream, not far away, piercing through the gathering gloom. She pressed the child tight against her chest and came out and watched the fire raging on the hill tops all around her. Was it the boom of a gun or the crackling sound of burned bamboo? She did not know and trembled from neck to feet. Her eyes opened wide and still she could see nothing except the red leaping flames. And she heard wild screams. She heard the desperate cries of cows and calves emanating from the burning cowsheds and let out a mad shriek. At her wit's end she ran over to Basan's courtyard, retraced her steps and looked everywhere for a weapon. The sparks from burning huts flew high up into the night sky like swarms of mad fire-flies and the enormous, greedy tongues of fire quickly approached her. She hugged the bewildered child and ran towards the bamboo thickets and then ran in the direction of the river Howrah. The old woman stumbled, fell down, rose again with the crying child clinging to her bosom and ran towards the river. The roar of the raging fire had almost drowned the cries of the slaughtered men and burning cattle but she heard the crazy chirping of the birds in the bamboo thickets. She ran through the thorny bushes, heaving and bleeding, and reached the main road. She heard an inhuman cry quite close at hand and entered a thick bush of long sharp grass the locals made their roof with. A half-burnt calf ran past them to nowhere and she gave a violent start. A painful numbness came over her entire frame and she did not know which way to go. Basan lay still, motionless on her broad shoulder, the warm saliva oozing out in unending stream bathing her cheek and neck. A bunch of arrows flew overhead, whistling and coming from every direction. She looked up for a while and then shut her eyes. God! God! God!

The old woman stood still for a moment's reflection and then started moving towards the town. A fearful realisation dawned on her suddenly and she came to an abrupt halt. The child in her arms belonged to a different community and the mad man-eaters in town would fling him into fire seeing his flat nose and narrow eyes. That bloody nose would give him away. She pulled at his nose fiercely and Basan cried out in pain. 'No, not to that hell of a town.' The old woman whirled around and made for the hills. The hillmen would surely kill her over there, she shuddered to think, turned and glared in the direction of the town. I'm safe in town and Basan is in the dark hills. She decided she would leave Basan in the hills and then run to the town for safety and loosened her grip on the inert child. Basan slipped down a little, yelled in panic and braced his chubby arms around her neck. Who could imagine those little hands possessed the strength of a giant? To him the old woman's bosom was the safest cage in a cruel jungle, offering him comfort and warm hope of life. For them, both the places were unsafe and they had nowhere to go. The frantic woman searched her mind for an answer and found none.

All of a sudden the strong beams of flashlights played on their faces from both sides, blinding them and startling them. The flashlights seemed to be like the blood thirsty eyes of wolves. The old woman ran away and the dark swallowed them.

Three days later the police found two corpses in a bush beside the narrow drain. A single spear had pierced through the two of them—an old woman and a child.

Translated from Bengali by Bonomali Goswami

LAWSOHTUN

Kynpham Sing Nongkynrih

You, who remain the city's backyard,
yet to feature in its postal map!
A town of taxi-drivers, squeezing passengers
like a sack of potatoes; of foul-mouthed drunks,
crawling about in the morning sun; of nocturnal
prowlers, who do not even spare drying underwear.

Having built my house on your slope
I am sad and happy.

You, who haven't come of age,
and yet to receive the services
of a gutter or the safety of a footpath!
Your pigeonhole shops can offer me nothing
but *waidong*[1] and children's edibles preserved
long after their expiry dates. And if my telephone
happens to be dead, you can offer me nothing
but frustration.

[1] A piece of betel nut sold together with lime-smeared betel leaf.

In the morning the wind comes from nowhere
like a malevolent spirit, pelts me with sleet
in summer, whips me with frost in winter. Here
the wind turns everything cold, except my temper.
My aunt, who spits at my car; my mother, who spits
at my cellphone; my cousins, who simply sulk; all
have been truly iced. And so have my
neighbours, their vicious tales dogging me everywhere.

At night the moon rises to show me your mermaid
rivulets dashing from the hills into your vile slime.
Under the moon, the pillars of the Indian Army
like white iron bars caging your cool hills
like captured beasts; turning the play fields
of my youth into forbidden and murderous spots.
Under the moon, squat tin roofs like monstrous
caterpillars troop into your woodland, devouring
tree after tree. Only sometimes could I spot the distant
Mangkashang,[2] sky-mark of a wandering tribe, basket
of secrets. Often I just mount the terrace to watch
gunmen blasting the night like *Diwali* crackers.
I would have packed up and left but
for a zealous mother, who would curse me
with a dog's life and your *dorbar,*[3] welcoming
me like a rainmaker.

No more will the city dwellers treat me like
a houseless migrant. Here we even grow
our own garden-fresh, pesticide-free vegetables.
In winter your slopes are flushed with the love
of cherries. In summer they wear the fair blooms
of plums and your numerous pears as if set
for a white man's wedding.

[2] Khasi name for the Himalayas. The name vaguely refers to an ever-visible landmark or even a basket of some sort.
[3] Khasi village council.

I never tire of their soft gazes and their
promise of dreams and redemption.

Maybe, after all, someone has to save your
streams and pine groves. Despite the cold
wind, there are times when I feel determined
to liberate your hills.

Translated from Khasi by the Poet

HOPE

Mitra Phukan

Unsure of themselves, hesitant yet determined, the two ladies who sat in our drawing room that sunny winter morning, looked as though they had made a long journey. Their tired eyes and casualness in attire indicated that they did not belong to this city, that they had come only recently.

Their 'out-of town' origins were also reflected in the timing of their visit. After all, nobody decides to drop in on a weekday morning, not even close friends. We all know, don't we, the 'value of time' as they say. To land up at nine in the morning in a frantically, and fashionably 'busy' household, is not just awfully inconvenient for the hosts, but also an admission that the visitors themselves are not nearly as modishly occupied.

The ladies were told that I was at breakfast, but they insisted, politely I believe, that it was all right, they would wait. Resigned to falling-behind my schedule, I went in to see what they wanted.

They sat close together on the sofa, as though they found comfort in proximity to each other. The older lady, a middle-aged person of maternal appearance, was dressed in a conventional white *mekhela-sador* with a maroon border, the usual dress of ladies of middle-class in the smaller towns. Her hair was pulled back in a bun, but strands framed her face, deepening the maternal look. Her skin was unlined, but there were, I noticed, signs of strain around her eyes, that were reflected in the nervous fidgeting of her hands with the end of her maroon-bordered sador.

The other person was much younger. If the broad swathe of sindoor in the parting of her hair had not announced her marital status, I would have taken her to be a college student. Slim and fresh-faced, she looked at me with wide eyes that had, however, none of the carefree look of youth. They did not look like mother and daughter. Mentally making a note that I would spare them not more than five minutes, I sat down.

They half rose from their seats, folding their hands in deep namaskars, smiling timidly at me. Timidity annoys me. But without showing my irritation, I joined my palms together in response, and said, in a neutral tone, 'Yes?'

The older lady, oblivious, it seemed, to the coldness of my tone, began to talk. Her voice was as soft as her looks, her gestures diffident.

'I'm Sewali Barua,' she began. 'Mrs Sewali Barua.' This, she gestured towards the girl next to her, 'is my daughter-in-law. Nandini. Nandini Barua.'

The girl smiled hesitantly at me. I nodded, without speaking.

'You are Rittika Choudhury?' asked Sewali Barua. My name on her tongue had the small-town intonation that my city-bred friends have changed to a more urbane manner of pronunciation. But it sounded sweeter on her tongue than it did on theirs. She looked anxiously at me, as though to verify whether I was indeed I, before she went on to the task in hand.

I told her that yes that was indeed my name. I couldn't help looking pointedly at my watch.

But Sewali Barua seemed to have missed the glance.

'We have come from Parbatpuri by the night bus. We arrived here an hour or so ago.' She continued in a firmer voice. 'We had to meet you …'

Parbatpuri. I knew the place. A small town, surrounded by hills on three sides, and bordered by the mighty Luit River on the fourth. Surrounded by mile upon mile of lush tea gardens, it is the headquarters of one of the remote districts of our state. But though it is a picturesque town, it is not for its beauty that Parbatpuri is in the news these days. We, at the newspaper office where I work, see the name often in the news dispatches that come in. Parbatpuri, these days, is the very nerve-centre of the fierce unrest that boils all around the district, the insurgency and violence that threatens to rip apart the very fabric of our lives, even in this distant capital-city of the state where I live.

I looked at them with greater attention. They returned my look innocently. Certainly there was nothing of the terrorist about them; nothing that my suspicious eyes could discern. Of course, these days, it is getting more and more difficult to ascertain, just from the first glance, who wields a gun and who does not. Young girls have them, yes, even middle-aged ladies have been known to possess firearms.

The other woman, the girl, Nandini Barua, spoke up. She had been rummaging around in her handbag, a well-worn artificial leather one, and had taken out a magazine. She now held it out for me to look at, saying, 'There is a story here, titled 'Death of a Dream'. You did write it, didn't you?'

I reached out and took the magazine from her hand. I recognised the name, the logo and the masthead. Her index finger was pushed through the pages. She flipped it open before my eyes. Even before I looked at it, I knew the story she meant. Yes. 'Death of a Dream.' It was illustrated with the line drawing of a man. His face was contorted with agony, his arms were out flung in front of his face, as though to ward off blows. Or bullets. The artist had dressed his creation in a mixture of Indian and Western clothes. Jeans, tough-looking shoes, but over them, a soft flowing, embroidered kurta. I turned the pages. Yes, certainly it was the same story. But I hadn't written it.

I gave the magazine back to her. 'I recognise the story, of course. But no, I didn't write it.'

Disappointment, or was it distress, flared on their faces. 'But your name, it's here …' pointed out the girl.

'As the translator, I translated the story. I didn't write it, though. Shyamol wrote it. Shyamol Borpujari.' I pointed out the bylines to her.

'Oh.' They looked helplessly at each other.

My impatience had abated somewhat, replaced by curiosity. 'What is it? I mean, why do you want to meet the author of the story?'

The two women turned towards me. Sewali Barua's hands still moved restlessly on her lap. Nandini Barua, who now had the magazine open at Shyamol Borpujari's story, stroked the page tenderly and repeatedly. The ladies looked placid enough on the surface, but it was obvious that there were undercurrents of tension within. It was the thought of fathoming these undercurrents, which made me settle down on the chair a little deeper.

Around me, the household hummed with the usual morning sounds. The children had already left for school; the man of the house was on tour. Pots clattered in the kitchen as the maid scrubbed the breakfast dishes. Ordinary, everyday sounds dissolved into the liquid golden winter sunshine that has inspired so many of our poets to lyricism and poetry. All of this was a far cry from the agony and anguish that I knew were contained in the pages that Nandini Barua now stroked gently in her lap. The anguish that was portrayed in the drawing of the man in the illustration was the agony that, we all knew, lurked beneath the surface of the golden glow of winter mornings, the murkiness that ticked mercilessly into newspaper offices, day and night, in the reams and reams or news stories and pictures, from all corners of this tormented land about killings, kidnappings, and extortions.

'What is it?' I asked again, gently. True, timidity irritates me, but these two women ... there was something about them, a trusting helplessness, and, yes, an indefinable air or something, sorrow perhaps, that hung around them, which made me unconsciously modulate my tone.

The older woman, Sewali Barua, spoke at last. Her voice was soft as falling feathers, but unfaltering. She looked steadily at me as she talked, her hands never ceasing to twist and crumple the edge of her maroon-bordered sador.

'The story that you wrote, I mean translated,' she said, 'was published in that magazine, the *City Review,* last month.'

I nodded. Yes, I had finished translating Shyamol's story about six weeks or so ago. It had been a difficult piece, not easily translatable. There were many culture-specific terms and phrases that had defied translation. Shyamol had written this story more than two years ago. It had appeared in an Assamese literary magazine about eighteen months ago. He had given it to me then, with a request that I translate it into English. I had dawdled over it, not because of laziness, but because it was difficult to translate. In the meantime, the original had won Shyamol a couple of literary awards. It was a tightly structured story, written in unadorned language about an escape from prison, where the escapee had been imprisoned for terrorist activities. While fleeing the police, the protagonist, Shankar, happened to take shelter in the unoccupied house of a music teacher. While the police outside tightened their cordon around the house, Shankar, seeing the violin and other musical paraphernalia in the absent musician's house, came to the realisation during the course of the night that, after all, violence was not the means to the creation of a just society. He read the diary of his absent host, full of longings for a time of peace, all of which awakened an echo in his mind. Yes, he, too, had had a dream, but unlike the musician, he had taken to arms in the pursuit of that dream, a dream that now lay shattered under the onslaught of a thousand bullets. The means had become an end—the goal was still a distant chimera, which had often disappeared from his field of vision as he had systematically conducted raids, killed people, all in search of a more just and better society. His dream, he realised as he paced around the musician's small, one-roomed house, listening to the strains of John Lennon's song 'Imagine' on the cassette player of the musician, had crumpled and died under the weight of violence. Finally, at dawn, Shankar, freshly bathed and dressed in the absent musicians clothes, went out of the house. Bullets rained all around him, as still humming 'Imagine', he fell.

'After we, I mean Nandita and myself and the rest of our family read it,' said Sewali Barua, 'we have been trying to locate you.'

'Didn't you read the original story in Asomiya?' I asked. After all, they did not look the sort who made up the readership of somewhat elitist English literary magazines.

Sewali Barua shook her head. 'No. In fact we were unaware of even this story, till a friend of my husband, whose son is a lecturer in English, brought it to us.'

This was getting rather complicated. But I was hooked. I wiped my mind clean of the other thoughts, the appointments that would be missed, the tasks that would have to be crowded into the rest of the day, and prepared myself to give them a patient hearing.

The girl spoke up. 'We wanted to ask you ... do you ... did you ... know the man?'

'Shyamol? Yes, quite well,' I replied. 'We work in the same office. He has already made a name for himself both as a journalist and a short story writer. He takes his stories from true-life incidents that he sees around him in his work as a newspaperman.'

But she shook her head. Her eyes, as they stared at me, had an intense, focused look, as though this was the most important question she would ever ask in her life.

'No, I don't mean the writer. I mean the person—Shankar, the hero of the story. Do you know him?'

I was taken aback. Confused, I looked towards the older woman for help. But she too was staring at me, as though their lives depended on my answer. Even the restlessness of her hands had stilled.

'But—it's a story ... I mean it is fiction, a figment of Shyamol's imagination. How can I ...?' Something about the way they sat, still and erect, as though they were holding their breaths, made me stop. In a firmer voice, I queried, 'Why do you ask?'

The two of them looked at each other, then at the magazine that Nandita was still cradling in her lap. They looked disappointed, yet not completely deflated. Haltingly at first, then, gradually with more sureness, they spoke to me of an event that had occurred six months ago.

'We are from Parbatpuri, as I told you,' said Sewali Barua. 'My husband retired two years ago ... he was a clerk in a tea garden. We have been living in the town of Parbatpuri since then. We are a small family ... my husband, myself, and'—she looked tremulously at me—'my son. He—my son—was awarded his engineering degree at the same time that my husband retired. He got a job here, in this city, a couple of months later. He was a good student; you see ... he always topped his class. Getting a job was no problem for him.' There was a note of pride in her voice as she said these last sentences.

She paused. It was obvious that she was not used to making long speeches. I waited for her to continue.

'He got married a year ago. She ...' she glanced at her daughter-in-law sitting beside her, 'she was his classmate. Yes, she is a qualified engineer, as well.'

This surprised me. Looking at Nandini's slim, almost frail frame, I would never have thought her to be a qualified engineer.

'He—my son—used to come home every weekend. Nandini had a job at Parbatpuri itself, in a small private firm. He, too, was trying to get a suitable one there, so that we all could live together in the same town, you know, under the same roof. He … my son …' she looked directly at me, and asked, 'Oh, I forgot. I haven't told you his name, have I?'

I shook my head, wondering why I needed to know her son's name.

'Shankar. His name is Shankar.' I looked quickly at her, but said nothing. It was the girl, Nandini, who took up the story again. Her voice was soft and persistent. She looked at me steadily as she spoke. Her eyes were, for the most part, expressionless, as though she was relating the story of some other person, a man she barely knew.

'He was not very happy with his job. There were tiffs with his boss, delays in salary payments, that sort of things, you know. If he had been happy, he would probably not have thought of shifting to Parbatpuri … Anyway,' she appeared to take a grip on herself, that evening, it was a Friday, he rang us up, saying that he would be coming home the next day, Saturday, as usual. But this time, he said, he would be coming home for good. He was giving up his job. He would look for something suitable in Parbatpuri, or thereabouts, or set up a small engineering concern of his own, our own. It was a dream we had, even while we were students … to acquire some capital by working at jobs for a while, and then set up something of our own, you know. Two mechanical engineers should be able to make a go of it.'

I nodded. Her voice, unwavering but soft, continued. Once or twice, she looked at her mother-in-law's face, equally expressionless, but she addressed her words to me.

'That was the last we heard from him.'

The words took a moment to sink in.

'But … haven't you made enquiries … the police …'

'Of course. We've done all the usual things that are done when a thing like this happens.' It was Shankar's mother who spoke this time, her voice empty of any emotion. 'Police. Rewards. Announcements in the newspapers, on TV. Large notices with his picture on them. Perhaps you saw them?'

I shook my head. How could I tell her that in these troubled times, we journalists, and, indeed, most citizens, were suffering from a 'crisis fatigue'. There were many tragedies taking place all around us. So many sons, husbands, brothers, sweethearts had gone missing. Some bodies were found, others were not. The papers were full of pictures of missing persons, mostly young men in the prime of their lives, who had suddenly vanished. How could we remember them all?

Of course I said nothing of all this to her.

'But there was nothing. No clue, no trace of his whereabouts … Nobody knew where he went. His colleagues in the office, his landlord … we talked to them all, so did the police, but there's nothing … it's as if he just vanished.'

I looked at her, speechless. What can be more heart wrenching for a mother than to have to speak these anguished words? Her son had been missing for the last six months. I understood the pain of her vacant face, the edge around Nandini's bland tone. They had reined in their emotions, tightly, for to relax their hold on them would have been disastrous. Horrors lurked beneath the surface of their minds, fed by the rumours that were everywhere, rumours about the fate of those who disappeared. If once that dam burst, and their dread came out in a tumultuous rush, if they once began to think that their Shankar … but no, in that line of thought lay disaster. Better to focus on the task at hand.

Nandini took over. It occurred to me that these two had gone through this routine many times before. When one left off, the other took up the thread of the narrative. When the mother needed to compose herself to calmness again, the daughter-in-law took over. When the younger woman was overwhelmed, the older one continued.

'We came to you because we thought that maybe you know something about him. About Shankar.' The vermilion in her hair was a blazing trail of hope, a hope that was reflected, suddenly, in her eyes now. It was the hope without which these two frail creatures would crumble and disintegrate just as surely as a broken dam crumbles under the weight of onrushing floodwaters.

'I? How … I mean why should I?'

'No, of course not. Now that we know that you translated the story, but did not actually write it … to tell you the truth, it never occurred to us that translators and writers could be different people, we saw your name … made enquiries …'

I said nothing. It was obvious that they had been blinded by hope. It was clearly written in the magazine that Shyamol was the writer, and I, the translator.

'You see,' she continued, 'there are so many similarities. Shankar, the name, of course. Then the fact that the Shankar in the story and my husband, both of them, they loved music. Especially Western music. And that song, 'Imagine'.' She looked fixedly at me. 'My husband loved that song. It was one of his favourites ... surely ...'

I knew what was coming. I waited.

'It cannot be a coincidence. It cannot.' The words were strong, but her tone was soft, still. 'Could you ... please ... could you ask the writer, where he got the story from? He's a journalist, you said so, and you said he bases his story on something that he comes across in his journalistic work. Please—can you ask him ...?'

I would have pitied them, this pleading wife and the stoic mother next to her, if I had not been so close to tears myself. The frailty of the straws that they were clutching at was so obvious to me, an onlooker. But they were drowning, and hope was all they had to hold on to. I could have pointed out that Shankar was a very common name, that, in any case, if the story had been based on truth, the first thing that a writer would have done would have changed the name of the protagonist. As for the liking for music, who doesn't like 'Imagine'? If a poll were to be conducted, I didn't doubt that the song would be the favourite of billions across the globe. Coincidences. But coincidences happen, they happen all the time. Coincidences that no fiction writer would dare to put into his work, for fear of being ridiculed as too lazy to concoct a plausible plot, are piled upon the lives of men and women as they go about their daily chores in such a careless manner that one is left gasping. And the events and preferences that the women in front of me elaborated just now were hardly coincidences. And as for the fact that their Shankar, and the hero of the story were both missing ... this was a time of unrest. And when such social upheavals take place, it is common for youths to go missing.

'Of course I'll put you in touch. But ...' I knew what I had to say might be futile, but I had to try. I did not want to be the one to snatch the straw away from them, but it had to be done. Without losing any time I made up my mind. 'In fact, instead of you going over to his house, why don't you speak to him on the telephone? I can get his number for you.'

The gratefulness in their eyes made me look away. Mechanically I asked, 'Your Shankar, he disappeared ... six months ago. Isn't that right?'

The two women nodded.

'This story,' I told them, gently, trying not to look into their trusting eyes, 'this story was written much earlier. More than two years ago, in fact. It is only this translated version that has appeared now, a month ago.'

They stared back at me, expressionless.

'Don't you see?' I asked, mildly exasperated. 'There can be no link between the two things. The story was written before your son—your husband disappeared. It's a coincidence, that's all that it is.'

It was Nandini who spoke first.

'I see. Yes.'

She looked at me, the sindoor glowing in the parting of her hair with the hope that was reflected in her eyes. Hope that refused to die, if it did, their lives, too, would be like flotsam in the mad rush of a river in torrential spate, without direction.

'But,' she continued, still in the same soft, unemotional tone, 'if it's not too much trouble, I mean, could you tell us where the writer, this Shyamol Borpujari, lives? After all, he is a journalist. He goes around, meeting all kinds of people, he may know something that the police do not. After all, people run away, they hide when they see the police. But a journalist ... surely he will know something.'

I could see it happening in front of my eyes. She was loosening her grip on one wisp of straw in the raging currents of the river that were swiftly carrying her away, only to clutch at another, equally fragile.

'In any case,' interrupted the older woman, 'we would like to meet him, the author, I mean ...'

Shyamol's voice was gruff with sleep when he answered the phone. I knew he was a late riser. I was also sure that the situation that had developed would intrigue him enough and he would not mind his missed sleep.

Quickly, I explained the situation to him in a low voice. The telephone was in the room next to where the two women were sitting, but I still found myself talking in a tone that was the opposite of my usual brisk, no-nonsense, rather loud voice.

Immediately, the sleepiness vanished from Shyamol's voice. I pictured him in my mind—his dark, mobile face, his sensitive mouth, his mop of receding hair, and his short, somewhat squat frame—as I spoke. Shyamol was an ordinary looking man. He had a pretty wife whom he loved dearly, and a six-month-old baby. His was a normal life. But there was a magnetism about him, a charisma that made people open up and pour out their life-stories to him, even though he was a total stranger. It was this quality in him that made him such a good journalist and a gifted short story writer. He took his material from life. But it was his deep imaginative ability that coloured facts, and transformed the stuff of everyday life into works of art that made readers, even in distant places, identify with the characters of his stories. He was an award-winning short story writer. I thought, perhaps, the presence of these two ladies in my drawing room as well as the identification of 'their' Shankar with the Shankar in 'Death of a Dream', was a tribute to the universality of the story written by Shyamol.

Our relationship has grown much beyond the usual office-colleague one. I have become very fond of him in the last couple of years since he had joined our office. He, too, looks on me as his elder sister, a person with whom he can share his thoughts, knowing well that I will not be judgemental. He often uses me as a sounding board for his stories as they develop in his mind. I feel privileged. For, though I put my expensive English-medium education to some use in my sub-editor's job, I know that I will never be capable of the kind of incandescent creativity that seems to be, Shyamol's second nature. At his urgings, I have tried my hand at translation, and have translated several of his stories into English. He, of course, writes in the vernacular. I am never satisfied with my translations that, I feel, do not do justice to the raw power and the compassion that inundate his stories. But Shyamol seems happy enough with my translations, and will consider no other person for the job. Perhaps he is blinded by his regard for me.

'They read the translation, you said?' he asked when I had finished. 'That appeared about a month ago. But their Shankar disappeared six months ago, whereas I wrote the story much earlier. So, obviously …'

'I know,' I told him. 'I've explained it all to them. The point now is not that they think you have written about their Shankar. They seem to have accepted that there is no link between the two incidents, or, rather, between the story and their lives. But they are desperately in search of something, some clue, some small spark of hope. You know how important it is ... something to keep them alive. And they seem to think that you will be able to give them that something.'

'Yes, I see,' replied Shyamol.

I knew he did. So many times, over the past deeply troubled decade, we had seen people coming to the offices of the newspaper. People with hope in their eyes, and perhaps a torn photograph, or a news item, or a scrap of paper, something which they thought was a link between some report that they had read in our paper, and a loved one of theirs, a person who was missing, or had gone away from their lives at some time in the past. They believed, for some reason, that there was something about the power of the Press that would give them succour. These people with despair in their hearts but a spark of hope in their eyes had already knocked on the doors of the law, of the police, and of justice, before they turned to us. The Press was usually the last resort. Just as, perhaps, for these ladies, Shyamol's story was one of the last straws of hope in the torrential flood of their lives.

'Just talk to them,' I urged him now. They seem to think that you know something about their Shankar, not because you wrote the story, but you are a journalist.'

Shyamol didn't hesitate. He knew it wouldn't be a pleasant task, this talk with the mother and wife of a missing man, but he said immediately, 'Of course. Put them on the line.'

One by one, the women came up to the telephone and spoke in their soft voices with Shyamol. I don't know what exactly it was that he told them, but when the telephone was finally put on the hook again, they looked at me, not at all as though their inquiries had led them to a dead end, but as if they had seen the light at the end of the tunnel.

'I asked him how he got the inspiration for this story,' said Sewali Barua, as she gathered her bag, preparing to leave. 'I mean, because of the similarities between his story and the events that had happened in our lives. He explained that it was imaginary, not based on any one incident, or any one person, but a kind of composite of what he had seen and heard, has been seeing and hearing, as a journalist.'

I refrained from saying I told you so. But I couldn't help being puzzled by the expression in her eyes. There was no disappointment; instead, they burned in an undaunted fire with a renewed blaze of hope.

Nandini took up where her mother-in-law had left off. 'We've made an appointment to meet him at his office in about an hour. We still have some time before we catch the return bus to Parbatpuri. He's agreed to talk to us.'

'What about?' I asked. What more, indeed, was there to talk about? Wasn't this going to be the end of this particular story, then?

Both women looked at me with mild surprise, as they would at a person who fails to understand the simplest statement. But Nandini explained to me, patiently, 'It's that 'seeing and hearing' that he, Shyamol Borpujari told us about. Surely, I mean, it's quite possible that he might have heard something about Shankar, something that the police had missed. He goes all over the state, into the remotest jungles and the furthest villages, in search of stories, he told us so himself. It is more than possible that he might have a clue about Shankars whereabouts. Isn't it?'

They looked at me without the expectation of an answer. In any case, I was too stupefied to give them one. How could I tell them that they were chasing chimeras? For the last six months, this was probably what had kept them sane. This pursuit of anything that they perceived to be a 'clue', this clinging to the belief that it would lead them to Shankar, even though, gradually, the clues had become slimmer and slimmer, and their hopes more and more unrealistic. Clutching at straws, yes, that was what they were doing. But there was nothing else that they could do to hold on to their sanity. Nothing at all. The State machinery had failed them; the social set-up of a so-called civilised society had failed them. How long would it be before they, too, were overwhelmed by the swirling ferocity of the flood waters that raged all around them, how long before they, too, got drowned?

They were polite in their farewells, and grateful for having been put in touch with Shyamol, who shone as a beacon of hope for them now. But it was obvious as they thanked me in their soft and polite voices that their minds were elsewhere. Nandini put the magazine back into her bag, as carefully and gently as though she was putting a child to sleep. Sewali smoothed the maroon border of her sador one last time before turning around and leaving my house.

I watched the two women walking away as if an untold sorrow had them in its grip. The tragedy of their situation, I knew, would make them move from person to person, place to place, searching for some tidings, some small morsel of news about the man who had dropped out so abruptly from their lives, till exhaustion finally overtook them, months, perhaps even years from now. As time would pass by, weariness would engulf them, for they might cling stubbornly to whatever they perceived to be hope. After many years, if she were lucky, Nandini would meet a man, a person who would offer her the chance of a new life. She would have to wait the mandatory time before it is legally possible for her to remarry, and start anew.

But always, at the back of her mind, even if she would be blessed with a full and active life in her later years, there would be a niggling worry. Even in the arms of the other man, she would wonder about Shankar. Where was he? Was he alive? And if indeed he was alive, why had he dropped out of their lives so abruptly? Was it something that she had done, some inadequacy in her that she was completely unaware of, but which, for him, was so totally unbearable that he had preferred to leave her, leave even his parents, his childhood surroundings, and had chosen the life of guns and violence that raged all around them? And if, indeed, he was dead, then, how had it happened? Was he alone when he took his last, shuddering breath? Was it her face that had stayed in his consciousness as he had slipped out of this world? What had he been thinking of? Was there something, some thought perhaps, or, something that he would have communicated to her if he had died in her arms? Till the end of her days, even if she were fortunate enough to be able to pass the sunset of her life surrounded by the laughter of happy grandchildren, even if she had a loving, caring man by her side, she would wonder.

And that wonder would keep her away from happiness always.

As for Sewali Barua, her life would take a much straighter route. She would never come to terms with the death of her only child. Never. Perhaps had it been a long and agonising illness that her son died of, she would have even been grateful that with Shankar's death, his suffering had ended. Even if he had been snatched away from her by a sudden accident, she would have eventually come to terms with his death. Perhaps she would have sought solace in religion, perhaps she would have found eventual peace through her work with other unfortunate ones, with destitutes, or abandoned children.

But the way Shankar had just disappeared, suddenly, without any warning whatsoever, from her life, there was no way that she would ever be able to forget. In all the remaining moments of her life, no matter what she was doing, she would always be alert for some news of Shankar, some inkling of his whereabouts. How could he be dead? It was impossible. In the serene, rural, almost idyllic world that she had grown up in, people did not just disappear. True, the newspapers of today were full of sudden, unexplained disappearances. But these things happened to other people, never to bright, happy, just-married young men like Shankar. He had never been involved with 'those' people; why should he even think of joining up with them? No, he was around somewhere, yes, somewhere quite near. Perhaps, without her being aware of it, he had even visited them once or twice, just to see that they were all right. And of course, he would be back. She would wait for his return, which could happen any moment, without warning. Perhaps his journey home had been interrupted by an unavoidable detour. She would cook at least a couple of his favourite dishes daily, right till the time that old age overpowered her ability to hobble around the kitchen freely. If he were to arrive without warning, he would not find his mother unprepared to welcome him with the kind of cooking that he loved.

And till the very end of her life, she would keep a lamp alight in her heart as she waited for Shankar to return home.

FOREBODINGS

Kynpham Sing Nongkynrih

When for the umpteenth time
the region's liberators
clamped a *bandh* on Republic Day
there was nothing else to do
but watch the grey winter sky
breeding ill will.

Over the rooftops
the outstretched branches
of a tall tree, straining
to break free.

By the window
two large buildings
like Sumo wrestlers
threatening my in-law's house.

And mocking from a clothes line
my neighbour's underpants
in their irreverent best.

Fear like a militant
had silenced every sound

and the timid afternoon
was slinking out like peace
from this town.
with the high branches, plummeted
homeward to my wife and the darkness.

Translated from Khasi by the Poet

KASHMIR

THE STORY OF A WOMEN'S COLLEGE IN KASHMIR

Neerja Mattoo

Through my long association with the Government College for Women, Maulana Azad Road, Srinagar, as a student as well as a teacher, from 1952 to 1995, I have been witness to its phenomenal role as an instrument of change. An institution that began small, housed in what was a 'Widow's Palace' in the time of the erstwhile 'Maharajadhiraj' of Jammu and Kashmir, it grew to alter a whole society's perspective on women. The graph of its success in empowering women, which had steadily gone upwards, suddenly took a plunge in the last decade of the twentieth century. This was the time when in the valley of Kashmir everything fell apart and no one was sure of the meaning or value of anything but the gun. But let us go back to the beginning.

It was a heady time. Not only because we were just into our teens, but because the world around us felt young, confident and exuberant—we were sure that things could only get better. Kashmir along with the rest of the subcontinent had been pronounced free only a few years back. Awami Raj they said it was—'People's Rule', and the sheen on that idea had not yet worn thin. Faith in the leadership had not yet taken a beating. And certainly things had changed for the better within an unbelievably short span. Lands had been distributed among the tenant farmers with no compensation to the absentee landlords. With one stroke of a purposeful pen the wretched of the earth had become owners of the land they had cultivated for generations for someone else. Bonded labour was abolished, the userers warned off. And a college for women set up, where admissions came abegging to every woman in pursuit of an education or vocation. The sky seemed to be the limit for women's aspirations.

The year was 1952 and the college was only two years old when I entered it. Had it been born earlier, our eldest sister, the brightest in the family, could also have gone to college after passing matriculation as a private student. She could not go beyond this step in her formal education because in 1941 there was only one college in Srinagar where her brothers went for higher education. The half a dozen girls on its rolls came from non-Kashmiri families, the 'advanced', 'modern' Punjabi girls, competing with whom was unthinkable for a 'respectable' Kashmiri Pandit girl. This even though her own father and future father-in-law (she was married the next year) were both professors in that college. If this was the unquestioned reality in an educated, comparatively 'emancipated' Kashmiri Pandit family, who not only had a far stronger tradition of learning—conventional as well as modern brought in by their English education—what the situation must have been for Muslim women can well be imagined. 'Steeped in ignorance' might be a cliche, but it was the truth. The poorer classes were, of course completely unaware of the need for education, but the upper classes—as well as the middle class in its unrelenting desire for respectability—would not encourage it for fear of throwing open the doors to subversion. The scales were heavily weighed against women. Only a few could break free from the mould in which they had been cast from birth. One such woman who did it with aplomb and made a difference, was Mahmuda Ahmad Ali Shah, the first Kashmiri woman to head a college in Srinagar. This tall sternly beautiful woman had a commanding personality. Her single-minded commitment to the ideal of Kashmiri women's emancipation was largely responsible for making this college an institution of academic and cultural excellence. One of her most repeated exhortations at the morning assembly was to ask the students to always walk with their heads held high as there was nothing that should cow them down as long as they were in the right. There was no confusion of course regarding what was right: doing their bit for creating a socialist, secular society where everyone was free to reach her potential in an atmosphere of freedom.

The years from 1950 to the 70s were the kind of years when everything seemed within reach, anything possible with hard work and determination. The achievements of women during these decades were so significant that that they altered the gender landscape of schools, colleges, offices, courts, police stations, hospitals, hotels and business establishments. Women were everywhere, making their mark in every field. This revolution had been brought about surprisingly, without there being an organized women's movement in the state. Women began to take the possibilities for their careers for granted. It had not occurred to them as yet that with their unrestrained expansion, the roads would get narrower and there would not be room for everyone—in the professional colleges, in other employment opportunities. Or that a time would come when the gift of freedom would be taken away with the same suddenness that it had been bestowed upon them and they would regress to the swaddling they had broken free from. But I am talking about a time when optimism was still in the air and expectations from 'progress' were raised to limitless heights. Of course it was an unreal situation, in hindsight. The events from the mid-'80s onwards, leading to the total collapse of the educational edifice in the '90s could be attributed, to some extent, also to the frustrations generated from these unnaturally high expectations of the rewards from free education.

The things I remember about the college today may sound incredible in today's devastated educational scene in Kashmir, but they are true nevertheless. My first vivid memory of the college is symbolically the most significant too. It is that of the rehearsal for a play we freshers saw when we ventured towards the little wooden hut-like structure that served as an auditorium in 1952. (The fully equipped large auditorium which we got from the government in the 1960s after so many drama festivals—an annual feature—had been staged in that very hut, was burnt down in the 1990s. Another instance of the cyclic nature of history perhaps!) The play was about Habba Khatoon, who we learnt to our amazement had been a poet and consort of a king of Kashmir. This was our first introduction to the history of Kashmir, which till then was not taught at any stage of our school or college education. The dialogue was in English as the play had been written by a professor of the college who did not know Kashmiri, while the lyrics were Habba Khatoon's own, set to music by the music department. That it was possible for our poor disdained, till then looked-down-upon Kashmiri language to rub shoulders with the awesome English language on equal terms was an overwhelming experience. This experiment, so new at that time, opened a door to a whole world of mutually enriching linguistic and cultural cross currents. Kashmir no longer felt small, nor was being called a Kashmiri an epithet of contempt anymore. In fact suddenly one felt proud to be a Kashmiri, yet secure enough to accept valuable lessons from other cultures. We did not realize then that this was an instance of what is now called Kashmiriyat, the word appropriated by those who know nothing about it.

Soon we too became a part of this cultural revolution, eclectic in our choice of plays to act in, be they the poetic plays of Tagore, translated into English and Kashmiri, the farce-like comedies of Moliere in Urdu, the socially relevant satires of Ramesh Mehta in Hindustani, Bernard Shaw's witty exposes of social and political hypocrisies, the sparkling, epigrammatic Restoration comedies or the powerful human dramas of Shakespeare. And then we did something really extraordinary, performed a folk opera celebrating a Kashmiri myth. It was the creation of two geniuses of modern Kashmir, the poet Dinanath Nadim and the music composer Mohanlal Aima. The attempt was so successful that it marked our entry into the first All-India Youth Festival held at Talkatora Garden in New Delhi in 1954. The cast included girls from orthodox families who had never ventured outside the valley of Kashmir, but such were the pursuasive powers of the teachers and the principal that they were allowed to go, in the belief that whatever was part of the college activity must be good. The faith reposed by parents in their daughters and giving them the freedom to travel without a male relative as escort, was indicative of how the times had changed within a short time! The experience of living for a whole week in tented accommodation with hundreds of men and women students from the premier universities of India, interacting with them on an equal footing was unforgettable. We never felt inferior to anyone in any way, even the likes of Bhupen Hazarika, Sharan Rani Mathur and Vijay Anand happened to be part of the Assam, Delhi and Bombay university contingents. In our unsophisticated innocence, we were not even conscious that in this prestigious platform we were representing an 'educationally backward' state!

The ease with which Kashmiri Muslim girls—most of them first generation literates—fitted into the routine of a modern college with its emphasis on sports, debating, NCC (National Cadet Corps), educational tours and cultural activities is unimaginable in today's benighted state. No parent protested when their daughters were asked to participate in a marchpast with students from the two boys' colleges in Srinagar every month, when the then Prime Minister Sheikh Mohammad Abdullah took the salute. Among them were married women, some of them mothers, who were primary school teachers deputed to attend college and get a degree to improve their prospects. No voices were raised against the girls wearing the army-like NCC uniform, or performing on the stage, reviving old Kashmiri folk song and dance forms, or travelling to places all over India in trains, the teachers roughing it out with them in IInd class compartments, learning about the history of India's past, without sermons being stuffed down their throats. We were engaged in a 'dialogue' all the time, without knowing it was a fashionable word!

Dramatics formed a very important part of our life in college. The whole gamut of stagecraft, without any formal training was appropriated by us, unselfconsciously. With what supreme self-confidence the girls played the part of great men characters from world drama, the only serious problem being their long hair! I remember the enthusiasm with which Muslim girls from extremely orthodox families were ready to wear basanti saris and flowers in their hair for a Tagore play or western costumes for an English period play. This great equalizer was aided by the fact that the college rules demanded that all students wear a uniform—beige kurta, white salwar and white dupatta. Thus there was nothing to distinguish one girl from another. In the college we were all equal, no matter from which economic class or caste, or urban or rural background we came from.

Religion, till 1990, was something that had no role to play as far as life in the college was concerned. Academic merit or achievements in other fields were what counted. The Student's Council with two representatives from all the sections of every class had a President elected directly by the students. Academic performance, participation in activities like debating, dramatics or editing the college magazine *Pamposh* were taken into account in this election. Of course it was not wholly democratic—the personal preference of the principal, conveyed through subtle hints and prodding played a part in ensuring the success of a 'deserving' candidate who might not have been a 'popular' choice, but religion and communal leanings had nothing to do with it. In fact in the early '80s, one of the presidents was a girl from Assam, whose father was an army officer posted in Srinagar. Kashmiri girls were secure enough to have an 'outsider' occupy the highest position that a student could aspire to in the college. Generally a girl who had the confidence of the staff and was popular for her social graces too, would get to occupy the prestigious position because her duties included welcoming distinguished personalities from the country and abroad. Every eminent person from the world of politics, art, literature, music, economics or science, who came to Kashmir would invariably be invited to the college to address the students or be introduced to the culture of Kashmir. These frequent encounters threw the windows wide open. If it was Jawaharlal Nehru one year, it could be Aneurin Bevan or Rajendra Prasad the next. The students who saw and heard Amartya Sen, Sardar Jafri, Begum Akhtar, or Stephen Spender in their college itself, did not need any more cosmopolitan exposure. No wonder they could hold their own when competing with the best products of the leading universities of India and the world. Even though it was only a government college where education was free, its reputation was no less than that of any elite college in Delhi. But I am talking of what is no more.

No one could have predicted the suddenness with which the liberal, humanist atmosphere, which had survived through several upheavals threatening to tear the social fabric of Kashmir apart, like the dismissal and imprisonment of Sheikh Abdullah in 1953, the infiltration of the mujahideen in 1965, the Pandit agitation of 1967, the tensions of the 1971 war, the politically and communally charged elections of 1983 and 1987, could be blown away. Something was certainly brewing in Kashmir, stealthily striking at the roots of the trust and bonhomie that existed between the communities, destroying the sense of a common future of all Kashmiris that had been their dream and pride. The sickness that had affected the world outside suddenly entered the college in a dramatic manner one day in the year 1989. Leaflets were dropped over the till then impregnable walls of the college demanding that the Muslim girls wear burqa and the Hindus wear a bindi to save them from 'unnecessary harassment'! It was the first time that a wedge was introduced to divide the students along communal lines. But at that stage the response of the students was heartening—they refused to follow the diktat. We did not realize that it was the thin edge of the wedge. Then there were rumours that a man with a stick was lying in wait outside college to hit any girl who did not cover her head. But even this threat was not powerful enough to beat them into submission. The gun had not yet been used to enforce it and when that happened, the scene in 1990 at the college reopening after the winter break was completely changed. There were hardly any Pandit students and the view was an unrelieved black, not figuratively but literally. Almost all the girls were now covered in a burqa of that colour, only some out of religious conviction, most out of fear, which was palpable, rampant.

There was no freedom anymore for any one, particularly not for women. For them it was a complete about turn. Humiliation and helplessness took the place of the earlier hard-won confidence. There was no question of holding one's head high, safety lay in abject submission, whether to the orders of the militants or the state. The mere act of attending college or any other educational institution required the courage of a mad woman and soon all institutions, whether government offices, schools or other institutions collapsed. No longer was there a commitment to anything. Terror was the only driving force. When bare survival is at stake, who can afford the luxury of a meaningful education? In fact, education was the first casualty. As schools and colleges were targetted, carefully built-up libraries and laboratories went up in flames, along with our auditorium which had been witness to so much of the history of our achievements in academic and co-curricular fields. A dark night had descended upon us, our little world which prided itself on a syncretic way of life, revelling in its diversity, was awash in a uniform black. More than this outward transformation was the transformation in attitudes and expectations. From a vibrant, forward-looking, multi-cultural community of women we had turned into something which is the worst manifestation of monoculture.

It took a couple of years, unrelieved in their bleakness and terror, for women's natural resilience to reassert itself. The synthetic polyester burqa gave way to a cotton chador, but the decline in educational standards was hard to remedy. Large numbers of competent, experienced teachers had migrated from the Kashmir valley to safety. Those who stayed back like me, had become irrelevant to the scene. Gradually our students did manage to sit for the examinations and even pass them, but hope of a better academic future was nowhere in sight as long as they were in Srinagar. Parents who could afford it—and provided the results were out in time—sent their children out for studies. The bright ones who stayed on were sucked into militancy in one way or another, some died and some were as good as dead. Violence to flesh and spirit continues unabated and hope finds it more and more difficult to sustain itself.

At present there seems to be a conspiracy of silence regarding the history of women's emancipation in post-partition Kashmir. Of course, girls are still attending schools and colleges but the air of freedom which we had the good fortune to breathe is gone. Instead of the brightness of hope illuminating their faces, a veil of fear clouds them. Not only do they need moral courage to defy diktats from various quarters, their life is in danger even when making a short trip, perhaps from a randomly flung grenade exploding in their faces or a humiliating search in the bus or being caught in crossfire—there are terrors at every step. But more than these is the colossal loss of a culture which revelled in diversity, the loss of a time when religious or linguistic identities did not have an aggressive face, when concerns were shared despite academic competitiveness. The present generation of students have no idea of what it was like before the madness of 'homogenization', unleashed by forces over which they have no control, overtook them. This essay is an attempt to address this very generation, in the hope that by understanding the past, they may get insights into the future and pull themselves out of the morass of despondency they are sunk in at present. Hence this story of the multi-dimensional life college education offered not too long ago.

I am thinking at this time of two outstanding Kashmiri Muslim students of mine, both with great potential. One had the good fortune of passing out in the seventies, while the other did so in the nineties. The former is now a highly successful lawyer in Washington, who has earned herself the sobriquet, 'Queen Bee', because she helps immigrant professionals with their B-1 visa problems. With no jobs available in Kashmir and private enterprise stifled, the other young woman, equally gifted and promising, is still waiting to find a useful, fulfilling role in Kashmiri society today.

WHO ARE THESE DURYODHANAS?

Somnath Zutshi

A huge clamour, heart-rending cries! It sounded like the dawn of Doomsday itself. The heavens had turned black at the very peak of day, as if an invisible force had drawn a thick sheet of black polythene over them. The only things visible were the two huge, hairy hands of this force, spreading the black polythene all over within the blinking of an eye. The first thing eclipsed was the sun. Its size began to shrink, light faded and it disappeared from sight. The day turned into a starless, moonless night, like the pitch-dark night of a new moon.

A roar of loud, beseeching cries. Is this the apocalypse? People barred their doors and windows in terror but darkness advanced into the rooms. They switched on the lights—nothing happened. They tried to light earthen lamps, but the wicks refused to burn. It grew bitterly cold. Hugging their infants to their breasts, mothers cried loudly. They were not cries, they were hollow shrieks without any life in them. Even crows who on other days would have been looking for food in fields, downs, marshes and plateaus, appeared numbed today. They just cawed on incessantly—some secret sense seemed to have told them that it was not the natural darkness of night, it did not smell right. They huddled together, their cawing growing louder and louder as if to say, 'No—it is not night as we know it'. In their thousands they flew in the darkness. Though they could not be seen in the abounding darkness, the flutter of their wings made a loud rustle. They were flying, not to their nests or roosting perches in the north, but just anywhere, in panic. God knows how many fell dead in flight.

Suddenly a proclamation rang out, 'Caution! Be warned! On your guard!' Stout staffs hit the gates of houses as the calls came. At this, life returned to the cowering humans—at least someone was alive! And the loud outcry rose to a crescendo. Countless hordes gathered in the field: some with broken visages, some half-dead. Out of the multitude came a powerful voice, 'Do not panic, countrymen! It is not night, in fact. This black pall will soon be lifted and there, will be light once again!'

Another cry rose to counter this claim, 'All lies! The sun is gone—how long can living things survive?' The first voice retorted with, 'Did not the skies once darken into night at mid-day during the Mahabharata war? I tell you there is no cause for panic.' 'But that was only a momentary night, brought about by Lord Krishna in order to destroy falsehood, whereas this night has lasted for hours now. Where will we find a Krishna to fold up this darkness? This night is much more cruel than that night in the *Mahabharata.*'

A third voice intervened, 'Absolutely correct. Lord Krishna will not be born again, certainly not in this *Kaliyuga* and that too to lift one curtain of darkness!'

A fourth voice shouted, 'Brothers! Do not let us waste any more time. We grow faint with weakness. Let us follow the birds, leave in the direction they have taken. Listen! Even now you can hear their wings—*sav, sav, sav, sav*! Thousands, millions have already taken flight.'

Everyone gave assent to this and began to leave. Again the loud cries! Holding their infants to their breasts, mothers joined the throng. The inhalation and exhalation of their breath itself sounded like a scream. In the bitter, freezing cold, all track of children was lost—they did not want to know whether they still had breath in them. In the buzzing darkness, they just stumbled along. Several collapsed by the roadside. 'Those who have fallen, have fallen—we must go on', exhorted a voice. 'How many of us will survive this nightmare to reach the destination?'

Before this question could be answered, the sound of a low one-voice religious chant was heard. Feeling with their outstretched hands and guided by the sense of smell, they guessed that they were in a forest—a holy man had to be around. 'Who's there?'

'Hush! Silence! The ascetic is practising yogic austerities,' a low voice answered the query.

'Ha!—the heavens are falling apart and he is practising his austerities? Seeking his own salvation, is he? Tell him, Creation is coming to an end! Let him demonstrate his yogic powers now.'

The ascetic heard the outburst, and from a distance came his advice: 'Come into this deep cave, perform deep penance and you will find salvation.'

The second man protested, 'Your holiness! We have hardly seen anything of this world yet, hardly having established ourselves on this earth, how can we ascend to the heavens? You are asking us to give up life and find redemption?'

The third joined in with, 'Why would the Lord Brahma have created this world? He certainly did not intend to finish it off midway! The sculptor does not break his beautiful idols after making them; create the sun, the moon, the stars, the earth, only to destroy them? No, he will not upset the balance of this universe—impossible!'

The first man screamed, 'Are you suggesting that Darkness will triumph over Light? Is the Mahabharata being played all over again only to ensure the victory of Duryodhana? To let untruth bring truth to its knees? Holiness, the Evil ones are just the chaff in the grain, just a fly in a cauldron of milk. You must punish them and we would find salvation in this life itself.'

The ascetic attempted a loud, mocking laugh, but it seemed to lack vigour. He frowned and said, 'Only the name of God is Eternal.'

'With no one left to chant that name? Is that what you mean?'

Again there was a huge outcry: mothers wailed with low moans. One man spoke up, 'It is the ascetics like him who took Duryodhana's side in the Mahabharata war then!'

Another one burst out in anger, 'Listen, everybody! This is no ascetic or *rishi*. He is either the disciple or preceptor of Duryodhana. He will survive us all and find *moksha* in his forest!'

A third man spoke up loudly, 'If you all have the strength, let us get hold of huge lances and pierce holes in this polythene. Raise your heads and give a huge roar in one voice—the blackened skies will crash open and the sun come out in all its glory. The other course is to follow the birds—take the path they chose. The choice is yours.' In answer, there came a huge roar, a full-throated roar.

A powerful cry came also from a house near the fields they had left behind. It was a cry from a youthful throat. In one leap the young man was out of his bed, trembling with rage. Light seemed to hurt his eyes, he rubbed them and found himself in the arms of his mother, hugging her tightly.

'Why did you cry out? You frightened me!' she was saying.

'Was it a full-throated, powerful cry or not?' he asked. The mother could make nothing of it. He rose at once and went to the window and opened it. The fallen leaves in the garden were being blown away by the wind: and they looked like small fragments of black polythene. But when his eyes found the roses in perfect bloom upon the rose bush, colour returned to his drawn face.

It was not evening yet. His heart was still filled with fear, anxious to see the crows return to their northern climes, to their nests in the *chinars* at sunset, beating their wings to the rustle of *sav, sav, sav* and joyfully setting up a clamour with an occassional chatter of, *tein, tein, tein*. He went back to bed muttering to himself, 'How many Duryodhanas are yet to be born?'

THE BURNT-OUT SUN

Anees Hamdani

From the distance came the sound of a siren. I don't know whether anyone else heard it or not but I heard it—not just heard the sound but recognised it too. It was the ambulance siren and its call was for me. That is why I came out. Excuses or arguments would serve no purpose. The matter had been settled at the top: I was sick and needed treatment. Within a few moments it drove up to where I was standing. Two men got out. They did not speak to me at all but I read the message very well from their faces. That is why I walked towards the ambulance fast. I entered it and the two followed me inside. One of them closed the door. The driver, between whose black teeth glittered a white cigarette, glanced at me. Something stuck in my throat and I could not swallow.

The wheels spun on the cold surface of the road. I don't know whether anyone else was aware of it or not but the wheels kept on whirring. I could not understand anything of what was happening. Neither did the men say a word. And I did not dare ask. When my glance fell on them accidentally it seemed that I had been watching them for ages. Sometimes they appeared to be deep in thought.

When the ambulance came to a halt they took my arms and led me to where they wanted. I found myself in a dark cell, where there was just one bed and on it lay God knows what. Spread on it I saw a blanket, red as though saturated with blood. That is why the things on the bed could not be discerned. And there were the stark, high, white-washed walls of the cell. I could not understand why they were painted white—perhaps to bring some light, I thought. But then where was the light? Here there was nothing but darkness. Why were the walls white? I thought I would enquire, but from whom? There was no one, but even if there had been, how could I ask? Then there came a sound—drip-drip-drip. This did something to me. My innards quivered under its shrill, piercing jabs. How long would it go on? And I in this room, in this situation? Nothing made sense. Was it sunny outside or was it raining? Where was the drip-drip-drip coming from? I wished I could dismantle the walls, and see what was happening outside. How long had I been inside? I knew nothing. I had been leading a quiet, harmless enough life. Why then did they put me in a strait-jacket? And why did they change my environment? Has sickness ever been cured by a mere change of place?

I have been here now for a long, long time. Sometimes I feel as if I have just arrived here. It is hard to keep count of the years.

What happened ultimately was something I had never imagined. Actually I have always been waiting for something that never happens. Through the wall the two of them came— the same wall through which they had forcibly pushed me in earlier—and advanced towards me. They said nothing. One of them removed the red blanket from the bed. Spread underneath was a white sheet. I cast one look at the white sheet and another at the white of the walls and then lifted my eyes to their faces. The same thought occurred to me once again: why did the walls have such white faces? To tell the truth, I did not have the courage to ask them. Perhaps they were cleverer than I was and that was how they read the unframed question on my face and one of them spoke, 'One must get acquainted with death before it comes. That is the reason why these walls are painted stark white.' They took charge of me and laid me down on the white sheet, face upwards, brought some instruments and cut my face into two. They left one half linked to my skeletal form and severed the other. One of the two brought a cloth and, wrapping the severed half of my face in it, put it in some safe place beyond my gaze. I could understand nothing of it at all. All was deathly still. They said nothing, nor did I venture to speak. Then they picked me up and put a chain around my neck. I looked down and felt a locket that was suspended from it. There was a number engraved on it. I tried very hard to read the number but could not. The fact was that my eyes had gone with the part of my face which had been removed so how could I read anything? Then they took me out of the room the same way as I had been brought in, through the wall. As we came out, one of the two said, 'Go, you are free now. You will never see an ambulance again, nor will you, ever be brought here.'

FINDING FACE
Images of Women from the Kashmir Valley

Sheba Chhachhi

IMAGES ARE PART OF THE ARSENAL

A pheran clad man, faceless, features almost completely obliterated by cap/muffler/scarf, holding an AK47. The caption says 'Militant in front of mosque, Srinagar'.

Two men in khaki uniform, faces shadowed under helmets, eyes trained on their task of reloading their machine guns in an amorphous landscape. Even though the caption says no more than 'Security forces face increasing attacks in Kashmir', we all know that this is the 'border'. In the mind of the ordinary citizen of India the image of Kashmir is dominated by sets of men with guns. They may be brave soldiers defending the nation against Islamic terrorists or conversely, depending on which of the two sides on offer you are on, courageous martyrs fighting a just and holy war against a brutal occupying army.

These images have remained virtually unchanged for the last 15 years. Repeated ad infinitum in the dominant media, they have become so familiar that they barely need to be seen to be recognized. Dead men—mutilated bodies, charred flesh and unidentifiable 'human remains'—occupy the space left over by armed men. Photographs of sites of violence accompany these stock images. Bomb blasts, damaged buildings, burnt down shrines, confiscated arms, and city streets under patrol. If these sites are inhabited at all, it is by those ubiquitous men with guns. Disturbing, even brutal images, seen so often that the reader/ viewer has long become inured.

Beneath this violent layer are other traces—childhood memories of summer holidays, film romances of the 50s and 60s, 'the vale of paradise'. Once in a while, this layer is leavened by the reappearance of that quintessential tourist postcard image, a *shikara* (boat) on the Dal Lake, in advertisements issued by the Government of Jammu and Kashmir, announcing the return of 'normalcy'. Appearing and disappearing on the same screen are the faces of politicians, leaders, men of varying persuasions and credibility, always accompanied by statements about who 'owns' Kashmir. In this visual narrative, ordinary men, women and children are non actors, (or at best part of a supporting cast brought on stage as victims of militant violence) a de-peopled representation of Kashmir affirming its unambiguous construction in the popular imagination as territory.

Within the Kashmir armed struggle, this selective depiction has created an almost grotesque use of the photograph as evidence of oppression and violence. Alongside heroic depictions of armed militants, local publications, videotapes, pamphlets etc., seem to engage in a competition of the horrific—one account of torture exceeded by the next. Photographs of mutilated bodies, defaced, anonymous corpses, the shattered corporal remains of victims blur into a vast repository of images that the modern mind has already received countless times. The displaced Pandit community has its own version, equally morbid. Sadly, rather than bringing home the extent of suffering more forcefully, this repeated showcasing of wounds defeats its own purpose. The human being disappears behind the propaganda—the initial shock and potency of these images of violence soon evaporates, leaving the viewer either numb or alienated.

Travelling in the Kashmir valley, we encountered another, curious form of local representation. Handed (sometimes surreptitiously) to potential supporters of the Kashmiri cause, these are images of people, but curiously depersonalized. The most common are postcard size photographs of crowds—a mass of villagers gathered around a dead body, numbers of mourners carrying the bier of a slain 'commander', a mob shouting slogans, a long row of young men in pherans lying on the earth, people crowded behind. Collaged onto these images of 'the people' is the ubiquitous man with the gun, now dead: the mangled remains of head and shoulders, bedecked with blood and flowers carefully cut out from another photograph and superimposed. The 'people' and the usually unrecognizable, defaced corpse graphically brought into the same frame. In more elaborate versions, a passport photo of the dead hero is included in the collage, texts extolling his martyrdom inked alongside. In the homes of dead militants, these are 'family photos'.

Unwittingly, these photographs—of armed men, dead men, leaders, faceless victims—repeat current tropes of Kashmir in the mainstream media.

In both discourses the victims are usually female. A grieving mother, wailing female mourners, a woman widowed by militants, are the protagonists of a few Sunday features. A small number of photographs of crowds of women protestors can be culled from 1990-91 files. These images are taken as an affirmation of women's support for the armed struggle, just as the image of the raped woman is a key ideological tool used by both the militants and the Pandits to justify their political positions. In a twisted adjunct the touristic trope of the beautiful 'Kashmir ki kali' still surfaces in 'boys talk' amongst army men, journalists and Republic Day floats.

Amidst the mass of ordinary Kashmiris without countenance, the bodies of Kashmiri women seem to achieve representation. In August 2001 an unprecedented number of images of Kashmiri women were published in the national dailies. This interest followed a diktat issued by a hitherto unknown militant group warning Muslim women in the valley to wear burqas or have acid thrown on their faces. Photographs of women (mainly in Srinagar) in or out of burqa, buying burqas, college students with guards at the gates, tailors sewing burqas, etc., etc., were repeatedly shown. Figures of women succumbing to the diktat were published, and added to the daily roll call of the numbers of the dead, the 'burqa watch'. A short-lived call for imposition of burqa in 1993 had received similar coverage. For a brief moment it may seem as though the rigid separation between private and public, the domestic and the political has been breached. On the contrary, these boundaries have only ossified further.

Notwithstanding apparently sympathetic motivation, the image of the burqa clad woman makes a satisfying congruence with that of the masked Muslim terrorist. The equation Kashmiri = Muslim = Fundamentalist = Terrorist, stands reaffirmed.

The hitherto unseen Kashmiri woman remains faceless, her body inscribed by Islamic retrogression, shrouded in otherness.

The erasure of the human from dominant representation of Kashmir is a powerful weapon serving, in the ultimate analysis, to maintain the conflict rather than provoke the seeking of resolution. Stereotypes, however vivid, do not suffer. People do.

'WHEN THE GUN IS RAISED, DIALOGUE STOPS ...'

The photographs and testimonies that follow seek to bring the human back into the discourse on Kashmir. These pages are an extract from a larger work, a photo-installation by Sheba Chhachhi and Sonia Jabbar: 'When the gun is raised, dialogue stops ... women's voices from the Kashmir valley'. The installation is a humble attempt to give space to the women of Kashmir whose voices have been obscured by the clamour of war and contention. First created in 1995, the installation has evolved and changed over the years. Each avatar, both in form and content, reflects the increasing complexity of our understanding as well as changes in the valley from our first visit in 1994 (Women's Initiative on Kashmir, report: 'The Green of the valley is Khaki') to Sonia Jabbar's intensive interaction from 1995 to 2000. The installation was last presented in August 2000, in New Delhi. Here the viewer is invited to step behind the screen of the dominant media and enter the private space of war. Humble materials—earth, brick, rice—evoke domestic space, creating two solemn rows, fifty feet long, of thirty-six low platforms. On each platform, thirty-six wooden *rihals* (bookstands), traditional holder of the Koran, the Gita and the Guru Granth Sahib, now hold sheets of rusted iron carrying black and white photographs and text. The viewer is slowed down and the usual mode of viewing photographs altered as she/he is drawn into intimate contact with each image/text. The images and text do not necessarily bear a literal one to one relation. The testimonies are culled from interviews with Kashmiri women over six years and a wide range of subjective positions finds articulation. Shia women, Sunni women. Pandit refugees. Pandits who have chosen to stay on in the valley, college students, peasants, housewives, workers, and academics. There are statements by women whose brothers or husbands are militants, as well as those who have suffered at the hands of militancy, just as there are those who have faced the violence of the security forces. What binds them across different religions, ethnicities and relationships to the war is an unambiguous rejection of violence. These voices are voices of reason, compassion and hope, despite great suffering; voices, which could, perhaps, prove to be the seeds for a solution to the present crisis.

I faced the power of his gun with the power of my mind. I felt no fear. I had the axe. Had the axe not been there; there was a rolling pin, a ladle. If I had a gun, they would have seized it long ago. These are my own implements. No one can take them away from me.

Jana, a carpet worker, who escaped molestation by
a Border Security Force soldier, Awanpora village

I knew my husband was a militant. I knew that some day he would be killed. I grieve, but I do not complain. When you are a militant, you are ready to die. But why did they kill the other seven men. They were innocent, they had not killed anybody. I have to bring up my children. Where does a woman go? What can she do? If women become militants, what will happen to the children? Who will look after them? Who wants all this killing? A woman cannot become a militant.

Jameela, Malangaon, Bandipora

'Will your son become a *mujahid?*' we asked, watching a ten year old child playing with his toy gun. The child of a freedom fighter will be a freedom fighter!' But then, caressing the cheek of her 17 year-old, she almost whispers, 'As soon as even a tiny bit of beard appears, I shave it off. I can't lose him as well'.

Saira, Bandipora

You must not believe everything that people tell you. You must not listen with your ears but with your heart.

Parveen, a doctor, Srinagar

Kunan Poshpora village is still remembered as 'the raped village' in Kashmir. In February 1991 security forces raped 30 women. Even three years later when we visited the village we found that the married raped women had been deserted by their husbands. A seventy year old woman had been thrown out by her son. The young women, raped or not, remained single. Girls told us that they were teased even by the village men: 'Did you enjoy it? Want some more?'

It was ten o'clock at night. In the mosque near our house there was a huge gathering of people making a great noise. Islamic slogans were being shouted. We had never heard or seen anything like this before. We became afraid. My husband phoned relatives and they said that the same was happening in their area. Our anxiety increased. What should we do? It carried on. On the fifth day they came and asked our men to join their procession. They were demanding azadi. But no one went.

Pandit refugee in Delhi, name withheld on request

The militants came in the middle of the night and demanded food and shelter. We have never been involved with any militant group nor with the azadi movement. But what could we do? They had guns. At dawn there was a raid. The *faujis* cordoned the place and as the two men ran out into the snow they were killed. Then the C.O. ordered all of us out of the house and started beating my teenage sons and husband until they bled. 'Keep militants here, do you? I'll teach you a lesson,' they said. They took my husband away warning us, 'If any of my men had been killed this village would have burnt like Pattan, remember that.'

Haleema, Buthu village. (Mohammed Wali Reshi, 55 years, was arrested under the Public Safety Act where a person can be detained without trial for a period of two years. The FIR for Reshi said 'Mohammed Wali Reshi incites militants against India'.)

Community makes nation. Silence the community and the nation dies. War takes place. In war, one side wins, the other loses. What neither wins nor loses, but simply dies as a result, is humanity. Human values, human relationships, faith, trust. I fear for the end of all of this. I fear that humanity will not survive.

A school teacher, Avanporgaon, Pulwama district

My father was so handsome and strong. He looked just like Rajesh Khanna. Everybody loved him because he was always laughing and he was a good person. He used to ride a motorcycle. The Hizbul Mujahideen had warned him about drinking but when he didn't care they killed him.

Benazir, a teenager, Bandipora

I asked them why have you come here in the middle of the night, is this how you do your duty? I told them to go away, my husband is not here.

They barged into my home, stuck a gun to my head and slapped me. 'Where have you kept the money?' they demanded. 'We have no money, we're *mazdoors,* daily-wage labourers.' They slapped me again and then searched the rooms, broke open the trunks. When they couldn't find anything they locked my children into the other room and raped me one by one. They were soldiers from the ITBP (Indo-Tibetan Border Police) camp. They were both drunk.

Rubeena, a Bengali woman who had come to Kashmir eight years before and married a Kashmiri. This testimony was given the day after the rape.

We were afraid but we thought it would blow over. First, B.K. Ganju, a junior engineer in the telecom department was brutally murdered. The women of his family were not even allowed to mourn. Then, several other prominent members of our community were killed. Terrified, we left en masse.

Pandit refugee in Delhi, name withheld on request

Those days my brother was underground. We hadn't seen him in months. That day just my mother and I were at home. I was only 16 then. The STF men were given a tip-off that there was a cache of arms hidden in the house. When they came we said there was nothing and they were free to search the house if they wanted. They ransacked the entire house from top to bottom. When they didn't find anything they first locked Mummy in one room. Then they picked me up and stuck my head in a large bin full of rice. I was choking and crying. Mummy was banging the door begging them to leave me. Finally, they stopped torturing me and pulled me out. But before leaving a *jawan* placed both his booted feet on my bare ones and ground them down until my toe nails came off. It took 18 months to heal.

'You must hate the security forces after what they did.'

'No, I can't truthfully say that all Indian soldiers are bad. Some are good and some are bad. Just as some militants are good men and some are bad.'

Amina, sister of a militant, Srinagar

My husband was abducted by militants seven years ago. We have no idea whether he is dead or alive. Every time the talk of my remarriage begins

in my family, we get a whiff of a rumour about his being alive. And so the wait begins again ...

Hamida, a half-widow, Bandipora. (Islamic law only permits the remarriage of widows after the death of the husband has been established conclusively.)

It was after years that we had all gotten together at a marriage—all of us women—Hindus, Muslims, Sardarnis. It was almost like the old days ... We laughed and danced late into the night. Then, as we prepared to go to sleep, I heard some of the Muslim women whispering among themselves in the next room: 'It's been such a lovely evening. It is true, isn't it, that a garden is only a garden of any worth when there are many kinds of flowers gracing it.'

Rajni, one of the 18,000 Pandits who chose to remain in the Kashmir valley

We always considered ourselves as first class citizens of Kashmir, but now I'm so confused. What do you think will happen? Do you think it will be safe for us to raise our children here?

Kanwal, a Sikh woman in Srinagar, after the Chittisinghpora massacre of 36 Sikhs

Suddenly my students began to wear veils ... such pretty girls. They said they were being pressurised by their brothers and the speeches from the mosques. Until then we had secular ways in the college—all the girls in uniform ... during the exams when I scolded a girl she turned around and said 'Madam, my cousin is a militant. How can you scold me?'

Mrs Jai Kishori Pandit, Professor, Government College for Women, Srinagar

Men go to mosques. We go to the *ziarats,* the shrines. There we weep together and unburden the load that sits heavily on the chest. We cannot face God on our own, so we ask the Pir buried there to intercede on our behalf.

I find great peace there. What are these men thinking when they burn down our shrines? Where will we go if this carries on?

Abida, Srinagar

My son never asked me, 'Ammaji, can I go to Pakistan and become a militant?' He simply left. I wept. That is the fate of the mothers of Kashmir.

When he crossed the border on his return he was caught and jailed for two years. When he was released the *tanzeem* (militant group) got after him because they felt he'd broken under torture.

So he joined the Ikhwan to protect himself. Either way he was trapped. I don't sleep at night because of the numerous attempts on his life. This is not life but hell.

Lala, Bandipora. Her son, the Ikhwan Area Commander was ambushed
and killed a few months later

I didn't decide to leave. We came here for a holiday. Everything was left behind. We had to start all over again ... from a spoon. Is this any way to live? Five of us in a rented room, no privacy, the heat, sleepless nights—this, after what we had been used to in Kashmir.

Prana, Refugee Camp, Delhi

Today the talk of separation hurts me. But what can we do? Our voice was not heeded properly. Kashmir was not part of India before 1947. After 1947 onwards a kind of cold war started. There was discontent which was not allowed outward expression. Those who wanted to speak were suppressed. We had started to participate in the election process, national games. We began to believe that India was our country. There was terrible rigging in the 1987 elections and once again everything shattered. Riggings, firings ... how could we feel this country is ours? People who do not come out of their homes much cannot differentiate between the government and the people. They began to feel that the Indian people are our enemies. In the midst of this dilemma this war started. Some people started to use guns instead of their minds. And what do we want? What do we want and how—those questions were left behind with the gun. When the gun is raised, dialogue stops.

Gulshafan, P.T. Instructor, Srinagar

NOTES ON CONTRIBUTORS

BANKIM CHANDRA CHATTOPADHYAY (1838–1894), Bengali poet, novelist, essayist, and journalist, is most famous for being the author of 'Vande Mataram' or 'Bande Mataram', the national song of India. Some of his major works include *Durgeshnondini*, *Kapalkundala*, *Mrinalini*, *Radharani*, *Chandrasekhar*, *Rajsimha*, *Anandamath*, and *Debi Chaudhurani*.

AUROBINDO GHOSE (1872–1950) was an Indian nationalist, scholar, poet, mystic, and evolutionary philosopher.

BHAGAT SINGH (1907–1931), an Indian freedom fighter, is considered to be one of the most influential revolutionaries of the Indian independence movement.

SARAT CHANDRA CHATTOPADHYAY (1876–1938) is one of the most popular Bengali novelists of the early twentieth century. His work represents rural Bengali society and the associated themes of superstitions and oppression. Some of his major works include *Baradidi*, *Bindur Chhele*, *Parineeta*, *Biraj Bou*, *Debdas*, *Choritrohin*, *Srikanto*, *Grihodaho*, *Pather Dabi*, *Ses Prasna*, and *Bipradas*.

RABINDRANATH TAGORE (1861–1941), also known as Gurudev, was a Bengali poet, Brahmo religionist, visual artist, playwright, novelist, and composer whose works reshaped Bengali literature and music in the late nineteenth and early twentieth centuries. He was awarded the Nobel Prize for Literature in 1913, making him the first Asian Nobel laureate. Among his best-known works are *Gitanjali*, *Gora*, and *Ghare-Baire*.

BAL GANGADHAR TILAK (1856–1920), an Indian nationalist, social reformer, and independence fighter, was the first and strongest proponent of 'Purna Swaraj' (complete independence) in Indian consciousness. Tilak, along with Gopal Ganesh Agarkar, Vishnushastri Chiplunakar, and some others, started two newspapers: *Kesari* and *The Mahratta*.

EDMUND CANDLER (1874–1926) was a journalist. Apart from *Siri Ram—Revolutionist*, his works include *The Unveiling of Lhasa* (1905) and *Abdication* (1922), among others.

MAHASHWETA DEVI (b. 1926) is an Indian social activist and writer. Some of her major works include *Jhansir Rani*, *Amrita Sanchay*, *Andhanmalik*, and *Hajar Churashir Ma*. She was awarded the Jnanpith Award by Sahitya Akademi in 1996.

TARIT KUMAR is a Hindi poet. His work has been published in *Thema Book of Naxalite Poetry*.

SAROJ DUTTA (1914–1971), born in a semi-landlord family of Jessore in East Bengal, was a journalist and a veteran member of the Communist Party of India (Marxist-Leninst). He was arrested from a hideout in Calcutta and shot dead by the police on 5 August 1971.

BANI BASU (b.1939) is a Bengali author, essayist, critic, and poet. Her major works include *Swet Pastharer Thaala*, *Ekushe Paa*, *Maitreya Jataka*, *Gandharvi*, *Pancham Purush*, and *Ashtam Garbha*. She was awarded the Tarashankar Award for *Antarghaat* and the Ananda Purashkar for *Maitreya Jataka*. She is also the recipient of the Sushila Devi Birla Award and the Sahitya Setu Puraskar.

ASHIM RAY (1927–1986) was an active participant in the independence movement influenced by leftist ideology. He later forayed into journalism and writing. Among his more famous books are *Ekaler Katha*, *Gopal Deb*, and *Shabder Khanchay*.

SAMRAT UPADHYAY is the first Nepali-born fiction writer writing in English to be published in the West. His books portray the current situation in Nepal. Upadhyay was awarded the Whiting Writers' Award for his first book *Arresting God in Kathmandu*.

LI ONESTO, a reporter for *Revolution*, was the first foreign journalist to travel deep into the guerrilla zones of Nepal in 1999. Her interview with Prachanda, the head of the Communist Party of Nepal (Maoist), has been circulated internationally—translated into Nepali, Spanish, Italian, French, Hindi, German, Pashtun (in Afghanistan), and Chinese.

SUSHMA JOSHI (b. 1973) is a writer and researcher in Nepal. She has co-edited *New Nepal, New Voices,* a collection of short stories from Nepal.

PANKAJ MISHRA (b. 1969) is an Indian essayist and novelist. He is particularly notable for his book *Butter Chicken in Ludhiana*, a sociological study of small-town India, and his writing for the *New York Review of Books*. Mishra writes literary and political essays for *The New York Times*, *The New York Review of Books*, *The Guardian*, and *New Statesman*, among other American, British, and Indian publications.

TENZIN TSUNDUE is a poet, writer, and a noted Tibetan freedom activist. He won the first-ever 'Outlook-Picador Award for Non-Fiction' in 2001. He has published three books to date, which have been translated into several languages.

JEAN ARASANAYAGAM (b. 1930 as Jean Solomons) is an English-language poet and fiction writer whose works concentrate on the ethnic and religious turmoil in Sri Lanka. Her major works include *Kindura* (1973), *Apocalypse '83* (1983), *The Cry of the Kite* (1984), *A Colonial Inheritance and Other Poems* (1985), *Fragments of a Journey* (1992), and *All is Burning* (1995).

A. SIVANANDAN (b. 1923) is the Director of the Institute of Race Relations (IRR) and editor of its journal *Race & Class* for over 35 years. From the 1960s, Sivanandan has written on race issues for the *Guardian, New Statesman*, and *New Society*, and also many articles for IRR's publications. His novel *When Memory Dies* won the Commonwealth Writers' Prize (First Novel Eurasia) and the Sagittarius Prize.

JESURASA, born in Jaffna, Sri Lanka, has published collections of short stories as well as of poetry. He was awarded a Sahitya Akademi award for his short story collection in 1974.

CHERAN (b. 1960 in Jaffna, Sri Lanka) is a poet, journalist, and academic committed to social justice. He was the deputy editor of the *Saturday Review*, the only independent English language weekly in Sri Lanka between 1981 and 1987. He has to his credit seven published anthologies of poetry in Tamil and his poems have been translated into English, German, Sinhala, Kannada, and Malayalam.

PASH (1950–1988) was the pen name of the Punjabi poet, Avtar Singh Sandhu. Deeply influenced by the Naxalite movement, he joined Punjab's Maoist front and became a very influential name in the Left and progressive movements in modern Punjabi literature. A fierce critic of the Punjab terrorists, he fell to their bullets in Jalandhar in 1988.

ANITA AGNIHOTRI is a poet and fiction writer. A civil servant by profession, she lives in Kolkata and writes in Bengali.

MOHAN BHANDARI, in a literary career spanning four decades, has produced as many as seven collections of stories. His works include *Til Chauli*, *Manukh Di Pairth*, *Kaath Di Latt*, *Moon Di Akh*, and *Tan Pattan*, among others. He has extensively translated from Urdu and other Indian languages. Among the many awards and honours he has received are the Sahitya Akademi Award, Chandigrfarh Sahitya Academy Award, and Kulwant Singh Virk Award.

KHUSHWANT SINGH (b. 1915) is a renowned journalist, author, and an authority on Sikh history. Some of his works include *The Mark of Vishnu and Other Stories*, *The History of Sikhs*, *Train to Pakistan*, *I Shall Not Hear the Nightingale*, *A Bride for the Sahib and Other Stories*, *Delhi: A Novel*, *Not a Nice Man to Know: The Best of Khushwant Singh*, *We Indians*, *Truth, Love and a Little Malice*, *With Malice towards One and All*, *Death at My Doorstep*, and *The Illustrated History of the Sikhs*. He was awarded the Padma Bhushan in 1974 and the Padma Vibhushan in 2007 by the Government of India.

KARTAR SINGH DUGGAL (b. 1917) has authored more than twenty collections of short stories, ten novels, seven plays, two poetry collections, and an autobiography. His works have been translated into several Indian and foreign languages. He has received many honours and awards, including the Padma Bhushan, Sahitya Akademi Award, Ghalib Award, Bharatiya Bhasha Parishad Award, Bhai Mohan Singh Vaid Award, and Soviet Land Award.

ROBIN S. NGANGOM is a bilingual poet who writes in English and Manipuri. A lyric poet and translator of long standing, he is a significant presence in the literature of North-east India.

NIRANJAN CHAKMA (b. 1951) has published six volumes of poetry in Chakma and Bengali. He was awarded the Ambedkar Fellowship by the Dalit Sahitya Akademi in 1997. He was formerly also the editor of *Tripura Sadak* published by the Government of Tripura.

BIMAL SINGHA (1948–1998) was a politician and writer from Tripura. He was killed by terrorists in 1998 while serving as the Minister of Health of the state.

MITRA PHUKAN is a well-known Assamese writer and contributes regularly to prominent English dailies in Assam. She is the author of a number of books for children and a committed member of the North East Writers' Forum and edits their journal, *New Frontiers*.

MAMANG DAI, a former member of the Indian Administrative Service, left the service to pursue a career in writing. She has to her credit numerous articles, poems, and short stories published in various journals, and is the author of *Arunachal Pradesh: The Hidden Land*.

KYNPHAM SING NONGKYNRIH belongs to the Khasi tribe and writes poems and short fiction in both Khasi and English. He is the editor of *Rilum*, the first poetry journal in Khasi. Awarded a 'Fellowship for Outstanding Artists 2000' from the Government of India, he was also the winner of the first North-East Poetry Award in 2004 from the North-East India

Poetry Council, Tripura. Some of his poems have been translated into Welsh, Swedish, and several Indian languages

SANJIB BARUAH is a professor of political studies at Bard College. His publications include *Durable Disorder: Understanding the Politics of Northeast India* (Oxford University Press, 2005) and *India against Itself: Assam and the Politics of Nationality* (1999).

NEERJA MATTOO (b. 1937) writes in English and translates from Kashmiri into English. She was Professor and Head of Department of English, Government College for Women, Srinagar. She has a number of published works to her credit, including *The Stranger Beside Me*, the first ever translation of Kashmiri short stories into English.

SHEBA CHHACHHI (b. 1958) is a photographer, installation artist, activist, and writer based in Delhi.

SOMNATH ZUTSHI (1923–1996) was a playwright, short story writer, and translator. He was a recipient of the Soviet Land Nehru award.

ANEES HAMADANI (1955–1989) worked as an agricultural scientist before joining Radio Kashmir as an editor. He wrote plays and short stories. Hamadani was hit by a bullet in 1989; his stories were posthumously published in a collection *Vijood Tu Thsayi*.

COPYRIGHT STATEMENT

The editor and publisher are grateful for permission to include the following copyright material in this volume:

I.—FREEDOM AND TERROR

II.—REVOLUTION AND TERROR

INDIA

MAHASHWETA DEVI, extract from *Mother of 1084*, translated by Samik Bandyopadhyay. Reprinted by permission of Seagull.

TARIT KUMAR, 'We Never wanted…'. Reprinted by permission of Thema.

SAROJ DUTTA, 'The Night of the Full Moon'. Reprinted by permission of Thema.

BANI BASU, extract from *The Enemy Within*, translated by Jayanti Datta. Reprinted by permission of Orient Longman.

ASHIM RAY, 'Auni', translated by Simita Ray. Reprinted by permission of Srishti Publishers.

NEPAL

SAMRAT UPADHYAY, 'A Refugee'. Reprinted by permission of Houghton Mifflin.

LI ONESTO, extract from *Dispatches from the People's War in Nepal*. Reprinted by permission of Pluto Press.

SUSHMA JOSHI, 'Waiting for the War to End'.

PANKAJ MISHRA, 'The People's War', *London Review of Books*. Reprinted by permission of the author.

TENZIN TSUNDUE, 'I am a Terrorist'. Reprinted by permission of the author.

III.—IDENTITY AND TERROR

SRI LANKA

JEAN ARASANAYAGAM, 'In the Garden Secretly'. Reprinted by permission of the author.

JESURASA, 'Your Fate Too', translated by A.J. Canagaratna. Reprinted by permission of Tsar Publications.

CHERAN, 'Amma Do Not Weep', translated by Lakshmi Holmström. Reprinted by permission of Tsar Publications.